The Well-being Transition

Éloi Laurent
Editor

The Well-being Transition

Analysis and Policy

Editor
Éloi Laurent
OFCE/Sciences Po
Ponts ParisTech
Paris, France

Stanford University
Stanford, CA, USA

ISBN 978-3-030-67859-3   ISBN 978-3-030-67860-9   (eBook)
https://doi.org/10.1007/978-3-030-67860-9

This Palgrave Macmillan imprint is published by the registered company Springer Nature
Switzerland AG.
The registered company address is: Gewerbestrasse 11, 6330 Cham, Switzerland

CONTENTS

NOTES ON CONTRIBUTORS

Rabia Abrar is Wellbeing Economy Alliance's (WEAll) Communications Lead. Based in Toronto, Abrar brings her experience delivering communications and marketing strategies for sustainable behaviour change campaigns to WEAll's communications and narratives work.

Fabio Battaglia is a PhD candidate at the University of Edinburgh, where he is undertaking research on the politics of well-being in Scotland and Italy.

Julien Caudeville is a researcher at the French Institute of industrial environment and risks (INERIS), expert in risk assessment and spatial statistics. His field of research deals with environmental health inequalities and environmental exposure modeling.

Stéphane Dion is a Canadian diplomat and has been Member of Parliament in the House of Commons of Canada (1996–2016), Minister of Intergovernmental Affairs (1996–2003), Minister of the Environment (2004–2006), President of COP 11 (2005), Leader of the Official Opposition (2006–2008) and Minister of Foreign Affairs (2016). This text is written in his personal capacity.

Michael Flood is a master's candidate at the National University of Singapore and Sciences Po, Paris. He was previously the Program Director of the Nova Scotia Quality of Life Initiative during 2018 and 2019.

Alessandro Galli is a macro ecologist and sustainability scientist; he is the Mediterranean-MENA Program Director at Global Footprint Network and project manager at the University of Siena.

Anders Hayden is an associate professor of political science at Dalhousie University in Canada. He is the lead editor of the forthcoming book *Towards Sustainable Wellbeing: Moving beyond GDP in Canada and the World*.

Amanda Janoo is the Knowledge & Policy Lead for the Wellbeing Economy Alliance (WEAll). Janoo is an economic policy expert who specializes in economic systems change for social and ecological wellbeing.

Florence Jany-Catrice is professor of economics at the University of Lille and a researcher at Clersé. In 2020–2021, she is Richard B. Fisher Member of the School of Social Science (2020–2021), Institute for Advanced Study, Princeton.

Jean Jouzel Laboratoire des Sciences du Climat/Institut Pierre Simon Laplace, CEA-CNRS-UVSQ, Research director (emeritus) at the CEA. Jouzel, a specialist of past climate changes, has been vice-chair of Working Group I of the IPCC from 2002 to 2015.

Éloi Laurent is a senior economist at OFCE/Sciences Po, a professor at the School of Management and Innovation at Sciences Po and Ponts ParisTech and a visiting professor at Stanford University.

Giorgia Dalla Libera Marchiori is biomedical researcher by formation, who is now studying a master in Sustainable Management at Uppsala University, Sweden. From January 2019, she has been the director of Swedish Organization for Global Health, a youth-led organization working to reduce health inequities in low-income settings.

Dominique Méda is Professor of Sociology and director of the Institute for Interdisciplinary Research in Social Sciences at the University of Paris Dauphine-PSL and joint holder of the chair in "Environmental restructuring, work, employment and social policies" at the Fondation Maison des Sciences de l'Homme (Collège d'études mondiales).

Raluca Munteanu is the Environmental Sustainability Manager at the Swedish Organization for Global Health.

Xavier Ragot is President of OFCE, Research Director at CNRS and Professor of Economics at Sciences Po.

Magali Reghezza-Zitt is a geographer, assistant professor at the École normale supérieure. Her research covers so-called natural disaster risk reduction, urban resilience and adaptation to climate change. She is a member of the French High Council for Climate.

Claire Sommer is Research Editor for the Wellbeing Economy Alliance, Communications Director for the Globally Responsible Leadership Initiative (GRLI), and a business writer.

Xavier Timbeau is an economist, researching on public policies, mainly environmental. Formally, he is Principal Director at OFCE, Applied Economics lab at Sciences Po Paris. He has been rapporteur for the Stiglitz Sen Fitoussi Commission in 2009.

Marie Toussaint is an environmental lawyer and activist, and Green Member of the European Parliament since 2019. Founder of the NGO 'Notre affaire à tous', she launched the International Alliance of Parliamentarians for the Recognition of Ecocide (www.ecocidealliance.org).

Denis Zmirou-Navier is Former Professor of Public Health, Lorraine University Medical School, Nancy, France, and chair of the Environmental and Occupational Health department at the EHESP School of Public Health, Rennes, France.

LIST OF FIGURES

LIST OF TABLES

CHAPTER 1

Introduction: A Roadmap for the Well-being Transition

Éloi Laurent

The Coronavirus disease 2019 (Covid-19) pandemic has shed a bright light on two realities of the twenty-first century. First, human well-being, starting with human health, is a widely shared value across societies around the world and very different political systems are willing and able to prioritize it over economic growth. Second, human prosperity is meaningless and can essentially vanish in a few years if it does not acknowledge its natural underpinning. If Covid-19 is a health crisis in its consequences, it is an ecological crisis in its causes (a zoonosis like SARS and Ebola) coming just a few weeks after the giant Australian fires fueled by climate change, as a reminder of the ecological conditionality of human prosperity. Contrary to a common belief, Covid-19 is not an external accident: it is deeply rooted in our economic systems.

One of the many and essential lessons of the current, far-reaching and long-lasting ecological-health-social-economic crisis is in fact that human

É. Laurent (✉)
OFCE/Sciences Po, Ponts ParisTech, Paris, France

Stanford University, Stanford, CA, USA
e-mail: eloi.laurent@sciencespo.fr

É. Laurent (ed.), *The Well-being Transition*,
https://doi.org/10.1007/978-3-030-67860-9_1

communities should better connect human well-being to resilience and sustainability via new ways to assess prosperity and bring those new visions to life by integrating them into new policies.

Actually, while the growth rate of gross domestic product (GDP) deeply influences government policy, and, in turn, the daily life of billions of citizens in the four corners of the planet, many facets of their existence are forgotten, neglected or sacrificed. More precisely, the three horizons of humanity in the twenty-first century—namely well-being, resilience and sustainability (Laurent 2018)—are almost completely overlooked by current economic measurement and policy.

The horizon of well-being stems from an immemorial question: What is the source of human felicity and development? Well-being can be measured objectively (through indicators that reflect the state of health or educational level) or subjectively (through the assessment happiness or trust) and at different scales geographically, it is individual and collective but in any event, it is a static metric that tells us nothing about human evolution in time.

For a dynamic approach that highlights not only the current state of well-being but also its future, we must turn to notions of resilience and sustainability. The question then becomes much more complex: Can we hope to maintain our well-being over time, and, if so, under what conditions, for how long, for whom?

Resilience, which attempts to determine whether well-being can withstand and survive shocks, is a first step in that analytical direction. Measuring and building resilience means trying to assess and improve the capacity of a community, locality, nation or the entire biosphere to cope with economic social or environmental shocks, such as the current one, without disintegrating.

The assessment of sustainability is even more ambitious and complex, as it aims to capture long-term well-being, both after the onset of shocks and in normal times. We can in this regard consider human societies as holders of a common legacy from which they derive benefits and which determines their long-term development: climate, biodiversity, natural resources, health, education, institutions, technological innovations, cities, infrastructures and so on. Attempts to assess sustainability consist in trying to understand under what conditions this legacy can be inherited, maintained and transmitted from generation to generation.

Alternative indicators to growth and GDP are about measuring and improving well-being, resilience and sustainability. A decade after the publication of the Stiglitz Report (Stiglitz et al. 2010), these alternative visions of our economic world, which flourished in the 1970s, have re-emerged from all corners of the world, at all levels of governance. Yet, GDP and growth remain very much dominant in defining public policies, influencing businesses and shaping imaginaries.

Therefore, at least two urgent tasks stand before us in order to make progress in the "well-being transition": first, connecting well-being to sustainability in a consistent framework highlighting their complementarity; second, operationalizing or institutionalizing well-being indicators, that is, integrating them into policy at all levels of governance in a democratic manner so that new insights actually lead to better outcomes. What matters ultimately are not well-being metrics but well-being policies.

The purpose of this volume is precisely to bring together key actors of the well-being community—pairing scholars with policy-makers—to advance those two agendas at a time when this progress has become a vital necessity and when the constructive criticism of GDP and growth is stronger than ever in academic and policy-making circles.

How to understand the first of these two tasks, that of a renewed integrated analysis of human and natural systems? There are at least three ways to represent and understand the ecological challenge of the first half of the twenty-first century. The first is the so-called planetary boundaries framework. The two articles by Rockström et al. (2009) and Steffen et al. (2015) that have popularized this approach have had a considerable impact (various versions of these papers having been cited to date nearly 10,000 times in the academic literature).

However, this model suffers from a serious flaw: the biospheric "limits" it considers and attempts to assess empirically, considered in isolation, are presented as falling within the scope of physics or chemistry (the authors speak of "biophysical thresholds" not to be crossed). However, our ecological crises are better understood not in terms of biophysical problems but rather in terms of social-ecological issues, bringing into play the differentiated responsibility and vulnerability of human groups confronted with environmental crises of which they are both the agents and the victims.

The 1.5 or 2 degrees of warming mentioned in the Paris Agreement are indeed chosen borders rather than objective boundaries, frontiers whose human design will determine the fate of hundreds of millions of people in coming years. Ecological crises are to be understood as social issues with two simple questions in mind: What social causes generate them? What social consequences do they induce in return? This is the whole point of the social-ecological approach.

This is where the framework of the "Donut economy" comes in. Initially proposed by Kate Raworth in an Oxfam working paper in 2012

(Raworth 2012), it purports to add a social floor (made up of 11 societal variables such as "food security, water and sanitation or health care") to the "ecological ceiling" (made up of the 9 planetary boundaries, including "core boundaries" such as biodiversity and climate change).

Between the floor and the ceiling, writes Raworth, there is a space—which is shaped like a donut—harboring an environmentally safe and socially just space in which humanity can thrive. She explains that her framework highlights the interconnected nature of the social, environmental and economic dimensions of sustainable development. But the interconnection is precisely, on the contrary, what is missing from this representation.

The challenge is to grasp and represent the interrelation, the articulation, the interweaving and not the simple juxtaposition or parallelism between social systems and natural systems. It is, therefore, necessary that the circles are put in contact in one way or another. The image of concentric circles, with the different dimensions of human well-being at the center and ecosystems at the periphery, already makes it possible to visualize the embedding of economic and social systems within the biosphere (Laurent 2018 and Laurent 2019).

But we can and should go further in attempting to integrate social and natural circles. One possibility is to sketch a social-ecological feedback loop (Fig. 1.1) which reproduces the mathematical symbol of infinity but

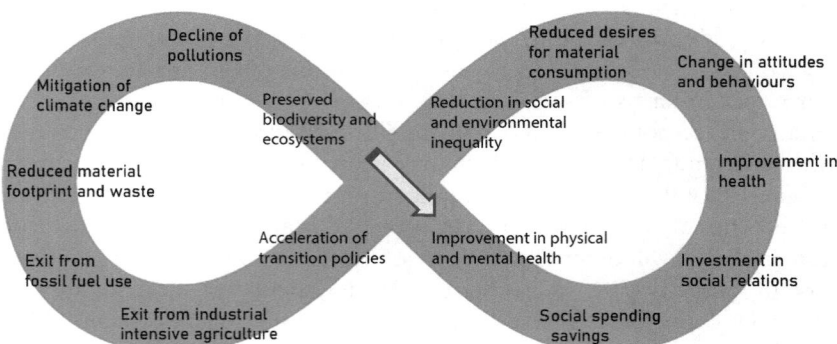

Fig. 1.1   The social-ecological feedback loop. Source: author

also evokes a "Möbius strip" (a figure that has inspired the recycling logo and by extension the circular economy).

This stylized representation puts in motion dynamic social-ecological synergies (that is to say, deep and lasting convergence between social and natural systems) and makes it possible to highlight two essential nodes or nexuses connecting ecological interdependence and social cooperation: the link between ecosystem health and human health; the link between social inequalities and ecological crises, or more positively, the sustainability-justice nexus.

The essential node of the social-ecological feedback loop links the health of ecosystems and the health of humans. Health appears to be the key to human development under ecological constraints because it is the interface between human systems and ecosystems. "Full health" (as we spoke in the twentieth century of "full employment") means human health understood in all its ramifications and implications (physical health, mental health, social ties, happiness, inequalities, social health, environmental health, environmental inequalities, ecosystem contributions). Full health is, therefore, understood as the health of a humanity fully aware of the vital importance of its environment and whose economic systems have meaning and a future only if they are embedded in the biosphere, which gave them life, nourishes them and will carry them in its collapse if it should happen.

Articulating social and natural systems highlights countless co-benefits. For example, investing in social relationships can have both health and ecological benefits. The link between the quality of social life and physical and physiological health is remarkably strong. The link between social isolation and materialism is less clear but nevertheless well established. There is, therefore, many reasons to believe that people living in a society centered on the quality of social ties and not the consumption of material goods will be in much better health, which will lead them to devote more attention and resources to the preservation of their environment, which is the ultimate guarantor of their health.

Full health also reconciles long- and short-time horizons, because it is also the best resistance here and now to the natural violence of ecological crises. Health is at once a compass and a shield that allows us to prepare for the future while facing the present. The devastating impact of the Covid-19 pandemic—the origin of which is the destruction of the environment—on a country like France, considered to be one of the most advanced countries in the world in terms of healthcare systems, offers a striking illustration of the health vulnerability in the face of ecological challenges.

But we can also, conversely, positively demonstrate the relevance of the essential link postulated at the heart of the social-ecological loop between human health and ecosystem health. Hundreds of meticulous and robust studies have resulted in a real mapping of the health benefits of biodiversity and ecosystems (Laurent 2020a).

The sustainability-justice nexus is the other key nexus in Fig. 1.1 (for an overview, see Laurent 2020b and Laurent 2021a), with justice understood as the lever and the goal of transition policies. The first dimension of the social-ecological approach to inequality may be described as integrated in the sense that it is aimed at showing that the environmental impact of the worsening of absolute forms of inequality (e.g., poverty), as well as relative inequality (e.g., income gap), is suffered, to a varying degree, by everyone (with the perimeter of the affected community being, however, subject to variation from the global to the local level). Thus, on the global level, the negative relation between poverty and preservation of biodiversity, empirically well documented, leads to a common impoverishment for humanity (the destruction of animal and plant species in the Amazon regions is damaging to the whole world). At the local level, the pollution of the water supply of a Chinese village because of the exorbitant power wielded, with the complicity of the local authorities, by a chemical plant established close by affects all the inhabitants. Social inequality indeed brings in its wake a host of harmful consequences now abundantly described in the academic literature on climate change, biodiversity and ecosystems.

But it is conversely necessary to recognize that environmental crises, fueled by inequality, themselves engender further inequality insofar as those hardest hit by them, on the international as on the intra-national level, are the most vulnerable sections of the population: this is the differential dimension of social-ecology. Observed from this standpoint, the emergence of environmental inequality calls for adequate social-ecological policy (again, see Laurent 2020b).

In sum, for the well-being transition to make significant progress on the analytical front, two nexuses of the well-being/sustainability relation have to be highlighted and explored further: the nexus between inequality and sustainability and the nexus between ecosystems health and human health. This is precisely what the chapters in the first part of this volume,

"Connecting Well-being to Sustainability: The Inequality and Health Nexuses", attempt to do.

Jean Jouzel and Stéphane Dion, key actors of climate science and policy for the last 30 years, first shed light on the "inequality and sustainability nexus". In "Climate Change and Climate Justice", Jouzel examines this link between climate change and inequalities both worldwide, through the IPCC perspective, and in France. In "Practicing Climate Justice: Negotiating Just Transitions in Canada and on the World Stage", Dion highlights the extent to which considerations of equity and justice are essential to forge collective action against climate change through four case studies in which he played a lead role.

The "Health and sustainability nexus" is then explored by Denis Zmirou-Navier in his contribution "Health and the Environment: Understanding the Linkages and Synergies". Zmirou-Navier reviews how public health, at local, national or world levels, is largely impacted by environmental factors and how public policies may alleviate, or aggravate, the health consequences of the current world economy pattern that deeply alters the environment. In "Toward Health-Environment Policy in a Wellbeing Economy", a group of scholars and activists convened by the well-being alliance (WEAll)—Éloi Laurent, Fabio Battaglia, Giorgia Dalla Libera Marchiori, Alessandro Galli, Amanda Janoo, Raluca Munteanu and Claire Sommer—attempt to develop and illustrate a co-beneficial approach between ecosystems and human systems sustaining a well-being economy, with health as the great connector. Finally, Julien Caudeville, in his contribution "Operationalizing the Health-Environment Nexus: Measuring Environmental Health Inequalities to Inform Policy" attempts to contribute to the development of policy-relevant environmental health inequality indicators.

But this revolution in how we see the world has to be accompanied by practical progress in how we can change it. The well-being transition should be a transition in institutions and policies.

In fact, it can be said that the criticism of economic growth is now in its third, political age (Laurent 2021b).[1] The first age, the age of philosophical criticism, is as old as the industrial revolution itself. It was born with the questioning by John Stuart Mill of the finality purpose of the economy. The question asked by Mill in Chapter VI of Book IV ("Of the Stationary State") of his Principles of Political Economy (1848) is that of

[1] This typology is taken from Laurent (2021b).

the fundamental purpose of economic activity: "To what goal? Towards what ultimate point is society tending by its industrial progress?"

In a series of papers published between 1972 and 1973, economists William Nordhaus and James Tobin contributed to the advent of the second age of growth criticism, the empirical age, picking up on the acknowledgment of Simon Kuznets himself, the inventor of GDP, that it was not a measure of human welfare. They indeed suggested that "growth" (understood as the increase of real gross domestic product or GDP in real terms) had become "obsolete" and attempted for the first time to offer not just an ethical or theoretical criticism of economic growth, but also a statistical alternative to GDP in the form of a "Measure of Economic Welfare (MEW)" (Nordhaus and Tobin, 1973).

This research and policy-making agenda has greatly expanded since then. In the last decade alone since the beginning of the "great recession", dozens of commissions have produced as many reports and hundreds of welfare and sustainability indicator proposals have emerged, some ready for use. As a culmination of this unprecedented effort, the United Nations adopted in September 2015 a scoreboard of 17 "Sustainable Development Goals" or "SDGs", designed to guide development policies in the coming years, where GDP plays only a minor role (as part of goal 8).

With the adoption of the SDGs has come the third age of alternative indicators: the age of institutionalization. This is what the chapters in the second part of this volume, "From Well-being Metrics to Well-being Policies", stand for.

"Building a well-being policy" opens with Anders Hayden's contribution "From Fantasy to Transformation: Steps in the Policy Use of 'Beyond-GDP' Indicators" that considers various steps in the use of beyond-GDP measurement, ranging from the "indicators fantasy"—the idea that simply producing alternative indicators is sufficient to generate substantially different policy outcomes—to transformative change involving a shift in societal priorities beyond growth or changes to other core features of the economic and social system. Florence Jany-Catrice and Dominique Méda, in their contribution "The Forum for Alternative Indicators of Wealth: Beyond GDP, Democratically", train a spotlight on a hybrid collective made up of academics and activists involved in the development of new indicators of wealth, known in French as the "Forum pour d'Autres Indicateurs de Richesse (FAIR)" which initial aim was to encourage the Stiglitz Commission to take into consideration citizens' expectations in its deliberations on the representation of "what counts". In "Building the

Transition Together: WEAll's Perspective on Creating a Wellbeing Economy", Rabia Abrar outlines the purpose for which the Wellbeing Economy Alliance (WEAll) was created, its evolution over time and examples of Wellbeing Economy policies being put into practice to shift the economic system toward a Wellbeing Economy, as these examples can serve as inspiration for how policy-makers can implement policies to make a Wellbeing Economy a reality. Finally, Éloi Laurent and Michael Flood, in their contribution "In Well-being We Trust: The Nova Scotia Quality of Life Initiative", present the Nova Scotia Quality of Life Initiative (NSQoL), led by Engage Nova Scotia using the Canadian Index of Wellbeing (CIW) measurement tool, as a leading example of the salience of subnational initiatives in advancing the well-being transition. They argue that a trust-based approach to well-being initiatives equates to their success and sustainability in the near and long term.

The last chapters' ensemble in the volume, "Well-being policies, from global to local" opens with a contribution from Xavier Ragot, "Can Global Capitalism Produce Global Well-being?" where Ragot distinguishes what is national in the well-being transition from what requires international coordination, the prime example of which is the ecological transition and argues that the perception of a fair distribution of efforts is essential, for both national and international coordination. Marie Toussaint, in her contribution "Integrating Environmental Justice into EU Policymaking", shows that if the EU sincerely intends to deliver on a well-being economy and pursue a just transition, it must embrace environmental rights and address environmental justice. Xavier Timbeau pleads for "European indicators and governance for the twenty-first century" and for the reform of European governance which must include new objectives, such as social issues or transition to a zero net emission society and new instruments better suited for efficient collective action. In her closing contribution, "Is Resilience Measurable?", Magali Reghezza-Zitt reminds us of the importance of resilience in the perspective of the well-being transition but also of its shortcomings and even perils.

The Covid-19 crisis and the subsequent lock-downs of large parts of humanity have triggered and renewed fundamental questions about the true finality not only of the economy but also of human existence, many of which were initiated well before this crisis. Among those, the need to define what is really essential to human well-being stands out: What do we really need? What can we actually do without? What should we do without? In closing of this volume with my contribution "Taking Care of

Essential Well-being in the 'Century of the Environment'", I try to shed light on these complex questions that will determine in the very short-run public policies and shape them for years to come, on the long road ahead of the well-being transition.

REFERENCES

Laurent, É. (2018). *Measuring tomorrow: Accounting for well-being, resilience and sustainability in the 21st century.* Oxford and Princeton: Princeton University Press.

Laurent, E. (2019). *Sortir de la croissance—Mode d'emploi.* Paris: Editions Les Liens qui Libèrent.

Laurent, E. (2020a). *Et si la santé guidait le monde? L'espérance de vie vaut mieux que la croissance.* Paris: Editions Les Liens qui Libèrent.

Laurent, E. (2020b). *The new environmental economics: Sustainability and justice.* Cambridge: Polity Books.

Laurent, E. (2021a). From the welfare state to the social-ecological state. In E. Laurent & K. Zwickl (Eds.), *The Routledge handbook of the political economy of the environment (forthcoming).* London: Routledge.

Laurent, É. (2021b). Integrating well-being indicators in budgetary procedures: Four shades of sincerity. In A. Hayden, C. Gaudet, & J. Wilson (Eds.), *Beyond GDP, toward sustainable wellbeing: International experiences, Canada's options.* Toronto: University of Toronto Press.

Nordhaus, W., & Tobin, J. (1973). *"Is Growth Obsolete?" in The Measurement of Economic and Social Performance,* ed. Milton Moss. New York: National Bureau of Economic Research.

Raworth, K. (2012). A safe operating space for humanity: Can we live within the doughnut, Discussion Paper, Oxford, Oxfam. https://www-cdn.oxfam.org/s3fs-public/file_attachments/dp-a-safe-and-just-space-for-humanity-130212-en_5.pdf

Rockström, J., et al. (2009). A safe operating space for humanity. *Nature, 461,* 472–475.

Stiglitz, J. E., Sen, A. K., & Fitoussi, J.-P. (2010). *Report by the commission on the measurement of economic performance and social progress.* Paris: *Commission on the Measurement of Economic Performance and Social Progress.*

Steffen, W., et al. (2015). Planetary boundaries: Guiding human development on a changing planet. *Science, 347,* 1.

PART I

Connecting Well-being to Sustainability: The Justice-sustainability Nexus

CHAPTER 2

Climate Change and Climate Justice

Jean Jouzel

Introduction

From 1994 to 2015, I have been deeply involved in the IPCC process as one of the lead author of the second and third reports and then as a bureau member for the fourth and fifth reports. My own field of research is about the reconstruction of past climate changes largely from the study of deep ice cores drilled in Antarctica and Greenland. In turn, my involvement with the IPCC was mainly at the level of working group I, dealing with the physical basis of climate change. Naturally, I have had during these 20 years—and still have—a profound interest for other aspects of climate change as assessed by working groups II about impacts, adaptation and vulnerability, in which these aspects dealing with inequalities are treated, and working group III which addresses mitigation of climate change. Moreover, I have had the opportunity to attend the sessions during which the summaries for policymakers of these reports have been approved.

J. Jouzel (✉)
Laboratoire des Sciences du Climat/Institut Pierre Simon Laplace, CEA-CNRS-UVSQ, Gif-sur-Yvette, France
e-mail: jean.jouzel@lsce.ipsl.fr

É. Laurent (ed.), *The Well-being Transition*,
https://doi.org/10.1007/978-3-030-67860-9_2

13

In fact, over the last 30 years, the IPCC has given increasing attention to the fact that risks associated with anthropogenic climate warming are unequally distributed and are generally more significant for underprivileged communities and people at all levels of development. In its fifth report (IPCC 2014), it has concluded that "people who are socially, economically, culturally, politically, institutionally, or otherwise marginalized are especially vulnerable to climate change and also to some adaptation and mitigation responses". One year later, this clear statement was echoed in the Paris Agreement (2015) though in a very weak manner simply noting "the importance for some of the concept of climate justice, when taking action to address climate change" and stating that this agreement "will be implemented to reflect equity… in the light of different national circumstances". Risks of inequalities associated with anthropogenic climate change are further explored in the IPCC special report "Global Warming of 1.5 °C" (IPCC 2018) with a dedicated chapter "Sustainable Development, Poverty Eradication and Reducing Inequalities" and, again, resounding statement: limiting global warming to 1.5 °C rather than 2 °C would make it markedly easier to achieve many aspects of sustainable development, with greater potential to eradicate poverty and reduce inequalities.

Indeed, there is little doubt that inequalities associated with climate warming will increase along with its amplitude. In this context, one can choose to define "climate justice" as aiming to do everything possible to stop global warming from increasing these inequalities (Jouzel and Michelot 2016). Obviously, given climate science, one should limit long-term future global warming well below 2 °C above preindustrial levels and pursue efforts to limit this temperature increase to 1.5 °C above preindustrial levels, the objective of the Paris Agreement. However, even limited to 2 °C, global warming will have consequences which our society will have to adapt to with, in the absence of measures, the risk of increasing inequalities between those who have the means to adapt and those who do not. In turn, for a successful well-being transition, the focus of this book, this objective of the Paris Agreement should be pursued in a spirit of "climate justice" this notion being defined as above, for example, with the objective to avoid increasing inequalities.

My participation in the French Economic, Social and Environmental Council (ESEC) gave me another opportunity to address this issue of climate justice. The IPCC and numerous other reports make us well aware of the vulnerability of certain countries and populations who hardly contribute to greenhouse gas emissions. But vulnerability also concerns developed countries in which the poor strata of populations could be the most vulnerable to climate change (IPCC 2014). Along with my colleague Agnès Michelot, an environmental law specialist, we attempted to analyze this risk of global warming through the lens of increasing inequalities within France and produced, on behalf of the section of Environment, the ESEC's opinion entitled "Climate justice: challenges and prospects for France" (Jouzel and Michelot 2016).

It is along these two lines, the IPCC assessments at the international level and the ESEC's opinion, at the national level, that I will examine in this chapter the link between climate change and climate justice.

CLIMATE CHANGE AND INEQUALITIES: A GLOBAL PERSPECTIVE

Changes in climate have already caused impacts on all continents and across the oceans and, with no surprise, future impacts and their consequences will be more important for larger warmings. This is clearly illustrated in IPCC (2014) that adopts a global perspective on climate-related risks under five categories associated with different "reasons for concern". For each of them additional risk due to climate change, when a temperature level is reached and then sustained or exceeded, ranges from undetectable to very high risk with intermediate levels, moderate and high.[1] All have impacts on human systems either directly or through their impact on natural systems which provide services for livelihoods. For example, there are risks due to storm surges, coastal flooding and sea level in low-lying coastal zones and small island developing states and other small islands, and due to inland flooding in some regions potentially affecting large urban populations. Risks also result from extreme weather events leading to breakdown of infrastructure networks and critical services such as electricity, water supply, and health and emergency services. Periods of extreme heat are associated with increased mortality and morbidity particularly for vulnerable urban populations and those working outdoors in urban or rural areas while risk of food insecurity and the breakdown of food systems are linked to warming, drought, flooding and precipitation variability and extremes, particularly for poorer populations in urban and rural settings.

---

[1] The definition of these five categories is fully explained in IPCC (2014) in which key risks are identified which contribute to one or more "reasons for concern".

Another example concerns the risk of loss of rural livelihoods and income due to insufficient access to drinking and irrigation water and reduced agricultural productivity, particularly for farmers and pastoralists with minimal capital in semi-arid regions.

Higher warming increases the likelihood of severe, pervasive and irreversible impacts. Global climate change risks are high to very high with a global mean temperature increase of 4 °C or more above preindustrial levels for all categories of risks. They include severe and widespread impacts on unique and threatened systems, substantial species extinction, large risks to global and regional food security, and the combination of high temperature and humidity compromising normal human activities, including growing food or working outdoors in some areas for parts of the year. The risk associated with crossing multiple tipping points in the earth system (thresholds for an abrupt and irreversible change) or in interlinked human and natural systems also increases with rising temperature.

The Paris Agreement has opened the possibility to avoid long-term global warming reaching up to 4 °C to 5 °C above preindustrial level but this is not warranted yet. And, even if all nationally determined contributions (NDCs) were fulfilled during the period covered by this agreement (2020–2030), this long-term warming could exceed 3 °C. Reaching the 2 °C objective will only be possible if these NDCs were globally multiplied by 3 over the coming 10 years, and by 5 for 1.5 °C. And carbon neutrality is required to stabilize global warming, between 2070 and 2080 for the 2 °C objective, and as soon as 2050 for 1.5 °C.

Even if limited at 2 °C above preindustrial levels, some risks are considerable and in this respect each half degree counts (IPCC 2018). Limiting warming to 1.5 °C rather than 2 °C could reduce the number of people exposed to climate risks and vulnerable to poverty by 62 to 457 million and this would also lessen the risks of poor people to experience food and water insecurity, adverse health impacts and economic losses, particularly in regions that already face development challenges (IPCC 2018). Avoided impacts between 1.5 °C and 2 °C warming would also make it easier to achieve certain Sustainable Development Goals (SDGs) including targets to reduce poverty such as those that relate to hunger, health, water and sanitation, cities and ecosystems. Even if long-term warming is limited at such levels, adaptation, which in some particular cases may entrench vulnerabilities and also have the potential to enforce inequalities, will be necessary.

IPCC reports (2014, 2018) point to the fact that many of the most vulnerable countries have contributed and contribute little to greenhouse gas emissions while climate change impacts are expected to exacerbate poverty in most of these developing countries. Intuitively, we understand that most of the risks we have briefly evoked will increase inequalities there. This is fully confirmed as climate change impacts are projected to slow down economic development, make poverty reduction more difficult, further erode food security and prolong existing poverty traps and create new ones, the latter particularly in urban areas and emerging hotspots of hunger. In addition, climate change interacts with non-climatic stressors and entrenched structural inequalities to shape vulnerabilities. However, although there is growing literature on climate change and gender as well as on indigeneity, other axes such as age, class, race, caste and (dis)ability remain underexplored.

Among the numerous examples that IPCC reports provide to illustrate how climate change will increase inequalities, one can cite two related to urban areas (IPCC 2014). First management such as the privatization of urban water supply and sanitation systems can advantage specific groups over others. Conversely, community-based solutions that also build social capital can be a component in generating urban resilience. However, even these solutions may exacerbate inequality at the city level, with only those local areas with strong levels of social capital being able to benefit most from community-led action or garner support from international and national partners. Second, population living in informal settlements will not be protected by insurance because of their low ability to pay and the high transaction costs for companies of administering many small policies. Low-income groups rely instead on local solidarity and government assistance when disaster hits. In addition, where risk levels exceed certain thresholds, insurers will abandon coverage or set premiums unaffordable to those at risk.

This anticipated increase of inequalities with the creation of new poverty pockets is not limited to the poorest countries on which the majority of research on the poverty-climate nexus remains focused. This risk also exists for developed countries and indeed very limited research examines climate change impacts on poor people and livelihoods in middle- to high-income countries. However, there is mounting evidence of observed impacts of climatic events on the poor in such countries, as documented for the European heatwave, the ten-year drought in Australia, and Hurricane Katrina in the USA. This example of Katrina clearly illustrates the propensity of natural disasters to victimize society's poorest and most vulnerable; these poorest populations were less well prepared before Katrina and had more difficulties to leave New Orleans during this devastating hurricane and, after it, all along the reconstruction phase (Mutter 2015).

I now examine this aspect of climate change and inequalities in developed countries through the ESEC's opinion on "Climate justice" (Jouzel and Michelot 2016).

CLIMATE CHANGE AND INEQUALITIES: THE CASE OF FRANCE

As a member of the Economic, Social and Environmental Council (ESEC)—the third constitutional assembly in France—since 2010, I am involved in its "section de l'environnement", chaired by Anne-Marie Ducroux. In December 2015, the notion of climate justice was included in the Paris Agreement and, at the initiative of my colleague Agnès Michelot, the idea of focusing an opinion on climate justice at the national level was proposed in early 2016 and was approved by the ESEC bureau. Our section was then tasked to draft an opinion on "Climate justice: challenge and prospects for France" and we were with Agnès Michelot appointed as rapporteurs. The full draft of this opinion has been adopted by 152 votes to 15 and 15 abstentions in September 2016. For the ESEC, which supports the fight against all forms of inequality, the key aim of this opinion was to contribute to public policies which will help to limit and, if possible, to reduce social and economic inequalities caused by global warming on a national level. Before focusing on these recommendations (see also Jouzel and Michelot 2020), it is useful to briefly review some characteristics of climate change in France and the associated risks of increasing inequalities.

Since the beginning of the twenty-first century, metropolitan France has experienced warming close to 1.3 °C higher than its global average value and in about 20 years, its climate will be characterized by an increase in average temperatures of between 0.6 and 1.3 °C, all seasons combined. Beyond 2050, much greater warming would be observed in the case of an emitting scenario with, at the end of the century, a sharp increase in average temperatures of up to 5 °C in summer (Ouzeau et al. 2014). The summer of 2003, about 3 °C warmer than the average summer of the twentieth century, would then become the norm in the second part of this century. During heatwaves record temperatures could, in certain regions, occasionally exceed 50 °C. In addition an urban heat islands is characteristic of large cities (in 2003, temperatures were, at the end of the night, 4–7 °C warmer in Paris than in the inner suburbs). Precipitation will tend to increase in winter and decrease in summer with a deficit that could exceed 50% around the Mediterranean Sea. Thus, drought episodes would increase in a large part of southern France, which does not protect these regions from "Mediterranean" events causing flash floods, episodes which could become more frequent and potentially more intense.

The rise in sea level will accelerate according to the rate of greenhouse gas emissions, with the risk of reaching up to one meter by 2100 in the case of an emitting scenario. Sea level rise would then become the main cause of the aggravation of the flood hazard: the regions of Languedoc, the Rhone delta and Aquitaine are particularly concerned but the rest of the Atlantic coast, certain coasts of Hauts de France and the plain of eastern Corsica are also affected. Up to a million people in these coastal regions could be affected by at least one flood every year from 2050. In practice, all the consequences identified on a global scale must be taken into account for our country: loss of biodiversity, modifications of natural ecosystems, reduction in agricultural yields, impacts on viticulture and forests, increase risk of forest fires, acidification of the ocean with consequences on oceanic productivity and on coral reefs. And that is just as worrying on the side of the populations: in the hypothesis of a warming of 3 °C, two-thirds of Europeans could be affected by climatic disasters in the absence of appropriate adaptation measures. Each year, around 350 million Europeans could then be exposed to harmful climatic extremes, 14 times more than at the beginning of the 2000s and the number of deaths associated with these extremes would increase considerably. Compared to the turn of the century, people living in southern Europe, Italy, Greece, Spain and southern France, with 64 times more deaths, should be the hardest hit. At the origin of 99% of deaths, heat waves are expected to have the deadliest effects.

As in metropolitan France, global warming will be perceptible in the overseas territories but generally at a slightly slower rate. As for tropical cyclones, their frequency should either not be changed or be reduced, but the most intense could become even more intense in terms of maximum wind speed and intensity of precipitation, especially those that will reach the coasts of America from North and Central America; this also applies to many islands in the Pacific.

To my knowledge, we have no quantitative estimates of the relative influence of these extreme events on low income with respect to high-income populations on a national basis, but intuitively, the former should be more affected in the majority of situations. For example, in the case of intense heatwaves in the Paris area, low-income populations have often no possibility to leave this area for a few days, or a few weeks. Populations living in flood-prone areas in departments such as Hérault, Gard and Aude subject to Mediterranean events which are likely to intensify do not have the means to leave their difficult-to-sell house and this could be also the case in certain coastal regions subject to the risk of submersion. And one can think that low-income populations were less well prepared and had more difficulty coping with devastating hurricanes like Irma, which in 2017 destroyed many homes on the islands of Saint-Martin and Saint Bartholomew (this vulnerability of low-income populations is well documented for Hurricane Harvey which devastated Houston area one week earlier—see Guivarch and Taconet 2020).

Note also that almost all sectors of our economy are concerned: health, water resources, biodiversity, natural hazards, agriculture, forestry, fishing and aquaculture, energy and industry, infrastructure and transport systems, urban planning and the built environment, tourism, financing and insurance and so on with consequences as increased unemployment rate which in many sectors affects more directly low-income population. Also, all of these sectors—some of which contribute to emissions of greenhouse gases—are more or less affected by climate change and must prepare for it by considering appropriate adaptation measures. However, some measures proposed or taken with the aim to diminish our emissions or to adapt to climate change can generate inequalities. The planned increase in the carbon tax, triggering the "yellow vests" crisis, provides an example. This increase was unfair in the sense that, in a relative way, it affects more, and was rejected, by the low-income population, in particular by people who have to take their car to get to work.

As noted by the Haut Conseil sur le Climat (2019), an increase of the climate-energy contribution at the level initially planned for 2022 coupled with the modification on the taxation of diesel would have represented an effort of almost 1% of disposable income for the poorest 10% of households against 0.3% for the top 10% richest.

In this context of increasing inequalities linked to climate change, the ESEC has built a definition of climate justice at the national level based on the objectives that climate justice must pursue in terms of the fight against inequalities, considering that the failure to take into account the impact of climate change in public policies could increase the risks of social divide. The recommendations included in this opinion (Jouzel and Michelot 2016) have the ambition to create synergies between economic, social and environmental policies.

In this perspective, the ESEC recommends that strategies for combating and adapting to climate change be integrated into the policy for combating poverty and be evaluated with regard to their benefits for the poorest 20%. The recommendations also concern the national adaptation plan (PNACC) which should account for the concept of climate justice—which has since been done—and should also be integrated into the policy of fight against poverty. The ESEC also recommends that the ecological transition is prepared and supported by the training of workers according to the sectors of activity and that the most disadvantaged populations can benefit from training and job creation linked to the implementation of the ecological transition.

The ESEC seeks to support better integration of social and intergenerational justice into investment programs and projects. This requires that impact studies take into account how the most disadvantaged populations are affected by climate change, and by revising the rules for socio-economic evaluation of investment projects that the State applies to its own financing. This involves supplementing the calculation of a net present value or an internal global rate of return with an analysis of the redistributive effects regarding the most disadvantaged people and by setting an adjustment rate which better takes into account the well-being of future generations.

For the ESEC, climate justice should make it possible to promote practices and investments that strengthen the quality of employment in sectors that hire people, such as construction, waste management or circular economy. From the perspective of social, financial and fiscal equalization, the ESEC recommends carbon taxation to be able to be adjusted socially through the establishment of a system of progressivity, which has not been the case for the initially planned increase of this carbon tax. Another area attracts the attention of the ESEC, that of insurance policies, because it is becoming urgent to prepare for reforming the cover of climate risks in general and of the natural disaster schemes in particular, both to maintain national solidarity and to allow the poorest people to access insurance.

The ESEC also points to the need for supporting research with a focus on the consequences of global warming at regional scales and on "Climate services" intended to facilitate the implementation of mitigation and adaptation measures, in particular the prevention of risks linked to extreme phenomena, heat waves, floods, droughts, cyclones in overseas territories. The interactions between these climatic extremes and the health of populations deserve to be better understood. Work on the evolution of jobs, on the link between poverty and climate change, and more generally on the evolution of our societies in the face of inequalities would also be very relevant. There is also a need for studies on gender vulnerability taking into consideration the realities in different territories and a more significant risk culture in overseas France.

Via their impact on public policies, in particular, these recommendations should help to limit, and if possible, to reduce social and economic inequalities caused by global warming on the French population.

CONCLUSION

The notion of climate justice that this chapter has tried to explore and illustrate goes beyond the global and national levels on which I have focused here.

First, this notion has been discussed at the European level—and I anticipate in many other national and international contexts—with an opinion of the European Economic and Social Committee (Lohan 2017) in which it is recognized that the most vulnerable and poorest in society often suffer the greatest impact of the effects of climate change, despite these people being the least responsible for the emissions that have driven the climate crisis.

Second, developed countries should not limit their actions in favor of climate justice to their national territory as their international investments can weigh heavily in the implementation of environmental policies abroad. The ESEC expressed in this perspective the hope that a significant part of French investments will be geared toward the most vulnerable populations and in this way engage with the "Climate justice" approach, which our country committed to during the Paris Conference. Moreover, the ESEC recommends that France supports a definition of investment within the investment treaties which incorporates the principles of "Climate justice" and policies fighting climate change.

Still, the highest priority should be given to the concrete implementation of climate justice goals at the national level. The proposals presented clearly indicate that France, like many other countries, has the means to enter into an operational dimension quickly, without waiting for any consensus on a unanimously accepted definition of the concept at the international level. The objective of carbon neutrality in 2050 was indeed adopted unilaterally by France. By the same token, the creation of a "Citizen's Convention on Climate" which involved 150 citizens drawn by lot whose mandate was "to define structuring measures to achieve, in a spirit of social justice, to reduce greenhouse gas emissions by at least 40% in 2030 compared to 1990", was a significant advance in recognizing the importance of climate justice as a solution to climate change. Climate justice is an essential goal so that young people of today and tomorrow can, in the second part of this century, adapt to climate change instead of being ruled by climate change.

References

Guivarch, C., & Taconet, M. (2020). Inégalités mondiales et changement climatique. *Revue de l'OFCE, 165*, 37–69.

Haut Conseil pour le Climat. (2019). Agir en cohérence avec les ambitions, rapport annuel.

IPCC, Climate Change. (2014). *Impacts, adaptation, and vulnerability. Global and sectoral aspects.* Contribution of Working Group II to the Fifth Assessment Report. Cambridge, UK and New York, NY: Cambridge University Press.

IPCC. (2018). Global warming of 1.5°C.

Jouzel, J., & Michelot, A. (2016). Climate justice: Challenges and prospects for France ESEC opinion.

Jouzel, J., & Michelot, A. (2020). Quelle justice climatique pour la France. *Revue de l'OFCE, 165*, 74–96.

Lohan, C. (2017). La justice climatique, Comité Economique et social européen, Avis d'initiative.

Mutter, J. (2015). *Disaster profiteers: How natural disasters make the rich richer and the poor even poorer.* St. Martin's Press, St. Martin's Publishing Group, 288 p.

Ouzeau, G., Déqué, M., Jouini, M., Planton, S., & Vautard, R. (2014). Sous la direction de Jean Jouzel. Le climat de la France, au XXIe siècle, Volume 4, Scénarios régionalisés pour la métropole et les régions d'outre-mer.

CHAPTER 3

Practicing Climate Justice: Negotiating Just Transitions in Canada and on the World Stage

Stéphane Dion

Twenty-one years of experience as a Canadian parliamentarian, followed by three years as a Canadian diplomat in Europe, have allowed me to participate in or observe various climate negotiations and debates in Canada, in Europe and on the international scene. Over these years in public life, one of my main goals has been to contribute to the development of an effective climate change policy in Canada, one which would decrease greenhouse gas (GHG) emissions and, at the same time, benefit the economy and the social fabric of my country. I pursued this same goal on the world stage, trying to contribute to the development of a global climate agreement that would meet the four criteria by which it should be evaluated: "environmental effectiveness, aggregate economic performance, distributional impacts, and institutional feasibility" (Stavins et al. 2014).

For both Canada and the world, I recognized that taking into account the issues of justice and equity were essential factors in the quest for

S. Dion (✉)
Canadian Dipomat, Ottawa, ON, Canada

© The Author(s), under exclusive license to Springer Nature Switzerland AG 2021
É. Laurent (ed.), *The Well-being Transition*,
https://doi.org/10.1007/978-3-030-67860-9_3

success. That is the point that I will highlight in this chapter. Indeed, one of the conditions for the successful negotiation of an action plan to address the climate change crisis is linked to the imperatives of justice. Negotiators will only be able to agree if they think that what is asked of each of them is fair and equitable compared to what is required of others.

In various capacities, I have participated in numerous debates regarding three climate plans in Canada, and I have chaired a Conference of Parties (COP), the yearly United Nations climate conference. I will succinctly review these four processes—one after the other—not to report their idiosyncratic details nor their ups-and-downs, but rather to highlight via these case studies how essential equity and justice considerations are to the success of climate negotiations. I am speaking about equity and justice between individuals, but also between national, regional and/or industrial entities. For the Canadian federation, the main entities involved are the federal government and those of the ten provinces and three territories, while the UN negotiations are played out between roughly 190 countries at different stages of economic development.

Once I will have brought to light the justice-related issues underlying these four processes, I will explore the reasons why the great efforts made to give birth to climate action plans have regrettably led to results far removed from what is actually needed to stop, or at least adequately slow, global warming. We will see that these reasons are closely linked to issues of equity and justice.

To build this argumentation, I will draw on my past writings and my observations as a Canadian diplomat in Europe over the last three years, as well as a Canadian federal politician, notably as Minister of the Environment (2004–2006), President of COP 11 in Montreal (2005) and leader of the Official Opposition (2006–2008).

Project Green (2005)

When I became the federal Minister of the Environment in 2004, Prime Minister Paul Martin entrusted me with the task of establishing, with my cabinet colleagues, a federal plan to reduce GHG emissions in Canada. We succeeded in this endeavor; however, I must confess that it was not an easy task. The main obstacle that we had to overcome was related to the geographic concentration of Canada's GHG emissions, which creates particularly thorny issues of fairness between geographic entities and between energy enterprises (Dion 2011, pp. 21a–46a).

Canada emitted 15.6 tons of equivalent CO_2 emissions per capita in 2017, more than three times over the global average, which was 4.8 tons per person (Ritchie and Roser 2019). However, the vast majority of Canadians live in provinces whose annual emissions levels per capita are not that different from the European average, in the ten-ton range. Canada's performance is considerably skewed by the exceptional outputs of two of its provinces, Alberta (67 tons per resident) and Saskatchewan (68 tons per resident). Together, in 2018, these two provinces represented 15 percent of the Canadian population, yet 48 percent of its GHG emissions (41 percent in 2005) (Environment and Climate Change Canada 2020a, p. 29).

The major GHG impact of these two provinces can be easily explained: this is where most of Canada's hydrocarbon production, including from the oil sands, originates. Furthermore, approximately 91 percent of electricity in Alberta and 83 percent in Saskatchewan are produced using fossil fuels. In contrast, electrical generation in Quebec and British Columbia is practically free of CO_2 emissions, since it essentially comes from hydroelectric power—at a rate of 95 percent in Quebec and 91 percent in British Columbia (Canada Energy Regulator 2020).

Such a geographic concentration of GHG emissions is unique to Canada and not found, at the same extent, in comparable federations like the United States, Germany or Australia (Boyce and Riddle 2009) (Macdonald et al. 2013, pp. 30, 59). Likewise, compared to Canada, the European Union (EU) is much more homogeneous, with its four largest countries emitting a relatively similar number of tons per resident: France 5.8 tons, Italy 6.0, the United Kingdom 5.8 and Germany 11.2. Although negotiations between the EU Member States are never an easy task, the relatively homogeneous level of their emissions helped to establish EU targets (first Kyoto, then Paris), as well as distribute between the Member States the GHG reductions needed to achieve them.

In 2005, each Canadian province fought aggressively for a distribution of the reduction effort based on fairness criteria favorable to their respective interests. This debate took place within the political framework of a decentralized federation, whose constitution gives the provinces jurisdiction over the development, conservation and management of non-renewable natural resources. Provinces with lesser and stable emissions favored the "polluter pays" principle, one where the heavy emitting provinces and industries will have to reduce their emissions more than others, in order to reach a uniform national target of GHG reduction. Some of those less-than-average emitting provinces promoted the principle of recognizing first movers, under which industries that have already reduced their emissions in the past should not be subjected to new reduction efforts; instead, they should be rewarded with offsets paid by heavier emitters.

The government of Alberta has always categorically refused such criteria. In its view, it is only fair that reduction efforts take into account the fact that the entire country benefits from the economic spinoffs of oil and gas extraction, as well as the fact that federal revenues raised in Alberta contributes to the revenues of most other provinces through federal equalization payments. The government of Alberta argues that taking additional money from Alberta will not be the way to come up with the billions of dollars needed to reduce its emissions.

The plan that the Government of Canada released on April 13, 2005, titled "Project Green/Projet vert", provided a coordinated set of policies supported by a GHG cap and trade system (Government of Canada 2005). It was a nationwide cap-and-trade system, with a set of mandatory regulated emission targets for heavy industry, including oil and gas, electricity generation, mining and energy-intensive manufacturing sectors, but with an intensity-based emissions reduction target and not an absolute one.

In other words, instead of being compelled to limit their emissions in comparison to the total quantity of GHG being emitted (absolute target), large final emitters were assigned maximum allowable emissions relative to some unit of economic output, such as, for example, per barrel of oil (intensity target). The choice between intensity targets and absolute targets is a fairness issue that the Government of Canada had to take into account, when developing its national plan.

As such, intensity limits are not less stringent than absolute limits. In fact, they are even more demanding in a context where output is decreasing instead of growing (Sue Wing et al. 2006). Indeed, a declining industry will obtain, because of its reduced production, an automatic reduction in its absolute volume of emissions, whereas it will still have to make special efforts to reduce them in units of production. Hence, the use of intensity targets accommodates industries with strong production growth, but is asking more from stable or shrinking industries.

Moreover, to add flexibility, Project Green allowed companies to meet their targets through a combination of reducing their own emissions, purchasing emission credits—that is, paying for emission reductions achieved elsewhere—or by payment to a Technology Investment Fund. Also, the plan created a Partnership Fund committing the federal government to fund projects with the provinces and territories aimed at reducing emissions.

Project Green, of course, did not receive unanimous support, and Alberta and the oil and gas industry continued to protest, but at least most were ready to step up to the plate. A broadly shared view was that rather than waiting for the perfect plan, Canada had to act quick with what was negotiated (Bramley 2005).

At the end of the day, however, Project Green was never implemented. The Liberal Party of Canada lost the 2006 federal election, and the new incoming government chose to disregard the plan.

The Green Shift (2008)

In 2006, I had the honor of being elected as the leader of the Liberal Party of Canada, and with this, I became the leader of the Official Opposition in Canada's House of Commons during its 39th Parliament. My aim was to provide Canada more economic prosperity, social justice and environmental sustainability in bringing these three objectives together. This led me to rethink the plan to reduce GHG emissions, in order to better link it to economic and social objectives. This is how the Liberal Party of Canada came to run in the 2008 federal election, under an ambitious plan to make Canada "richer, fairer and greener" (Liberal Party of Canada 2008a). The centerpiece of its 2008 platform was a fiscal program called "The Green Shift/Le Tournant vert" (Liberal Party of Canada 2008b). It involved setting a fair price for carbon emissions by introducing a federal carbon tax, and using accrued revenue to reduce personal and business income taxes.

It would have been a revenue-neutral fiscal reform, where every cent raised would have been returned to Canadians through tax cuts. Seventy-five percent of Canada's GHG emissions would have been taxed at up to C\$10 a ton of equivalent CO_2 in 2009, gradually rising to C\$40 by 2012.

This Green Shift would have led to substantial cuts to business income taxes, as well as tax credits for green investments and R&D, all funded out of carbon tax revenues. Hence, these business tax reliefs would have greatly stimulated investment and green innovation. Furthermore, broad-based, progressive income tax cuts would have made the tax system fairer for middle- and low-income Canadians, reducing poverty in Canada by 30 percent and, through a new universal child tax benefit, cutting child poverty in half within five years. Refundable tax credits would have supported lower-income households who, because they pay little or no income taxes, would not benefit from reductions in tax rates alone. Besides, without granting any exemptions whatsoever, the Green Shift, still using carbon tax revenues, would have provided targeted support for various groups in their efforts to reduce their emissions. That is why the plan included a Green Rural Credit, a Northern Allowance, special credits for farmers, foresters and fishers, tax benefit for low-income workers and low-income Canadians with disability, as well as credits for not-for-profit and charitable organizations.

These social measures were aimed to make the plan fair. Since carbon pricing policies increase the cost of fossil fuels, they are likely to have negative impacts on social equity, if corrective measures are not adopted. Indeed, a cap-and-trade system or a carbon tax could be rather regressive in developed countries, given that low-income households ordinarily spend a large proportion of their income on heating and transportation (Congressional Budget Office 2007, pp. 246–257) (Dorban et al. 2019) and are exposed to energy poverty (Green et al. 2016). This is particularly true in a country such as Canada, with its cold climate and great distances (Krechowicz 2011) (National Round Table on the Environment and the Economy 2009, p. 76) (Lee and Toby 2008). The Green Shift avoided this type of inequity through an aggressive progressive fiscal policy. For middle- and low-income Canadians, higher energy costs caused by carbon pricing were more than offset by broad-based progressive tax cuts. These benefits would have not only mitigated the impact of a carbon tax on low-income Canadians, but would have helped lift them out of poverty.

The idea was that, in addition to being a moral obligation, tackling climate is also an economic and social opportunity that Canada should seize, reforming its tax system in order to encourage behavior that benefits our society, like hard work and ingenuity, and discourage behavior that harms it, like pollution and waste. Businesses would have been incited to reduce the amount of greenhouse gases they emit into the atmosphere as well as to invest in innovation. The tax system would have promoted a more inclusive society with less poverty, allowing more Canadians to use their skills and talents in the workforce. In short, the aim was to tackle climate change effectively and to boost investment, innovation and social inclusion.

Economists and environmentalists agreed—for once—to approve the basis of this comprehensive fiscal reform, combining environmental, economic, and social goals, a triple dividend the government would have used to concurrently fight climate change, promote social fairness and improve the competitiveness of the economy. However, I was unable to convince Canadians of the merit of the plan and to counter the Conservative Party's effective campaign against what they called "the tax on everything". The Green Shift was also attacked by the left-wing New Democratic Party, which argued that only big business should be subject to emission-reduction targets and that ordinary taxpayers should be exempt from them—notwithstanding the fact that cap-and-trade systems, like the one proposed by that party, have first-degree impacts on individuals and families and disproportionately burden low-income households.

What also did not help the cause of the Green Shift was the fact that, just before the campaign, the price of a barrel of oil reached a historic high of US$148; this significantly decreased public support for a carbon tax. Then, during the election campaign, the Great Recession of 2008 began. The sharp rise of economic concerns did not foster an appetite for a new green action plan, unprecedented and easily spun as too radical given the circumstances. In the end, the Liberals lost the 2008 election. The re-elected Conservative federal government did not adopt any carbon pricing policy.

I remain convinced that the Green Shift tax reform was the right one for my country and inherently fair. Moreover, it was infinitely simpler to understand than the climate plans of the other parties, which were based on complicated cap-and-trade mechanisms. However, it was the Green Shift that was criticized for being too complex. I think that it is because cap-and-trade systems are opaque, mysterious concepts, so complex that nobody will even try to understand them except for a few experts and stakeholders, while a fiscal reform involving a carbon tax is simple enough to be politically attacked, even for its alleged complexity (Dion 2013, pp. 291–323).

The best is sometimes the enemy of the good. The set of fiscal measures by which the Green Shift intended to improve social justice in Canada appeared to be lacking in clarity. Simply promising to send a green rebate of the same amount for each Canadian might have won more votes. Under a so-called Tax & 100% Dividend scheme, the government would tax carbon emissions and return the totality of the proceeds back to the public on a per capita basis—making sure to stress that every citizen would receive the same amount (Hanson 2009). Perhaps more salable politically, the Tax and 100% Dividend has, however, a much weaker positive impact than the

Green Shift in terms of redressing social inequalities, as high-income and low-income taxpayers would receive the same amount before tax.

THE PAN-CANADIAN FRAMEWORK ON CLEAN GROWTH AND CLIMATE CHANGE (2016–)

The Project Green of 2005 and the Green Shift of 2008 were not replaced and so Canada remained without any federal carbon pricing policy. Then, the Liberal Party of Canada won the October 19, 2015, federal election, under the leadership of Justin Trudeau. One of the Liberal Party's electoral commitments was to establish a carbon pricing policy for Canada.

When the new federal government began its mandate, Canadian climate policy had become driven largely by provinces. A major difference compared to the context of 2005 or 2008 is that by 2015, provinces had made progress in implementing their programs to combat climate change. The newly formed federal government had to take this reality into account. The four most populous provinces, representing 86 percent of the Canadian population (Ontario, Quebec, British Columbia and Alberta) had or were planning to have carbon pricing regimes in place. Alberta's plan especially was praised in an OECD report released in 2017: "In this challenging context, the province has become one of the first fossil-fuel based economies in the world to implement ambitious carbon pricing" (OECD 2017b, p. 139). However, on April 16, 2019, the Alberta general election resulted in a new provincial government that rejected part of this plan and, in particular, repealed its provincial fuel charge. Similarly, on July 3, 2018, the newly elected government of Ontario ended the climate plan of its predecessor, including its cap-and-trade pollution pricing system.

However, back in the fall of 2015, the support of the provinces seemed encouraging. After a year of negotiations with the ten provinces and three territories, the federal government announced, in December 2016, the "Pan-Canadian Framework on Clean Growth and Climate Change/Le Cadre pancanadien sur la croissance propre et les changements climatiques" (Government of Canada 2016). At that time only one province, Saskatchewan, opposed it. The plan was detailed in the law that followed, the 2018 Greenhouse Gas Pollution Pricing Act, and via a series of regulations (Government of Canada 2019b).

One of this plan's primary objectives is to enable Canada to achieve the GHG reduction target that it committed to under the 2015 Paris

Agreement, which is, reducing GHG emissions by 30 percent below 2005 levels by 2030. According to the OECD, "this is demanding in terms of reducing emissions intensity", considering that under a business as usual scenario—that is without any additional measures—Canada's annual GHG emissions, which in 2015 were 722 megaton (MT) of CO_2e (carbon dioxide equivalent), would reach 815 MT in 2030, while the reduction target by 2030 is 511 MT (OECD 2017b, p. 20).

Like the aforementioned 2005 and 2008 plans, this new federal initiative covers all the essential aspects of a comprehensive GHG emissions reduction plan: a new standard for the use of biofuels; strict regulation of emissions of short-lived climate pollutants such as methane, hydrofluorocarbons and black carbon; zero energy-ready building codes; increased carbon storage in forests and agricultural lands; phase-out of coal power plants; and major investments in clean technology, renewable energy, low carbon economy, green infrastructure, urban transit, net zero-emission vehicles deployment and adaptation initiatives.

In addition, the Pan-Canadian Framework calls for the establishment of systems of carbon pricing across Canada. This carbon pollution pricing framework has two parts: first, similarly to Project Green, an intensity-output-based pricing system for large industrial emitters; second, similarly to the Green Shift, a pollution price on fuel. The fuel charge started at C$20/ton of CO_2e in 2019, rising by C$10 per year to C$50/ton in 2022. This new carbon pricing model differs from Project Green and the Green Shift in terms of its approach toward both the provinces and Canadian citizens.

Regarding the provinces, the Pan-Canadian Framework does not establish a uniform federal carbon pricing policy across the country. Rather, federal intervention happens only as a mandatory substitute in any province or territory where there is an absence of an adequate price system. The aim is to set stringent federal standards to ensure that pricing across Canada is fair and efficient, while allowing flexibility for provinces and territories to develop their own systems.

Provinces and territories may keep or set up the form of carbon pricing of their choice: either an explicit price-based system (such as a carbon tax or carbon charge and performance-based emissions system) or a cap-and-trade system. The jurisdictions that choose to opt into the federal system will decide the usage of revenues generated by the carbon pricing policy. In each jurisdiction that fails to align with the federal benchmark, the federal government will return output-based pricing revenues to the jurisdiction in which it was collected.

Regarding the citizenry, as was the case with the Green Shift, households receive a rebate to offset the cost of the fuel charge. However, this only occurs in provinces where the provincial government chooses to levy a fuel charge or where the federal benchmark applies. The federal government is returning approximately 90 percent of the direct revenues from the federal fuel charge to residents of the province via an annual carbon rebate, called Climate Action Incentive payments, and which vary by household size. The remaining proceeds will support municipalities, small and medium-sized businesses, schools, hospitals, universities and colleges, not-for-profit organizations, and indigenous communities in the given jurisdiction.

Like in the Green Shift, the plan includes supplements for residents of small and rural communities, farmers and fishers, in recognition of their increased energy needs and reduced access to public transit.

Hence, the amount of the rebate varies by province, instead of being universal across the country like in the Green Shift. Furthermore, this amount is not being paid out based on a particular household's income. Instead, it varies by household size (Government of Canada 2020).

The federal government calculates that eight in ten households in these provinces will receive more money back than what they would pay in increased costs (Government of Canada 2019a). The less GHGs a household emits, the more it will profit from these rebates. Since low-income households tend to emit less than high-income ones as they consume less, and since they pay no or few taxes on the rebate compared to high earners, they are thus more likely to benefit. In this way, the system remains fiscally progressive even if it does not take household income into account when calculating the payment. After verification, the Parliamentary Budget Officer confirmed these governmental calculations: with the exception of the highest income quintile, nearly all households will be better off on a net basis because the rebate exceeds the household carbon cost (Office of the Parliamentary Budget Officer 2020b).

In 2017, the OECD carried out a comprehensive review of this Pan-Canadian Framework. It touts it as "a well thought-out strategy" and points out that "putting in place Canada-wide pricing, a key pillar of the framework, will be essential". Noting that carbon pricing would apply to between 70 and 80 percent of total emissions, the OECD observes that "this is a higher share than under the European Union Emissions Trading

System, for example". The OECD sees in the Framework an occasion to strengthen the Canadian economy: "Carbon pricing and new procurement policies will help boost demand for eco-innovations in Canada, while a new emphasis on public investment in research and development (R&D) and skills should help increase supply" (OECD 2017b, pp. 38–39).

One province (Prince Edward Island) and two of the three Territories (Yukon and Nunavut) opted in the federal output-based pricing system. In four provinces (Alberta, Saskatchewan, Manitoba and Ontario), the federal policy will prevail in whole or in part, since they chose not to implement a carbon pricing regime aligned with the federal standards. The governments of these provinces vehemently protested against the implementation of a federal backstop against their will. The fact is that despite the exceptional amount of effort deployed by the federal government to rally the provinces, its carbon pricing system faced fierce opposition from some of them and from part of the public. Almost as much as was the case in 2008 around the Green Shift, carbon pricing became a significant ballot box issue during the federal 2019 election. The Liberal Party was re-elected, but as a minority government, and without winning a single seat in Alberta or Saskatchewan.

Carbon pricing became an issue at the ballot box but also in court, since some provincial governments decided to legally challenge the Greenhouse Gas Pollution Pricing Act, claiming that it infringes on provincial jurisdiction. By split decisions, the Saskatchewan Court of Appeal (May 5, 2019) and the Ontario Court of Appeal (June 28, 2019) determined that the Act is constitutional. However, on February 24, 2020, a 4-1 majority in the Court of Appeal of Alberta held that the Act is unconstitutional. Ultimately, the Supreme Court will have to decide the issue.

COP 11 (2005)

If negotiating the distribution of efforts to reduce greenhouse gas emissions in a developed country like Canada is, as we have seen, not a simple task, then it is by no means less complex negotiating such a climate agreement in the global arena, amongst roughly 190 countries, at very different stages of development. This is what I endeavored to do, as President of the United Nations Annual Conference on Climate Change, held in Montreal in 2005, the 11th Conference of the Parties (COP 11) of the UN Framework Convention on Climate Change.

In 2005, the time had come to adopt the operating arrangements of the Kyoto Protocol, the global climate agreement of the time, and to prepare its second phase; neither of these two operations was simple.

When the Kyoto Protocol was negotiated at COP 3, in 1997, it was decided that the first phase would end in 2012 and that discussions respecting the post-2012 period would be initiated in 2005, in order to complete them in good time and enable all countries and industry to be well prepared for the move to the second phase in 2013.

For two weeks, between November 28 and December 9, 2005, at the Palais des congrès de Montréal, delegates of 189 countries, watched by more than 10,000 participants, had to decide whether they would agree to extend the life of the Kyoto Protocol beyond its 2012 first phase. All knew that a failure to do so would have had a debilitating effect on the continuation of the first phase. In other words, the challenge of COP 11 was the survival of the Kyoto Protocol.

The main controversial issue amongst the countries was the allocation of binding targets for the reduction of greenhouse gas emissions. For Phase 1, it was decided that only 37 developed countries (and the European Union)—the so-called Annex 1 countries—would have to agree to bindings targets. They committed themselves to reduce their annual carbon emissions for the years 2008–2012, to an average of 5.2 percent below 1990 levels. No specific action was required of developing countries, though they were invited to set voluntary reduction targets. Developing countries could also participate in the Clean Development Mechanism, under which their certified emission-reduction projects would be supported by, and then credited to Annex 1 countries to help Annex 1 countries to reach their binding targets.

The distinction between Annex 1 countries and others was based on the principle of common but differentiated responsibilities. This principle acknowledges that individual countries have different capabilities in combating climate change owing to varying levels of economic development. It also takes into account the fact that developed countries are historically responsible for the current levels of greenhouse gases in the atmosphere.

In 1997, when the Kyoto Protocol was agreed, Annex 1 countries were emitting the majority of greenhouse gases. The problem though was that this was no longer the case by 2005, due to major growth in greenhouse gas emissions in emerging economies, notably China as a result of its spectacular industrial boom. In 2001, the United States, at that time the largest emitter with approximately a quarter of the world's GHG emissions, withdrew from the Kyoto Protocol, claiming that it weakened its economic competitiveness in the face of a rapidly emerging China, which did not have binding emissions reduction targets to achieve.

With the United States out of Kyoto, the other Annex 1 countries no longer saw why they should continue beyond 2012 to be the only ones holding allocated binding targets when, together, they represented less than one-quarter of global GHG emissions. From the point of view of an effective global fight against climate change, their position was understandable.

However, the developing and emerging countries had a completely different opinion. They were adamant in sticking to the original Kyoto distinction between them and Annex 1 countries. They were determined to not be assigned reduction targets, arguing that doing so would be contrary to the principle of common but differentiated responsibilities. They asserted their right to economic development and emphasized the historic responsibility of the developed countries, the great beneficiaries of 150 years of industrialization based on fossil fuels. "You did it, you fix it" was their point of view and they did not want to change position. The major emerging economies—countries such as China, India and Brazil— strongly shared this view, fearing that emissions targets under Kyoto would hamper their rapidly developing economies.

During the months that preceded COP 11 in Montreal, my team and I made many bilateral and multilateral visits. Throughout, we were careful to consult and include the developing countries. At a conference of African environment ministers in Nairobi, they told me that in their experience, such levels of consultations were unprecedented ahead of a COP. We were convinced that the G77+China grouping—about 130 developing countries—were not a monolithic group and, so, if we engaged each of them properly, they would not necessarily follow the lead of their most reluctant members (including petroleum-producing countries).

In a case of highly unfortunate timing, a few days before the Conference, the Canadian Government was defeated in the House of Commons. We were in an election! I will not elaborate here, but suffice it to say that this political context did not simplify matters.

When the Conference started, the G77+China considered, at their initial caucus meeting, pulling out of the Conference right there and then, to avoid a discussion of a reallocation of binding targets after 2012. But then our months of pre-consultations, travel and personal/bilateral workmanship paid off: many said that the Canadians were their friends, had worked hard and had shown respect and fairness.

The US delegation said they would not interject on Kyoto's future since they were not part of it, but they insisted throughout the negotiations that they opposed any new process under the Convention, as they steadfastly opposed any mandatory caps on their emissions. At one time, during the very last days of the Conference, the US delegation walked out. I was, however, able to convince them not to leave the Conference. I was helped by massive public pressure including many US citizen groups and critical media coverage. A bipartisan group of 24 senators wrote to President Bush, urging the United States to "at a minimum refrain from blocking or obstructing" discussions. As the *Economist* described it: "America's chief negotiator stormed off in a huff, throwing the meeting into chaos. The talks looked destined to fail. Then something odd happened that persuaded the elephant to dance. (…) Finding itself isolated, the American delegation reluctantly returned to the negotiating table" (The Economist 2005).

US opinion notwithstanding, a consensus painfully emerged among the delegations for the establishment of a two-track process to be followed in the years ahead: an ad hoc group would be set up under the Kyoto Protocol umbrella, to review countries' commitments; and a dialogue would be initiated on future implementation of the UN Framework Convention on Climate Change, with four supporting working groups (sustainable development, adaptation, technology and market-based opportunities). At 6:16 a.m., on Saturday, December 10, I gaveled the meeting closed to the sound of wild applause and ovations, and the sight of flying briefing papers!

Painstaking preparations throughout the year, the mobilization of an outstanding team, numerous visits to all continents, a broad and intense diplomatic effort, carefully managed negotiations and admittedly a little luck—although as in hockey, you make your own luck—enabled COP 11 to both rescue the Kyoto Protocol and revive the international movement to address climate change. I described the Montreal Action Plan as a "map for the future". Comments on the Montreal agreement were very positive. After fearing the worst, the world was relieved, even confident. Elizabeth May, then executive director of the Sierra Club of Canada, praised this "set of agreements that may well save the planet". "This is a major, major deal and a major historic day, to see this agreement going ahead", said Catherine Pearce, a climate change campaigner with Friends of the Earth International (CBC News 2005).

In another paper, I described in detail the work undertaken made in order to bring the parties together and get them to support a joint action plan (Dion 2010). From the perspective that interests us most here—that of the importance of considering equity and justice throughout the negotiations—I cannot overstate enough its fundamental consideration. A COP President, without becoming an expert of all the technicalities, must handle the principles of justice and fairness at play as well as the substance of the issues under negotiation, the rationale behind the different views and the domestic constraints of her/his interlocutors. On this basis, she or he must anticipate the different scenarios and the likely alliances to strategize means to mitigate the disagreements.

The President must engage, listen, be well aware of the consequences of climate change in the regions of her/his interlocutors and explore what kind of additional action they could take now and in the future in the context of an appropriate international regime. In short, the President should emphasize the opportunities rather than the constraints, and invite each country to explore what it would be able to do instead of wallowing in criticism of others.

A successful COP is not an outcome obtained without intense preparation. Personal ties and trusting relationships need to be put in place well before the Conference. The President must also make her/himself known to the global climate change movement—green activists, scientists, businesses, artists, NGOs, the public—in order to give the COP process a human face and to build a broad alliance. As much as possible, the President must be well-perceived by everyone—negotiators as much as observers—without creating unrealistic expectations.

The President cannot do this alone. She or he must assemble a strong team, made up of hard-working, experienced experts, advisors, negotiators, diplomats and managers. The President must develop a positive relationship with the Secretariat of the United Nations Framework Convention on Climate Change, which offers strong and professional support. Of course, the President should have the full support of her/his government. Throughout the year before the two-week conference, the Head of State, the Head of Government, ministers and top officials must engage their counterparts around the world.

After COP 11, the world was counting on Canada to widen the opening created in Montreal. The Kenyans, in particular, were counting on our cooperation to make COP 12 a success in Nairobi. It was vital that the two processes we had initiated—one under the umbrella of the Protocol and the other under the Convention—come together gradually, to finally become one under an international agreement well before 2012. A key deadline was 2008, the end of the Bush Administration.

Then, the Liberal government was defeated during the 2006 Canadian federal election. My current status as a non-partisan Canadian diplomat prevents me from commenting on the role that the Government of Canada played over the years that followed in the global climate negotiations. Everyone will nonetheless remember that in 2011, Canada became the first signatory to announce its withdrawal from the Kyoto Protocol. By 2015, however, Canada was once again being appreciated for the constructive role it played during the negotiations of the Paris Agreement.

THE PATHS TO CLIMATE JUSTICE

In this chapter, so far, I have attempted to report on the considerable efforts that were made, by many talented and determined people, to achieve three Canadian GHG reduction plans comprising carbon pricing systems and, in the international arena, to rescue the global Kyoto Protocol. Each time, we have seen how fundamental the considerations of justice and equity were to achieving such a result.

Should industrial emissions be capped in intensity or in absolute? Does a revenue-neutral fiscal reform, which taxes carbon emissions, offer opportunity to correct social inequalities? Should a country have the same carbon price policy over its entire territory or should it be adjusted according to its regions? Worldwide, how can all countries be brought into play while taking into account the differences in level of development and historical responsibilities? Reasonable people may answer these questions differently, depending on their interests and experiences, by referring to values, principles of justice and fairness, as well as considerations of efficiency. One cannot bring them to collective action without mitigating these differences on the basis of common ground and political leadership.

What remains to be explained now is why such considerable efforts and goodwill, rather than solving the problem, have led to results so far removed from what it would take to stem the threat that climate change poses to humanity.

One can consider the case of the Pan-Canadian Framework on Clean Growth and Climate Change. We know that under a business as usual scenario, Canada's annual GHG emissions would be set to increase from 722 MT in 2015 to 815 MT in 2030, while the Paris Agreement target is to reduce them to 511 MT by 2030. The federal government foresees that the measures currently contained in the Framework should reduce annual Canadian emissions to 588 MT by 2030. It will, therefore, be necessary to find 77 MT of additional reductions to reach the Paris target of 511 MT (Environment and Climate Change Canada 2020b). To help close this gap, the Parliamentary Budget Officer recommends further raising the carbon price (Office of the Parliamentary Budget Officer 2020a). However, we have seen to what degree the federal government is, on the contrary, under pressure to weaken its plan and scrap from it the carbon pricing system. The government is resisting these pressures, which can be expected only to increase due to the Coronavirus Disease 2019 (COVID-19) crisis, which has devastated the economy and public finances and has shifted priorities and mass funding to countless emergencies. In fact, in December 2020, the government courageously announced that the carbon price will increase from C$50 in 2022 to C$170/ton in 2030.

Now, take the Paris Agreement. Like so many other participants at COP 21, held in Paris in 2015, I witnessed how President Laurent Fabius and his team were able to give birth to the Paris Agreement. It was undeniably a diplomatic feat that a former COP president can appreciate. I was also proud of the active contribution of the Canadian delegation, led by Prime Minister Trudeau and then Minister of the Environment and Climate Change Catherine McKenna.

And yet, it is a well-known fact, officially admitted by the United Nations, that the current nationally determined contributions (NDCs)—as set out in the Paris Agreement, are insufficient as they would lead to a global warming of 3.2 °C above preindustrial levels by 2100, with warming continuing after. As we know, the Paris target is to keep global warming well below 2 °C. The current pledges would need to be roughly tripled for the 2 °C threshold to hold, and a fivefold increase in collective current commitments would be needed to stay below 1.5 °C (United Nations Environment Program 2019).

With the current pledges, global CO_2 emissions will remain on a slow upward trend until 2040. But, in order to hold global warming below 2 °C, CO_2 emissions should be peaking now, around 2020, and subsequently enter in a steep decline, to land at about half of today's level by 2040 and to be on course toward net-zero emissions by 2070 (International Energy Agency 2018).

Things will get even worse if the Paris pledges are not honored. Canada is far from being the only country in need of strengthening its climate plan in order to reach its 2030 reduction target. Most countries are facing this challenge, including the European Union (Climate Action Tracker 2020)

(Climate Transparency 2019) (European Environment Agency 2019). In other words, we are facing a double gap: an implementation gap between the current policies and the NDCs, and an ambition gap between the current NDCs and the Paris target of below 2 °C (Roelfsema et al. 2020).

Recently, some developed economies, including the European Union and Canada, pledged to be carbon neutral by 2050, and China by 2060. This is encouraging. It is fair to say, however, that while these projects are precise on the deadline and on the target to be reached, they are still vague as to the means of reaching them, including their costing. We all know too well that as new policies become more concrete and precise, and regulations developed, with explicit financial costs and carbon pricing systems, the more one may anticipate swift opposition by different lobbies and vested interests.

The gap is growing between what we are actually doing and what science says we should do to properly tackle climate change. How can we explain that? Why do we have so much difficulty in filling this gap between ambitions and achievements?

The easy answer, which we have all heard, is to blame the politicians: "how dare you do not do more!" Having been one of these politicians, having lost an election in 2008 on a climate plan, and being, as I write this chapter, an ambassador and special envoy representing a government proposing a courageous climate plan, I find this blame game too simplistic. After all, in democracy, politics is the responsibility of all citizens not just of the politicians.

In reality, the core of the problem is that, for humankind, avoiding the ravages of climate change is not only a vital obligation but also an immense and politically difficult task, involving tricky considerations of justice. In fact, two dimensions come into play here: the diffused nature of the problem, and its magnitude.

The diffused nature: people see and feel their need for gasoline and coal, but cannot see or feel a ton of CO_2; it has no color, no odor, no shape. Politicians cannot even commit to their voters that any additional effort to reduce their fuel consumption will be rewarded by immediate protection against global warming damage; no politician can credibly promise this. If the cities of Montreal or Paris were able to decrease their GHG emissions by half, this accomplishment in and of itself would not have any noticeable effect on these cities' climates. As GHG emissions have no borders, they spread around the world. They also spread over time, over decades, if not centuries.

The truly diffused global and non-localizable nature of the greenhouse effect adds considerably to the enormity of our task, because it exacerbates a problem well-known to theorists of collective action, namely the free-riding effect. This dilemma is encountered whenever, although the collective interest to act is known, the individual incentive to act is weak, because those who do nothing (the free riders) benefit from the efforts of those who act. As a corollary, those who are mainly causing the problem (here the large emitters of GHGs) are not the only ones to incur the costs, and indeed transfer a large part of the negative consequences to those who have almost nothing to do with it. This weakness of individual incentives results in an enormous collective action problem, because everyone can find a reason to be a free rider, that is, to do the least they can get away with while benefiting from the actions of others.

Fighting climate change and effecting an ecological transition are major tasks. It requires considerable effort. But who should make this effort? Each one of us of course. But if I make a substantial effort, and the others do nothing, or almost nothing, then what will it give me... or anyone? So I'm free-riding to some extent, because I know you are going to free-ride too. With everyone having an interest to reason this way, obtaining effective collective action will rely almost exclusively on moral pressure, linked to trusted mutual commitments, a sense of collective responsibility facing an emergency and a sense of equity between the participants. The development of a collective action plan becomes a huge challenge for negotiators, for results which are likely to be very disappointing.

The way to counter this free-riding effect is to change the rules of the game in order to strengthen individual incentives to act. In the case of combating climate change, the best way to stimulate this incentive to act for individuals, companies or countries would be to agree on a global carbon pricing system, which would make it beneficial for everyone to reduce their GHG emissions. Thus, "the less I emit, the less I pay" would become a universal rule against which no one could free-ride anymore. We could also channel part of the income from this world carbon pricing to support the most affected and vulnerable populations, which would add a measure of justice.

Alas, though carbon pricing is a well-admitted and needed tool to decrease emissions, most global energy-related CO_2 emissions remain cost-free (Carbon Pricing Leadership Coalition 2019) (Clarke et al. 2019) (Lagarde and Gaspar 2019) (International Monetary Fund 2019) (Metcalf and Stock 2020) (The New Climate Economy 2018) (OECD 2018)

(Pachauri and Meyer 2014) (United Nations Environment Program 2018), more specifically, 70 percent of them, according to the OECD (OECD 2019). Current global negotiations on carbon markets, stemming from Article 6 of the Paris Agreement, are widely perceived as "a real disappointment" so far (Stavins 2019). Article 6 allows countries to meet, in part, GHG reduction targets through market mechanisms such as carbon markets and pricing. Negotiators are far from being able to even discuss a possible world carbon pricing system, which many consider a necessary solution and which can be conceived as fair for all countries, whatever their level of development (Dion 2015) (Dion and Laurent 2012).

The problem posed by GHG emissions caused by human activity is not only diffuse, it is also enormous. The global industrial revolution was based on fossil fuels, by far the largest source of GHG emissions: coal, oil and natural gas. Despite all our efforts, fossil fuels continue to provide 84.7 percent of global energy consumption in 2018, a ratio that has not really budged since 1990 (88.1 percent) (Ritchie and Roser 2020). In other words, we are talking about changing nothing less than the material basis of our civilization: energy produced through burning fossil fuels. Concretely, that means that people are using fossil fuels constantly, in their daily lives, for transport, goods, heating, everything.

Aggressive climate policies face not only climate skepticism and formidable pushback from powerful interests in a fossil fuel-base economic system, but also voter concerns about possible higher energy costs. It is true that public pressure is mounting for action on climate change and this is a welcome development. Presently, in most democracies, no party can expect to win an election without some version of an—at least seemingly—credible climate plan. However, while many voters are casting their ballot to fight climate change, others are worried about how climate policies will consequently affect tax levels and fuel costs. Often, these conflicting concerns are regionally concentrated, as we have seen in Canada, with oil and gas extraction being quite significant for the economies of Alberta and Saskatchewan.

It is true that we need to act now, without delay, otherwise it will be too late to avoid the terrible impacts of climate change. At the same time, we need to act fairly, in order to keep voters on board, as their present daily life is so closely linked to the use of fossil fuels. I will end this chapter by giving a concrete example of the difficulty combining swift and fair action: the phasing out of coal.

The biggest single step that humanity can take to fight climate change is to address our long-standing burning of coal, the most carbon-intensive form of energy. To this end, Canada and the United Kingdom launched the Powering Past Coal Alliance in 2018, at COP 23, in Bonn. Humanity needs to wean itself of traditional coal, no later than 2030 for developed countries and 2050 for the rest of the world, which means stopping now the building of new coal power plants and accelerating the retirement of existing ones (International Renewable Energy Agency 2019).

To our own detriment, this is not the path the world is taking. In 2019, an estimated 6697 coal-fired plants were producing 40 percent of the electricity around the world; another 1046 new plants were planned or in construction (Global Coal Plant Tracker 2020).

Managing the necessary global phase out of coal will be a considerable challenge. First, we will need to replace, in a fair, affordable and reliable way, the immense energy power currently generated by coal. Second, we need to make the transition socially just for the people most directly affected, in a world where global energy demand is set to increase by nearly 50 percent between 2018 and 2050 and where one in nine of the world's population has still no access to electricity (US Energy Information Administration 2019) (International Bank for Reconstruction and Development/The World Bank 2019). The people affected include the coal miners and employees of generating stations, their families, their unions, the employers, contractors and suppliers, as well as the communities whose existence is threatened. The most labor-intensive form of fossil-fuel extraction, the coal sector, employs a global workforce of at least nine million people (Global Commission on the Geopolitics of Energy Transformation 2019).

These workers, unions and communities deserve much respect. They are women and men proud of their legacy and contribution to their community and country, having provided affordable and reliable electricity for generations. They do not appreciate having their work, their traditions and skills in producing coal being denigrated as "dirty". Any sign of lack of respect and consideration to these people will only give ammunition to the too numerous populist politicians who are trying to boost their support by attacking climate change policies.

In Canada, in Germany, in the EU, just transition plans are being developed and deployed to provide tailored financial and practical support to workers, regions and sectors most affected in moving away from fossil fuels, notably coal. These plans must be successful. We need to keep these workers, their unions and their communities on board for the fight against climate change and as part of the solution for a socially just transition.

Conclusion

The impacts of the climate crisis are already affecting us severely (World Meteorological Organization 2019). A 3 °C—or more—of global warming is not a world that we want to pass on to the generations to come. No population will be immune—least of all the poorest and most vulnerable—from the worst of the effects of climate change, including growing intensity of extreme meteorological events, rising ocean levels and salinization of land and water, acidification and alterations in seawater chemistry and in fisheries ecology, extinction of animal and plant species, damage to infrastructure and human habitat, prolonged droughts and heat waves with record temperatures at around 50 °C, more frequent dust storms and desertification, food scarcity and water stress, and more wildfires and damage to soils (Guivarch and Taconet 2020, pp. 35–70) (Buis 2019).

One must never lose sight of the fact that climate change comes in addition to many other environmental challenges. Even without climate change, we would still face an ecological crisis. After all, it is not climate change that causes pollution by chemicals, overfishing, over-harvesting forests, depleting soils, discharging 80 percent of wastewater without treatment, emptying groundwater or sending vast quantities of plastic into the oceans. What climate change is doing is exacerbating all these ecological disturbances, to the point of risking undoing "the last fifty years of progress in development, global health, and poverty reduction" (United Nations Special Rapporteur on Extreme Poverty and Human Rights 2019).

The crisis of climate change induced by human activity is all the more difficult to resolve in that it shakes nothing less than the very material foundation of our civilization: energy from fossil-fuel combustion. It is true that decarbonization policies may be cost-efficient, even without taking into account the major costs in delayed action. A lesson from global financial crises that occurred before COVID-19 shows that "green stimulus policies often have advantages over traditional fiscal stimulus" (Hepburn et al. 2020, p. 8) (Derviş and Strauss 2020). It is more and more proclaimed, even at the heart of the political and economic establishment, that the transition toward a low- or zero-carbon economy, including the phasing out of coal, presents ample opportunities on which countries must capitalize (OECD 2017a) (Baily et al. 2020). However, the vigorous collective action that is necessary to truly seize this opportunity and counter the climate crisis is hard to mobilize, precisely because the climate improvements obtained by each of these actions will always be diffused, unnoticeable, spread out in space and time, and easy to free-ride upon regardless of the efforts made.

Under these circumstances, our current initiatives are not without merit. However, they remain clearly insufficient. All governments have unsatisfactory records regarding environmental sustainability. There are two sides to this reality, which I have experienced over the years and described in this chapter: on the one hand, the considerable and often admirable efforts deployed by numerous pragmatic, talented and committed politicians, officials, diplomats and negotiators; on the other hand, the meagerness of their results compared to what must be done. Alongside others, I have for a long time but so far unsuccessfully proposed, as a key to the solution, a world carbon pricing system.

Time is running out. We must continue to support and encourage those decision-makers willing to do more, in the development of innovative and socially just solutions, and who, above all, understand that the imperatives of justice and equity are necessary conditions for success.

REFERENCES

Baily, A., Carney, M., & Villeroy, F. et al. (2020). The world must seize this opportunity to meet the climate challenge: As current and former central bankers, we believe the pandemic offers a unique chance to green the global economy. *The Guardian*. Retrieved from https://www.theguardian.com/commentis-free/2020/jun/05/world-climate-breakdown-pandemic.

Boyce, J., & Riddle, M. (2009). *Cap and dividend: A state-by-state analysis*. Political.

Bramley, M. (2005). *Meeting our Kyoto obligation: Canada's essential implementation steps in 2005*. Pembina Institute. Retrieved from https://www.pembina.org/reports/Kyoto20050613_Meeting_Kyoto.pdf.

Buis, A. (2019). *A degree of concern: Why global temperatures matter*. NASA, Global Climate Change. Retrieved from https://climate.nasa.gov/news/2865/a-degree-of-concern-why-global-temperatures-matter/.

Canada Energy Regulator. (2020). *Provincial and territorial energy profiles*. Government of Canada. Retrieved from https://www.cer-rec.gc.ca/nrg/ntgrtd/mrkt/nrgsstmprfls/index-eng.html.

Carbon Pricing Leadership Coalition. (2019). The Economic Potential of Article 6 of the Paris Agreement and Implementation Challenges. September. Retrieved from https://www.ieta.org/resources/International_WG/Article6/CLPC_A6%20report_no%20crops.pdf.

CBC. (2005). Climate-change conference ends with key deals. Retrieved from https://www.cbc.ca/news/canada/climate-change-conference-ends-with-key-deals-1.568142.

Clarke, L., Edmonds, J., Forrister, D., et al. (2019). *The economic potential of article 6 of the Paris agreement and implementation challenges.* International Emission Trading Association and the University of Maryland. Retrieved from https://www.ieta.org/resources/International_WG/Article6/CLPC_A6%20report_no%20crops.pdf.

Climate Action Tracker. (2020). CAT Climate Target Update Tracker target update. Retrieved June 2020, from https://climateactiontracker.org/climate-target-update-tracker/.

Climate Transparency. (2019). Brown to Green: The G20 Transition toward a net-zero Emission Economy 2019. Retrieved from https://www.climate-transparency.org/wp-content/uploads/2019/11/Brown-to-Green-Report-2019.pdf.

Congressional Budget Office. (2007). *Trade-offs in allocating allowances for CO_2 Emissions.* CBO Economic and Budget Issue Brief. Retrieved from https://www.cbo.gov/sites/default/files/110th-congress-2007-2008/reports/04-25-captrade.pdf.

Derviş, K., & Strauss, S. (2020). *The carbon tax opportunity.* Project Syndicate. Retrieved from https://www.project-syndicate.org/commentary/low-oil-prices-opportunity-for-carbon-tax-by-kemal-dervis-and-sebastian-strauss-2020-05.

Dion, S. (2010). The 2005 Montréal conference on climate change: successful summit, wasted opportunity. Paper presented at the millennium summit 2020, Quebec, April 20, 2010

Dion, S. (2011). The fight against climate change: Why is Canada doing so little. *The Tocqueville review/La revue Tocqueville, 32*(2), 21a–46a.

Dion, S. (2013). Carbon taxes: Can a good policy become good politics? In A. Himelfarb & J. Himelfarb (Eds.), *Tax is not a four-letter word; a different take on taxes in Canada* (pp. 291–323). Waterloo: Wilfrid Laurier University Press.

Dion, S. (2015). A world price for carbon; a necessary condition for an effective global climate Agreement. In *Harvard International Law Review* (Spring 2015 edition). Retrieved from https://carbon-price.com/wp-content/uploads/2015-05-St%C3%A9phane-Dion_A-World-Price-for-Carbon.pdf.

Dion, S., & Laurent, E. (2012). From Rio to Rio: A global carbon price signal to escape the great climate inconsistency. In Working papers OFCE (2012–16). Retrieved from https://www.ofce.sciences-po.fr/pdf/dtravail/WP2012-16.pdf.

Dorban, I., Jakob, M., Kalkuhl, M., et al. (2019). Poverty and distributional effects of carbon pricing in low- and middle-income countries—A global comparative analysi. *World Development, 115*, 246–257. Retrieved from https://www.sciencedirect.com/science/article/pii/S0305750X18304212.

Economy Research Institute, University of Massachusetts. Retrieved from https://www.peri.umass.edu/fileadmin/pdf/other_publication_types/green_economics/CapDividend_PERI.PDF.

Environment and Climate Change Canada. (2020a). *National inventory report 1990–2018: Greenhouse gas sources and trends in Canada*. Canada's Submission to the United Nations Framework Convention on Climate Change. United Nations Climate Change. Retrieved from https://unfccc.int/documents/224829.

Environment and Climate Change Canada. (2020b). *Progress towards Canada's greenhouse gas emissions reduction target*. Government of Canada. Retrieved from https://www.canada.ca/content/dam/eccc/documents/pdf/cesindicators/progress-towards-canada-greenhouse-gas-reduction-target/2020/progress-ghg-emissions-reduction-target.pdf.

European Environment Agency. (2019). Trends and projections in Europe 2019. Tracking progress towards Europe's climate and energy targets. EEA Report (15/20191994–2019). Retrieved fromhttps://www.eea.europa.eu/publications/trends-and-projections-in-europe-1.

Global Coal Plant Tracker. (2020). *Coal-fired units by country (units)*. Global Energy Monitor. Retrieved June 2020, from https://docs.google.com/spreadsheets/d/1JKJJa-jwK6YpkEQKP2bcENHR2yoS40ur8baQnIXHtIU/edit#gid=0.

Global Commission on the Geopolitics of Energy Transformation. (2019). *A new world: The geopolitics of the energy transformation*. International Renewable Energy Agency. Retrieved from https://www.irena.org/publications/2019/Jan/A-New-World-The-Geopolitics-of-the-Energy-Transformation.

Government of Canada. (2005). *Moving forward on climate change: A plan for honouring our Kyoto commitment*. Government of Canada. Retrieved from http://webarchive.bac-lac.gc.ca:8080/wayback/20060202163923/http://www.climatechange.gc.ca/kyoto_commitments/report_e.pdf.

Government of Canada. (2016). *Pan-Canadian framework on clean growth and climate change: Canada's plan to address climate change*. Government of Canada. Retrieved from http://publications.gc.ca/collections/collection_2017/eccc/En4-294-2016-eng.pdf.

Government of Canada. (2019a). *Fall 2019 update: Estimate impacts of the federal pollution pricing system*. Government of Canada. Retrieved from https://www.canada.ca/en/environment-climate-change/services/climate-change/pricing-pollution-ow-it-will-work/fall-2018-update-estimated-impacts-federal-pollution-pricing-system.html.

Government of Canada. (2019b). *Pricing carbon pollution from industry.* Government of Canada. Retrieved from https://www.canada.ca/en/ environment-climate-change/services/climate-change/pricing-pollution-how-it-will-work/industry/pricing-carbon-pollution.html.

Government of Canada. (2020). Climate Action Incentive Payment Amounts for 2020. Retrieved from https://www.canada.ca/en/department-finance/ news/2019/12/climate-action-incentive-payment-amounts-for-2020.html.

Green, K. P., Jackson, T., Herzog, I., & Palacios, M. (2016, March). *Energy costs and Canadian households: how much are we spending?* Frazer Institute. Retrieved from https://www.fraserinstitute.org/sites/default/files/energy-costs-and-canadian-households.pdf.

Guivarch, C., & Taconet, N. (2020). Inégalités mondiales et changement climatique. *Revue de l'OFCE, 165*(2020/1), 35–70.

Hanson, J. (2009). Carbon tax & 100% dividend vs. tax & trade. In *Testimony given at scientific objectives for climate change legislation to Committee on Ways and Means.* United States House of Representatives. Retrieved from http:// www.columbia.edu/~jeh1/2009/WaysAndMeans_20090225.pdf.

Hepburn, C., O'Callaghan, B., & Stern, N., et al. (2020). Will COVID-19 fiscal recovery packages accelerate or retard progress on climate change. In Smith School Working Paper (20-02). Retrieved from https://www.smithschool. ox.ac.uk/publications/wpapers/workingpaper20-02.pdf.

International Bank for Reconstruction and Development / The World Bank. (2019). Chapter 1: Access to electricity. In *Tracking SDG7: The energy progress report 2019.* Retrieved from https://trackingsdg7.esmap.org/data/files/ download-documents/chapter_1_access_to_electricity_rev030320.pdf.

International Energy Agency. (2018). IEA Publications. Retrieved from https:// www.iea.org/reports/world-energy-outlook-2018.

International Monetary Fund. (2019). Fiscal policies for Paris climate strategies—From principle to practice. In International Monetary Fund Policy Paper (19-010). Retrieved from https:// www.imf.org/en/Publications/Policy-Papers/Issues/2019/05/01/ Fiscal-Policies-for-Paris-Climate-Strategies-from-Principle-to-Practice-46826.

International Renewable Energy Agency. (2019). Global energy transformation: A roadmap to 2050. Retrieved from https://www.irena.org/publications/2019/ Apr/Global-energy-transformation-A-roadmap-to-2050-2019Edition.

Krechowicz, D. (2011). The effects of carbon pricing on low-income households and its potential contribution to poverty reduction. In *Sustainable prosperity.* University of Ottawa. Retrieved from https://institute.smartprosperity.ca/ sites/default/files/effect-carbon-pricing-low-income-households-and-its-potential-contribution-poverty-reduction.pdf.

Lagarde, C., & Gaspar, V. (2019). *Getting real on meeting Paris climate change commitments.* International Monetary Fund Blog. Retrieved from https://blogs.imf.org/2019/05/03/getting-real-on-meeting-paris-climate-change-commitments/.

Lee, M., & Toby, S. (2008). *Is BC's carbon tax fair? An impact analysis for different income levels.* CCPA. Retrieved from https://www.carbontax.org/blog/2008/10/31/is-bcs-carbon-tax-fair-an-impact-analysis-for-different-income-levels/.

Liberal Party of Canada. (2008a). Richer, fairer, greener: An action plan for the 21st century.

Liberal Party of Canada. (2008b). The green shift: Building a Canadian economy for the 21st century.

Macdonald, D., Monstadt, J., & Kern, K. (2013). *Allocating Canadian greenhouse gas emission reductions amongst sources and provinces: Learning from the European Union, Australia and Germany.* University of Toronto. Retrieved from https://www.researchgate.net/profile/David_Gordon18/publication/271850017_Allocating_Canadian_Greenhouse_Gas_Emissions_Reductions_Amongst_Sources_and_Provinces_Learning_from_the_European_Union_Australia_and_Germany/links/54d4e0c30cf25013d02a1536/Allocating-Canadian-Greenhouse-Gas-Emissions-Reductions-Amongst-Sources-and-Provinces-Learning-from-the-European-Union-Australia-and-Germany.pdf.

Metcalf, G. E., & Stock, J. H. (2020). The macroeconomic impact of Europe's carbon taxes. NBER Working Paper No. 27488. Retrieved July 2020, from https://www.nber.org/papers/w27488.

National Round Table on the Environment and the Economy. (2009). *Achieving 2050: A carbon pricing policy for Canada.* Government of Canada. Retrieved from http://publications.gc.ca/site/fra/9.651590/publication.html.

OECD. (2017a). *Investing in climate, investing in growth.* Paris: OECD Publishing. Retrieved from https://www.oecd-ilibrary.org/docserver/9789264273528-en.pdf?expires=1586277404&id=id&accname=ocid54006162&checksum=7B470BED73AA7EF9AD590C2C14109DC7.

OECD. (2017b). *OECD environmental performance reviews: Canada 2017.* Paris: OECD Publishing. https://doi.org/10.1787/9789264279612-en.

OECD. (2018). Effective carbon pricing rates. Retrieved from https://www.oecd.org/tax/tax-policy/few-countries-are-pricing-carbon-high-enough-to-meet-climate-targets.htm.

OECD. (2019). Taxing energy use 2019. Using taxes for climate action. Retrieved from https://www.oecd-ilibrary.org/docserver/058ca239-en.pdf?expires=1586092173&id=id&accname=ocid54006162&checksum=3FA64E4A4D3CE0D587C30A32BECDBE44.

Office of the Parliamentary Budget Officer. (2020a). *Carbon pricing for the Paris target: Closing the gap with output-based pricing.* Government of Canada. Retrieved from https://www.pbo-dpb.gc.ca/web/default/files/Documents/Reports/RP-2021-019-S/RP-2021-019-S_en.pdf.

Office of the Parliamentary Budget Officer. (2020b). *Reviewing the fiscal and distributional analysis of the Federal carbon pricing system.* Government of Canada. Retrieved from https://www.pbo-dpb.gc.ca/web/default/files/Documents/Reports/RP-1920-024-S/RP-1920-024-S_en.pdf.

Pachauri, R. K., & Meyer, L. A. (2014). Climate change 2014: Synthesis report. Contribution of working groups I, II and III to the fifth assessment report of the intergovernmental panel on climate change. Intergovernmental Panel on Climate Change. Retrieved from https://www.ipcc.ch/report/ar5/syr/.

Ritchie, A., & Roser, M. (2019). CO_2 and greenhouse gas emissions. In Our world in data. Retrieved from https://ourworldindata.org/co2-and-other-greenhouse-gas-emission.

Ritchie, H, & Roser, M. (2020). Energy. In Our world in data. Retrieved from https://ourworldindata.org/energy.

Roelfsema, M., Soest, H., & Harmsen, M. (2020). Taking stock of national climate policies to evaluate implementation of the Paris Agreement. *Nature Communications, 11*(2096) https://doi.org/10.1038/s41467-020-15414-6.

Stavins, R. (2019). The Madrid climate conference's real failure was not getting a broad deal on global carbon markets. *The Conversation.* Retrieved from https://theconversation.com/the-madrid-climate-conferences-real-failure-was-not-getting-a-broad-deal-on-global-carbon-markets-129001.

Stavins, R., Zou, J., & Brewer, T., et al. (2014). International cooperation: agreements and instruments. In *Climate change 2014: Mitigation of climate change.* Contribution of Working Group III to the Fifth Assessment Report of the Intergovernmental Panel on Climate Change. Cambridge University Press. Retrieved from https://www.ipcc.ch/site/assets/uploads/2018/02/ipcc_wg3_ar5_chapter13.pdf.

Sue Wing, I., Ellerman, A., & Song, J. (2006). Absolute vs. intensity limits for CO_2 emissions control: Performance under uncertainty. MIT Joint Program on the Science and Policy of. *Climate Change, 130.* Retrieved from http://web.mit.edu/globalchange/www/MITJPSPGC_Rpt130.pdf.

The Economist. (2005). Pricking the global conscience. Retrieved from https://www.economist.com/science-and-technology/2005/12/14/pricking-the-global-conscience.

The New Climate Economy. (2018). *The 2018 report of the global commission on the economy and climate.* The Global Commission on the Economy and Climate. Retrieved from http://newclimateeconomy.report:443/2018/.

U.S. Energy Information Administration. (2019). *International energy outlook 2019*. US Department of Energy. Retrieved from https://www.eia.gov/out-looks/ieo/.

United Nations Environment Program. (2019). *Emissions gap report 2019*. United Nations. Retrieved from https://wedocs.unep.org/bitstream/han-dle/20.500.11822/30797/EGR2019.pdf?sequence=1&isAllowed=y.

United Nations Environment Programme. (2018). *Emission gap report 2018*. United Nations. Retrieved from https://wedocs.unep.org/bitstream/han-dle/20.500.11822/26880/EGR2018_launch.pdf?sequence=1&isAllowed=y.

United Nations Special Rapporteur on Extreme Poverty and Human Rights. (2019). Climate change and poverty. Paper tabled at the forty-first session of the human rights council, United Nations, 24 June–12 July 2019. Retrieved from http://www.guninetwork.org/files/unsr-poverty-climate-change-a_hrc_41_39.pdf.

World Meteorological Organization. (2019). The global climate in 2015–2019. Retrieved from https://library.wmo.int/doc_num.php?explnum_id=9936.

PART II

The Health-sustainability Nexus

CHAPTER 4

Health and the Environment: Understanding the Linkages and Synergies

Denis Zmirou-Navier

INTRODUCTION

The World Health Organization defines the environment, as it relates to health, as "*all the physical, chemical, and biological factors external to a person, and all the related behaviours*" (WHO 2006), this definition applying to both built and natural environments. For the US Office for Disease Prevention and Health Promotion, environmental health "*is a branch of public health that consists of promoting quality of life and preventing or controlling disease, injury, and disability related to the interactions between people and their environment*" (ODPHP 2020).

These definitions underline that environmental health is not only concerned with exposure to risk factors such as hazardous substances in air, water, soil, food, other consumer products, or in occupational settings and processes; with consequences of natural and technological disasters; or with direct or indirect effects of climate change or loss in biodiversity.

D. Zmirou-Navier (✉)
Lorraine University Medical School, Nancy, France

EHESP School of Public Health, Rennes, France

É. Laurent (ed.), *The Well-being Transition*,
https://doi.org/10.1007/978-3-030-67860-9_4

This branch of public health is also interested in factors that promote good health, such as green spaces in cities or access to well-preserved natural sites.

Considerable research efforts have been devoted in all continents to improve our understanding of these negative or positive impacts of the environment on human well-being and to convert this large body of knowledge into information amenable to decision makers and to the many stakeholders, in view to contemplate the best courses of action, at international, national or local levels.

This chapter is composed of three sections. The first one offers a brief view of the public health stakes of the quality of the environment, based on its contribution to the global burden of disease. The second section stands that these stakes encompass the consequences of the degradation of the ecosystems and of the climate change. In the third section, the longest, several aspects of inequalities in exposure to environmental risk factors or in access to beneficial environmental conditions are exposed, in a view to underline their systemic dimensions.

Environmental Risk Factors: Major Contributors to the Global Burden of Disease

In the 2016 update of the 2006 seminal WHO report "Preventing Disease Through Healthy Environments", (Prüss-Ustün and Corvalán 2006), Anette Prüss-Ustün and her colleagues estimated that environmental risk factors were responsible worldwide for 12.6 million deaths, representing 23% of all annual fatalities (Prüss-Ustün et al. 2016). Extending this mortality toll to disability associated with diseases caused by these risk factors, the estimated fraction of the Global Burden of Disease (GBD) due to the environment amounts to 22%. These figures are in line with the estimates from the GBD 2016 risk factors group (GBD 2016 Risk Factors Collaborators 2017) where, among 84 behavioural, environmental (including occupational) and metabolic risk factors, the combination of environmental and related behavioural factors totals 22% of the GBD (those for which the current state of science allows to assess the contribution of known causes) (Table 4.1).

At a global level, air pollution (both indoor and outdoor, ranking 5th among the 84 risk factors), followed by unsafe water, poor sanitation and handwashing (9th rank), then occupational risks (12th), counted for the

Table 4.1 Global
DALYs attributed to 84
health risk factors in
2013, worldwide (men
and women)

Risk factors	Rank
Dietary risks	1
High systolic blood pressure	2
Child and maternal malnutrition	3
Tobacco smoke	4
Air pollution[a]	5
Others	...
Unsafe water, sanitation and handwashing	9
Others	...
Occupational risks	12
Others	...

[a]**In bold:** environmental health risks

Source: GBD 2016 Risk Factors Collaborators 2017

most important environmental contributors to the disability-adjusted life-years (DALYs[1]), a measure of the GBD. Yet, risk categories are not water-tight: the third ranking cause of DALYs was child and maternal malnutrition, for which environmental conditions (e.g. access to water for irrigation) have an important influence. The relative contribution of the different risk factors has changed over the last decades in relation with the rapid transformation in the demographic structure of the low-income and middle-income countries and with the environmental consequences of the economic development models adopted across countries and continents. During this period, extreme poverty has declined worldwide, particularly in Asia and South America. In parallel, the health impact of the forms of pollution associated with these very deprived environments (i.e. mainly indoor air pollution due to the usage of wood, charcoal and agriculture residues for heating and cooking in poorly ventilated housings; and microbial contamination of drinking water due to absence of managed water and sanitation systems) was reduced. Yet, these environmental stressors are still present in traditional rural areas and urban slums. On the other side, air pollution steadily increased in the urban areas of developing

[1] DALYs for a disease or health condition are calculated as the sum of the Years of Life Lost due to premature mortality in the population and the Years Lost due to Disability for people living with the health condition or its consequences (https://www.who.int/healthinfo/global_burden_disease/metrics_daly/en/).

and industrializing low-income and middle-income countries, and now endangers the health of billions of inhabitants (Landrigan et al. 2017).

A GLOBAL PERSPECTIVE: DEGRADATION OF ECOSYSTEMS AND CLIMATE CHANGE

The Well-being Toll of Degraded Ecosystems

Ecosystems are the planet's and thus humanity life-support systems (Corvalan et al. 2005). The lines to follow illustrate how they are severely affected by the current capitalist economy pattern dictated by the obsession of "GDP growth" and of short-term monetary yield. This model consumes ever more natural resources (petroleum, gas and other forms of fossil fuels; all categories of metal ores extracted from the soil—soon from seas—for the production of goods; natural forests that are converted into industrial agriculture and forestry fields; oceans fish livestock etc.).

The footprint of this economic model takes many forms. Two are of high concern in terms of long-ranging health consequences. One is industrial agriculture, with extensive usage of pesticides and fertilizers. It offered during some decades an important increase in crops' yield. It now, more and more, confines farmers in a vicious circle to cope with the erosion of soil fertility (EU 2020; IPBES 2019) and the gradual extinction of pollinating insects, while the costs incurred by machines and chemical inputs rise. These serious negative impacts jeopardize food production and the capacity to meet the needs of growing populations in many parts of the world. Another consequence of inappropriate pesticides and fertilizers usage is the contamination of watersheds and of surface water that feed the drinking water systems, and eutrophication of rivers. Also, peasants and their families are directly exposed to noxious chemicals, a situation that is particularly frequent in developing countries where access to information and assistance for proper usage and storage of pesticides is difficult (Caldas 2016).

Decline of the forest cover is another major negative footprint of this unsustainable model (Song et al. 2018). One consequence is the depletion of the role of forests in the absorption of carbon dioxide from the atmosphere, a process that is a major greenhouse gas sink. This depletion enhances the ongoing global warming (Natural Resources Canada). Further, destruction of natural forests to be replaced by industrial forestry and extension of agriculture and livestock, along with the need for land in response to growing populations in developing countries, lead to ever more close encounters between humans and forest wild animal species. These changes in land use facilitate the transmission of viruses and other pathogens yet unknown to humans (UNEP/ILRI 2020). Some recent zoonoses[2] had severe consequences (e.g. the Ebola virus that posed a global threat in West Africa in 2014–2015; the Zika virus, transmitted by mosquitoes, which caused numerous cases of congenital microcephaly in South America in years 2017–2018). The "forest origin" of the SARS-CoV2, the cause of the current Covid-19 pandemic, is still under debate when writing this chapter. When combined with the explosion of international trade and travels, this phenomenon favours massive transmission of pathogenic organisms from animals to humans. Other local or regional epidemic or pandemic episodes are extremely likely to occur in the future and will pose great challenges for public health and the global economy.

Other sources of microbial risks are intensive livestock and poultry production methods and genetic changes of disease vectors or pathogens induced by humans (e.g. mosquito resistance to pesticides or emergence of antibiotic-resistant bacteria). This globalization of health risks reflects the importance of the human–animal–ecosystem interfaces in the evolution and emergence of pathogens (Destoumieux-Garzón et al. 2018).

Public Health Impacts of Climate Change

Global warming already affects important sectors such as agriculture, freshwater quality and sea level or public health. These impacts will increase along the century, and new ones will emerge (Melillo et al. 2014, The Third National Climate Assessment, USA). Public health effects are, or will be, direct consequences of the turmoil of the environment humanity will have to confront with (e.g. injuries and fatalities due to extreme weather events and wildfire emissions whose frequency is projected to increase worldwide; or air pollution-related diseases). Climate change will also have severe public health indirect consequences, such as malnutrition caused by reduced agriculture yield, or fatalities from internal or international conflicts in relation with access to water.

---

[2] Zoonoses are a group of infectious diseases naturally transmitted between animals and humans (WHO: https://www.who.int/foodsafety/areas_work/zoonose/en/).

According to WHO, between 2030 and 2050, climate change is expected to cause approximately 250,000 additional deaths per year, from malnutrition, malaria, diarrhoea and heat stress (WHO 2018a). Hazards and conditions associated with global warming encompass a wide spectrum. The following are exposed in the review on "Climate Effects on Health" (CDC 2020). Air pollution will show rises in ozone concentrations (as a result of increases in daytime heat, of higher concentrations of precursor chemicals and of methane emissions) and in particles (wildfire and air stagnation episodes). Higher temperatures will favour pollen and production of other allergens and longer pollen seasons. It will also influence the geographic and seasonal distribution of insect vectors that cause the spreading of diseases (such as fleas, ticks and mosquitoes). Food production and quality may be threatened by local climate changes, along with more severe and longer shortages of water in arid areas or, conversely, with flooding caused by heavy precipitations or elevated sea levels in estuary and river delta crop areas. Waterborne diarrheal diseases will occur in relation with more frequent meteorologic events that will disrupt sanitation systems and alter drinking water quality. Extreme heat events will be more frequent and intense in coming decades; vulnerable groups, who will suffer from a variety of cardiovascular and respiratory failure events associated with heat waves, are the elderly, infants, those living in poor housing and the marginalized. Many of these situations are stressful; for instance, extreme weather events can affect mental health and induce high levels of anxiety, post-traumatic stress disorders and depression.

One important feature of global warming is that not everyone is equally at risk of bearing its deadly consequences. What is more, countries that will experience the most dramatic changes are not those that have most contributed to the accumulation of greenhouse gases along the last century. At local scales, communities who have little capacity to adapt to these changes (such as poor farmers in arid areas, indigenous groups, dwellers of housings with little protection against heat waves or hurricanes, low-income people living in coastal regions) already pay the greatest toll, and this will worsen in the future. According to the Internal Displacement Monitoring Centre, there were 18.8 million new disaster-related internal displacements recorded in 2017, most being related to consequences of climate change (IDMC 2018). Most of these refugees remain within their national borders and increase the pace of expansion of slums and insane peripheral zones of metropolitan areas in developing countries. However, hunger and despair also lead many to cross borders and seas, often in relation to situations of conflict or violence.

ENVIRONMENTAL HEALTH INEQUALITIES

Environmental health inequalities refer to health hazards that are disproportionately distributed among different segments of a population (Gouveia 2016). When these differences are avoidable, that is, subject to mitigation policies and actions that are not undertaken, these inequalities are unfair and the term inequities is appropriate in that they almost always affect the vulnerable social groups, the poor and/or members of discriminated minorities.

Inequalities (or inequities) deal with uneven exposure to hazards or with smaller access to environmental goods. Another notion is that of vulnerability, whereby individuals and groups are differentially susceptible to environmental hazards, thereby shaping their ability to cope, adapt or resist when exposed to given environmental stressors; they have reduced resilience (Bolte et al. 2011).

Environmental factors disproportionately affecting the poor combine unequal exposures and unequal vulnerabilities. According to The Lancet Commission on pollution and health (Landrigan et al. 2017), nearly 92% of pollution-related deaths occur in low-income and middle-income countries and, in countries at every income level, disease caused by pollution is most prevalent among minorities and the marginalized.

Another dimension of environmental inequities is intergenerational inequity. Generations to come will have to tackle the consequences of climate change and the accumulation of persistent pollutants in the environmental media, as a legacy of current production and consumption patterns (Ganzleben and Kazmierczak 2020). Children and youth have a greater vulnerability to the impacts of climate change. The disproportionate risks faced by children in developing countries and the challenging adaptations to climate-induced changes that youth will have to face worldwide, and particularly in these countries, can be viewed as issues of structural violence, including through exposure to direct interpersonal violence, civil war or regional conflicts due, in particular, to shortage of food and water and to forced migration (Sanson and Burke 2019).

Let us examine a few examples of these environmental health inequalities, respectively at international, national and local levels.

The latest WHO assessment of the worldwide impact of outdoor air pollution showed that, in 2016, 91% of the world population was living in places where the WHO air quality guidelines levels were not met, causing 4.2 million premature deaths (WHO 2018b). A considerable proportion (92%) of those deaths occurred in low- and middle-income countries, with the greatest numbers in the South-East Asia and Western Pacific regions of WHO. The Global Health Observatory data of WHO[3] exhibit a high heterogeneity in the world distribution of ambient air concentrations of PM2.5[4] where the vast majority of cities with high levels (defined here as annual average concentrations above 30 $\mu g.m^{-3}$, when the WHO guideline is 10 $\mu g.m^{-3}$) are located in the Middle East and Asia (in particular the Arabic peninsula, Iran, Pakistan, India and China), with also several cities in Africa and Central and South America. This situation is a consequence of the considerable development of industry and electricity generation using coal or petroleum, and of the gas oil and diesel fleet of vehicles for goods and persons in the large metropolitan areas of these countries, activities that emit into the air large quantities of particles and other pollutants. Important drivers of this evolution during the last three or four decades were, on the one hand, the quest of cheap labour force and of mass production (allowing economies of scale) by globalized companies from "Western" countries and, on the other hand, the absence of, or low-level of, labour and environmental regulations in "Southern" countries whose elites are eager to achieve "development" at an accelerated pace, with little consideration for occupational health and security and for environmental pollution (Kanemoto et al. 2014).

Large inequalities also exist regarding access to managed drinking water and sanitation systems. The situation described by the Pan-American Health Organization (PAHO) 2016 report regarding access to water and sanitation is an illustration of the remaining huge contrasts between rural and urban areas, and within the latter, between the modern and central well-equipped zones where middle- and upper-classes inhabitants reside, and the suburbs and slum peripheral areas (PAHO 2016). While important progress had taken place between 1990 and 2010, such that the

---

[3] https://www.who.int/gho/en/.

[4] PM2.5: suspended particulate matter with an aerodynamic diameter of 2.5 μm or less is the indicator of air quality that shows the greatest association with severe health effects and premature mortality. Most data shown in the 2018 WHO air quality assessment maps were collected during the years 2014, 2015 and 2016.

WHO Region of the Americas had reached the Millennium Development Goal (MDG) Target 7c for water,[5] and was on track to meet MDG Target 7d for sanitation[2] by 2015, usage of unimproved drinking water and absence of basic sanitation are still concentrated in the poorest populations. More so, the PAHO report acknowledged that the social gap between the better-off and the worst-off had widened. Worldwide, as well, the number of people living in urban areas without access to improved sanitation is increasing because of the rapid growth in the size of urban populations and of lack of well-sized efforts to confront this demographic pressure (MDG 2018). Large fractions of the South and Central American population have simply been out of the scope of public policies regarding this aspect of environmental health that, in the history of humankind, has been the core of the most important achievements in health. Everywhere in the world, and since the very initiation of modern environmental health in the first half of the nineteenth century, access to safe water and to sanitation correlates with life expectancy at birth, with infant mortality, with childhood mortality under 5 and with maternal mortality. Yet, an evaluation of the achievement in 2017 of the Sustainable Development Goals (SDGs), which superseded the MDGs in 2015,[6] assessed that 45% of the world population had yet no access to safely managed sanitation services (SDG indicator 6.1.1) with more than half of the population experiencing this situation in 29 countries (9 in Latin America; 7 in Sub-Sahara Africa; 7 in Northern Africa and Western Asia; 4 in Central and East Europe and North America; and 2 in Oceania) (UN Water 2020).

Public policies and action at the local level are also key to tackle environmental inequalities, for instance with respect to access to urban green spaces. Access to good-quality green areas improves health and well-being and makes the places in which one lives or works attractive (Morris and Saunders 2017). An array of mechanisms contribute to these "salutogenic" effects. Important factors are the provision of venues for physical activity, promotion of social contacts and their impacts on mental health (Gelormino et al. 2015); reduction of noise levels, abatement of

[5] MDG Target 7c for water aims for the following target: "By 2015, halve the proportion of people without sustainable access to safe drinking water and basic sanitation". MDG Target 7d for sanitation aims to "achieve, by 2020, a significant improvement in the lives of at least 100 million slum dwellers".

[6] This evolution from MDGs to SDGs translates the aim of the United Nations 2030 Agenda for Sustainable Development to give more importance to equity and inclusiveness as core policy principles.

air pollution and creation of fresh areas are also favourable effects of the presence of trees that provide shade and humidity, thus reducing the health impacts of heat waves. But important inequality exists in the spatial distribution and quality of green spaces across and within cities. People living in the most deprived areas are less likely to have a green area close to their dwelling compared with people living in the least deprived ones (Public Health England 2014). Furthermore, existing green spaces in low-income areas are often smaller, less pleasant and, hence, less used, particularly by women, the elderly and children, because of fear for security. Planning the development of green spaces is not sufficient; they also should be designed with the participation of the inhabitants and associated with promoting and marketing programmes (Hunter et al. 2019). This pattern aligns with the general observation of a strong heterogeneity in the spatial location of where different social and/or ethnic groups reside in cities and metropolitan areas, with only a few examples of mixed profiles. This is a legacy of historical industrial development and a result of how the housing and the labour markets operate, along with differential migration of those who can afford to move away from places that are affected by environmental burdens. This is all the more true that environmental burdens add up. Noisy and polluted areas, with rare green spots and poor access to good-quality food shops, or even flood-prone or near dumping sites areas: such places are where the most disadvantaged groups concentrate (Fairburn et al. 2009). Low-income and minority groups tend to possess less political power to oppose the location of sources of environmental hazards in their proximity, and experience economic discrimination in the housing market, which increases residential segregation.

As defined previously, vulnerable groups react more strongly to environmental hazards and nuisances and, consequently, are more susceptible to develop health effects. Extreme age is a well-known factor of vulnerability and the elderly, infants and pregnant women may be more severely affected. For some categories of hazards, health symptoms may manifest themselves later in the life span of individuals exposed during pregnancy of early childhood; this is, for example, the case for chemical substances that have endocrine-disrupting properties whose effects may appear at adolescence or further on. Another vulnerable category is people with pre-existing health limitations.

In the city of Paris, inhabitants residing in census blocks (2000 people on average), whose socio-economical profile was the most disadvantaged and where the long-term level of air pollution was the highest (using the nitrogen dioxide air quality indicator), died more frequently after short-term air quality episodes than those from more well-off census blocks (Deguen et al. 2015). Different explanations can shed light on this obviously unfair situation. A first set of reasons relates to cumulative exposure over the life span: groups with a lower socio-economic status are more likely to live (and have lived since childhood) in houses where the indoor air quality is poorer (because of insufficient ventilation, in particular in order to reduce energy costs); also, since they are often blue-collar workers and from other modest social categories, they are more likely to be exposed to specific occupational pollutants. Another set of reasons has to do with the higher prevalence of chronic conditions among these groups with limited economic and educational resources, in relation with the consequences of this cumulative exposure issue and with other risk factors such as smoking, unhealthy nutritional habits and obesity, and lack of physical activity. Finally, these social groups have less recourse to medical services, unless already seriously affected. By these processes, disadvantaged populations present a "predisposition" to the development of health conditions that might result from any additional environmental insult (in this case, short-term air pollution episodes). Efforts to document, in each city setting, where this type of summation of risk factors arises and who might cumulate these disadvantages is important to design appropriate mitigation and preventive public policies. Beyond this particular illustration in the context of France, the synergistic effects of the combination of factors often de-multiply in countries where social and environmental disparities are sharper, where the welfare state is less developed, and where the democratic debate on public policies at national or local levels is more limited.

A recent report on environmental health inequalities in the WHO European region (WHO Euro 2019) showed that environmental health inequalities have tended to persist or even increase over time (despite the improvement of environmental conditions in most countries in the region, an observation particularly true for energy poverty, thermal comfort, damp homes and noise perception (this conclusion was backed by another work from the EU environmental agency on social vulnerability to air pollution, noise and extreme temperatures; EEA 2019).

CONCLUSION: WELL-BEING BEYOND THE ABSENCE OF DISEASE AND INFIRMITY[7]

According to Morris and Saunders (2017), well-being can be defined as a measure of what matters to people in every sphere of their lives. A good physical state is an important element, but mental health and social integration are also essential components, underscoring how important social interactions count for well-being. Well-being has to do with experiencing one's capacity to seize opportunities (e.g. for education, employment, friendship or civic participation) and living in places that offer access to a safe and wholesome environment (good-quality green or blue spaces, well-maintained urban areas, proximity and access to commodities and to natural life—forest, mountain etc.). Well-being is also closely related to fairness: it declines when individuals and social groups feel that the economic and social benefits are disproportionally captured by others. Well-being should thus be extended to align with a multi-dimensional vision of human development that includes fairness. It should also be embedded in a wider approach integrating ecosystems.

In fact, because interactions between biodiversity, health of ecosystems, animal health and human health and well-being are so strong, both positively and negatively, the relevant framework to analyse their synergies should be labelled "ecological public health", a concept that echoes that of "One Health" promoted by WHO, FAO and UNEP since inception of the twenty-first century.

To realize that public health must now be considered from an ecological perspective means that its relation with the environment must be viewed on a broad spatial and temporal scale. The economic model that has developed along the twentieth century and expanded during the past three or four decades has driven profound changes to the ecosystems and planetary processes (Rockström et al. 2009; Steffen et al. 2015) that have already deeply degraded biodiversity, and now jeopardize the health and well-being of humankind. To understand this is a prerequisite to devising and implementing policies aiming to reduce the pace of these transformations and, in the long run, to stabilize the situation. As stated by Morris and Saunders (2017), "*It is now inconceivable that health, well-being, health*

[7] Preamble to the Constitution of WHO adopted by the International Health Conference, New York, 19 June–22 July 1946: "Health is a state of complete physical, mental and social well-being and not merely the absence of disease or infirmity".

care, and equity (...) can be delivered without rediscovering an environmen-
tal conceptualization of public health for the 21st century. It will demand
pursuit, through policy and action, of outcomes that recognize a 'quadruple
bottom line' measured in health and well-being, environmental quality,
equity, and sustainability".

REFERENCES

Bolte, G., Pauli, A., & Hornberg, C. (2011). Environmental justice: Social disparities in environmental exposures and health: Overview. *Encyclopedia of
Environmental Health, 2,* 459–470.

Caldas, E. D. (2016). Pesticide poisoning in Brazil. Reference Module in
Earth Systems and Environmental Sciences. https://doi.org/10.1016/
B978-0-12-409548-9.10282-9.

CDC. (2020). Climate effects on health. Retrieved August 28, 2020, from
https://www.cdc.gov/climateandhealth/effects/default.htm.

Corvalan, C., Hales, S., & McMichael, A. (2005). Ecosystems and human
well-being: health synthesis: A report of the Millennium Ecosystem
Assessment: WHO, Geneva. Retrieved from https://apps.who.int/iris/
handle/10665/43354.

Deguen, S., Petit, C., Delbarre, A., et al. (2015). Neighbourhood characteristics
and long-term air pollution Levels modify the association between the short-
term nitrogen dioxide concentrations and all-cause mortality in Paris. *PLoS
ONE.* https://doi.org/10.1371/journal.pone.0131463.

Destoumieux-Garzón, D., Mavingui, P., Boetsch, G., et al. (2018). The One
Health concept: 10 years old and a long road ahead. *Frontiers in Veterinary
Science, 5.* Retrieved from https://www.frontiersin.org/article/10.3389/
fvets.2018.00014.

EEA. (2019). European Environment Agency. Unequal exposure and unequal
impacts: Social vulnerability to air pollution, noise and extreme temperatures in
Europe, EEA Report No 22/2018. Copenhagen.

EU. (2020). Protecting soil in the CAP. Retrieved August 18, 2020, from https://
ec.europa.eu/info/food-farming-fisheries/sustainability/environmental-
sustainability/natural-resources/soil_en.

Fairburn, J., Butler, B., & Smith, G. (2009). Environmental justice in South
Yorkshire: Locating social deprivation and poor environments using multiple
indicators. *Local Environment, 14(2),* 139–154.

Ganzleben, C., & Kazmierczak, A. (2020). Leaving no one behind – Understanding
environmental inequality in Europe. *Environmental Health, 19,* 57.

GBD 2016 Risk Factors Collaborators. (2017). Global, regional, and national
comparative risk assessment of 84 behavioural, environmental and occupational,

and metabolic risks or clusters of risks, 1990–2016: A systematic analysis for the Global Burden of Disease Study 2016. *The Lancet, 390*(10100), 1345–1422.

Gelormino, E., Melis, G., Marietta, C., et al. (2015). From built environment to health inequalities: An explanatory framework based on evidence. *Preventive Medicine Reports, 2*, 737–745.

Gouveia, N. (2016). Addressing environmental health inequalities. *International Journal of Environmental Research and Public Health, 13*(9), 858.

Hunter, R. F., Cleland, C., Cleary, C., et al. (2019). Environmental, health, well-being, social and equity effects of urban green space interventions: A meta-narrative evidence synthesis. *Environment International, 130*, 104923.

IDMC. (2018). Internal Displacement Monitoring Centre Global Report on Internal Displacement 2018. Retrieved from https://www.internal-displacement.org/global-report/grid2018/.

IPBES. (2019). Global assessment on biodiversity and ecosystem services. Retrieved from https://ipbes.net/global-assessment.

Kanemoto, K., Moran, D., Lenzen, M., et al. (2014). International trade undermines national emission reduction targets: New evidence from air pollution. *Global Environmental Change, 24*, 52–59.

Landrigan, P. J., Fuller, R., Nereus, J., et al. (2017). The Lancet Commission on pollution and health. *The Lancet, 386*(10006), 1861–1914.

MDG. (2018). Millennium Development Goal 7: Ensure environmental sustainability. Retrieved from https://www.who.int/news-room/fact-sheets/detail/millennium-development-goals-(mdgs).

Melillo, J. M., Richmond, T. C., & Yohe, G. W. (Eds.). (2014). *Climate change impacts in the United States: The Third National Climate Assessment.* U.S. Global Change Research Program.

Morris, G., & Saunders, P. (2017). *The environment in health and well-being.* Oxford Research Encyclopedias, Environmental Science, Oxford University Press.

Natural Resources Canada. Retrieved October 25, 2020, from https://www.nrcan.gc.ca/climate-change/impacts-adaptations/climate-change-impacts-forests/forest-carbon/13085.

Office for Disease Prevention and Health Promotion. (2020). Retrieved August 18, 2020, from https://www.healthypeople.gov/2020/topics-objectives/topic/environmental-health.

PAHO. (2016). Environmental gradients and health inequalities in the Americas. Access to Water and Sanitation as Determinants of Health. Washington, DC. Retrieved from https://iris.paho.org/bitstream/handle/10665.2/31404/9789275119136-eng.pdf?sequence=1&isAllowed=y.

Prüss-Ustün, A., & Corvalán, C. (2006). *Preventing disease through healthy environments: Towards an estimate of the environmental burden of disease.* Geneva, Switzerland: WHO.

Prüss-Ustün, A., Wolf, J., Corvalán, C., et al. (2016). *Preventing disease through healthy environments. A global assessment of the burden of disease from environmental risks.* Geneva: WHO.

Public Health England and UCL Institute of Health Equity. (2014). *Local action on health inequalities: Improving access to green spaces.* London: PHE.

Rockström, J., Steffen, W., Noone, K., et al. (2009). Planetary boundaries: Exploring the safe operating space for humanity. *Ecology and Society, 14*, 32.

Sanson, A., & Burke, S. (2019). Climate Change and children: An Issue of Intergenerational Justice. *Children and Peace*: 343–362.

Song, X. P., Hansen, M. C., Stehman, S. V., et al. (2018). Global land change from 1982 to 2016. *Nature, 560*, 639–643.

Steffen, W., Richardson, K., Rockström, J., et al. (2015). Planetary boundaries: Guiding human development on a changing planet. *Science, 349*, 1286–1287.

UN Water. (2020). Monitoring SDG6 water and sanitation. Retrieved August 23, 2020, from https://www.sdg6monitoring.org/indicator-611/.

UNEP/ILRI. (2020). United Nations Environment Programme and International Livestock Research Institute. Preventing the next pandemic: Zoonotic diseases and how to break the chain of transmission. Nairobi, Kenya.

World Health Organization. Preventing disease through healthy environments. Geneva, Switzerland: WHO; 2006

WHO. (2018a). Climate change and health. Retrieved August 28, 2020, from https://www.who.int/news-room/fact-sheets/detail/climate-change-and-health.

WHO. (2018b). Ambient (outdoor air pollution). Retrieved August 20, 2020, from https://www.who.int/news-room/fact-sheets/detail/ambient-(outdoor)-air-quality-and-health.

WHO Euro. (2019). *Environmental health inequalities in Europe.* Second assessment report. WHO Euro, Copenhagen.

CHAPTER 5

Toward Health-Environment Policy in a Well-being Economy

Éloi Laurent, Fabio Battaglia,
Giorgia Dalla Libera Marchiori, Alessandro Galli,
Amanda Janoo, Raluca Munteanu, and Claire Sommer

INTRODUCTION: WHY THE HEALTH-ENVIRONMENT NEXUS MATTERS FOR A WELL-BEING ECONOMY

We urgently need to move away from considering natural resources and creatures as entries on a balance sheet where monetary economic value trumps all other values. Even with landmark studies proving the opposite, a cost-benefit approach has been the dominant way we think about—and account for—the value of a healthy environment.

É. Laurent (✉)
OFCE/Sciences Po, Ponts ParisTech, Paris, France

Stanford University, Stanford, CA, USA
e-mail: eloi.laurent@sciencespo.fr

F. Battaglia
University of Edinburgh, Edinburgh, UK
e-mail: s1516840@sms.ed.ac.uk

© The Author(s), under exclusive license to Springer Nature Switzerland AG 2021
É. Laurent (ed.), *The Well-being Transition*,
https://doi.org/10.1007/978-3-030-67860-9_5

But this is a false premise. There is no trade-off between "saving the economy" and "saving lives" nor between "the economy" and "the environment": If we degrade our environment, we will harm our health and destroy our economy. The real trade-off we face is choosing between the joint preservation of these three valuable dimensions of human existence or all three degrading into irreparable loss. To make this reality more tangible for policy-makers, new ways of thinking are needed.

A reckoning happened on April 7, 2020. On this day, half of the planet's governments, representing half of humanity, were in lock-down due to the COVID-19 pandemic. In doing so, these state representatives decided that health—connected to our environment—was superior to economic growth.

This chapter asserts that human health and the environment form a nexus and the support system, that *makes a Well-being Economy possible*. After describing the health-environment nexus, we illustrate it with five areas that show these interconnections.

THE HEALTH-ENVIRONMENT NEXUS: EVIDENCE FROM SCIENCE

Scholars have long highlighted the positive impact that protecting the environment can have on people's health and well-being. While it may feel intuitive to some, there is value in describing what scientists have concluded through research.

G. D. L. Marchiori
Swedish Organization for Global Health, Stockholm, Sweden

Uppsala University, Uppsala, Sweden
e-mail: directors@sogh.se

A. Galli
Global Footprint Network, Oakland, CA, USA

University of Siena, Siena, Italy
e-mail: Alessandro@footprintnetwork.org

A. Janoo • C. Sommer
Well being Economy Alliance, London, UK
e-mail: amanda@well-beingeconomy.org; claire@weall.org

R. Munteanu
Swedish Organization for Global Health, Stockholm, Sweden
e-mail: healthy_planet@sogh.se

From a micro-perspective, several different benefits of being exposed to, or of carrying out, certain activities in nature, as opposed to indoor or synthetic environments, have been repeatedly found. These include lower levels of negative emotions such as anger, frustration and sadness, reduced mental fatigue, stress and cortisol levels, reduced incidence of respiratory diseases such as asthma and reduced mortality from stroke, increased physical activity, happiness and self-esteem as well as many other cognitive, psychological and physiological benefits.[1] This is in addition to a vast category of other benefits: social (e.g. easier interaction), economic (e.g. increased value of properties surrounding areas such as parks) and spiritual (e.g. increased inspiration).[2]

A pioneer study carried out in 1984 found that even just looking at nature had a positive impact, with patients recovering earlier and requiring less strong drugs if their hospital room window faced leafy trees instead of plain bricks.[3] More recently, some studies are also starting to investigate the extent to which technological advancement and modern devices could increase human interaction with nature, although this field is still under development and many questions are still unanswered to this day.[4]

From a macro-perspective, the nexus among health, development and the environment has been the subject of several books and reports in the 1960s and 1970s—notably Rachel Carson's Silent Spring and The Club of Rome's The Limits to Growth. Also, a conference on the Human Environment, which also happened to be the first global environmental governance conference ever, was organized by the United Nations in 1972.

Yet, it is perhaps the publication of the *Our planet, our health* report by the WHO in 1992 that really marked a turning point. Tasked with the responsibility of analyzing the interconnection between health and the environment at the international level, the authors stressed very clearly the importance of having healthy ecosystems for a healthy life—or, to put it differently, of respecting the environment to improve people's health conditions.[5] With so many issues affecting both developed and developing countries, they called for greater cooperation to prevent deaths due to

---

[1] See Bowler et al. (2010), Hartig et al. (2014), Keniger et al. (2013), Sandifer et al. (2015), Tzoulas et al. (2007).

[2] Again, see Sandifer et al. (2015).

[3] Ulrich (1984).

[4] Frumkin et al. (2017).

[5] WHO (1992).

pollution and other diseases such as malaria, to ensure everyone had access to basic resources, and to reduce risks from biological or chemical hazards.

From that moment on, and particularly since the 1994 Helsinki Declaration and its annexed Charter,[6] the WHO has continued to stress the importance of promoting what it has been referring to as environmental health.

More recent publications, such as the 2019 Lancet Countdown Report, have widely re-affirmed the deep interconnectedness between health and the environment.[7] The authors focused particularly on climate change, arguing that despite growth experienced in fields such as those of renewable and low-carbon energies, "current progress is inadequate".[8] This could "result in a fundamentally altered world" where the health conditions of people of all ages are affected,[9] thus reinforcing previous work indicating that the passing of key planetary thresholds could trigger a series of cascade effects causing continued warming of the Earth climate despite reductions in human Greenhouse Gases (GHGs) emissions.[10] One clear example is that of heat waves, whose consequences can affect both the elderly (e.g. with heart failures) and younger people (e.g. with respiratory diseases). Given the large health benefits of healthier ecosystems, the authors thus see tackling the climate emergency as a "transition from threat to opportunity"[11] and indeed external commentators framed it as "the greatest global health opportunity of the 21st century".[12]

The strong nexus between health and the environment was also at the heart of the World Happiness Report (WHR), published in March 2020, in the midst of the COVID-19 pandemic. The WHR re-launched first of all the findings of a World Gallup Poll which showed that a large majority of respondents consider the environment as a policy priority and global warming as a threat to them and their families. The authors then showed how higher PM10, PM2.5 and maximum temperature levels decrease people's overall life satisfaction ratings in OECD countries. Using London as a case study and analyzing the Happiness data set, they also showed that walking, doing sports or gardening outdoors significantly increase

[6] See WHO (1994).
[7] Watts et al. (2019).
[8] *ivi*, p. 1387.
[9] Ibidem.
[10] Steffen et al. (2018).
[11] *ivi*, p. 1838.
[12] Wang and Horton (2015).

people's happiness, as do temperatures above 25° (whereas windy and rainy days act the opposite way).

In light of all the benefits of living or working in a natural environment discussed so far and pollution being still the cause of almost half-a-million deaths every year in the sole European Union, the European Environment Agency recently called for "systemic change through visionary policies" in order to protect the environment and improve the health and well-being of European citizens.

SHIFTING ANALYSIS FROM COST-BENEFIT TO CO-BENEFITS

In this chapter, we offer and illustrate an alternative to the cost-benefit approach that dominantly underpins decisions about human health and the environment. We suggest instead a co-beneficial approach between ecosystems and human systems sustaining a well-being economy, with health as the great connector. This approach stems from a priority order: The strength of the Biosphere—our environment (1)—permits humans' capacities (2) that together allow economic activities (3). It just does not work the other way around.

For instance, considered from the point of view of cost-benefit analysis by mainstream economists,[13] depending on more or less heroic assumptions, mitigating climate change does not seem an urgent task because its potential damage is dwarfed by future gains in economic growth. Yet, considered from the point of view of co-benefits analysis, mitigating climate change underpins human well-being and brings about considerable social savings resulting from preserved health, as well as social gains associated with the creation of an estimated 24 million new jobs by 2030 (ILO 2018). Figure 5.1 highlights the links between the environment, health and the economy defined by five co-benefits areas.

---

[13] See, for instance, Nordhaus (2017).

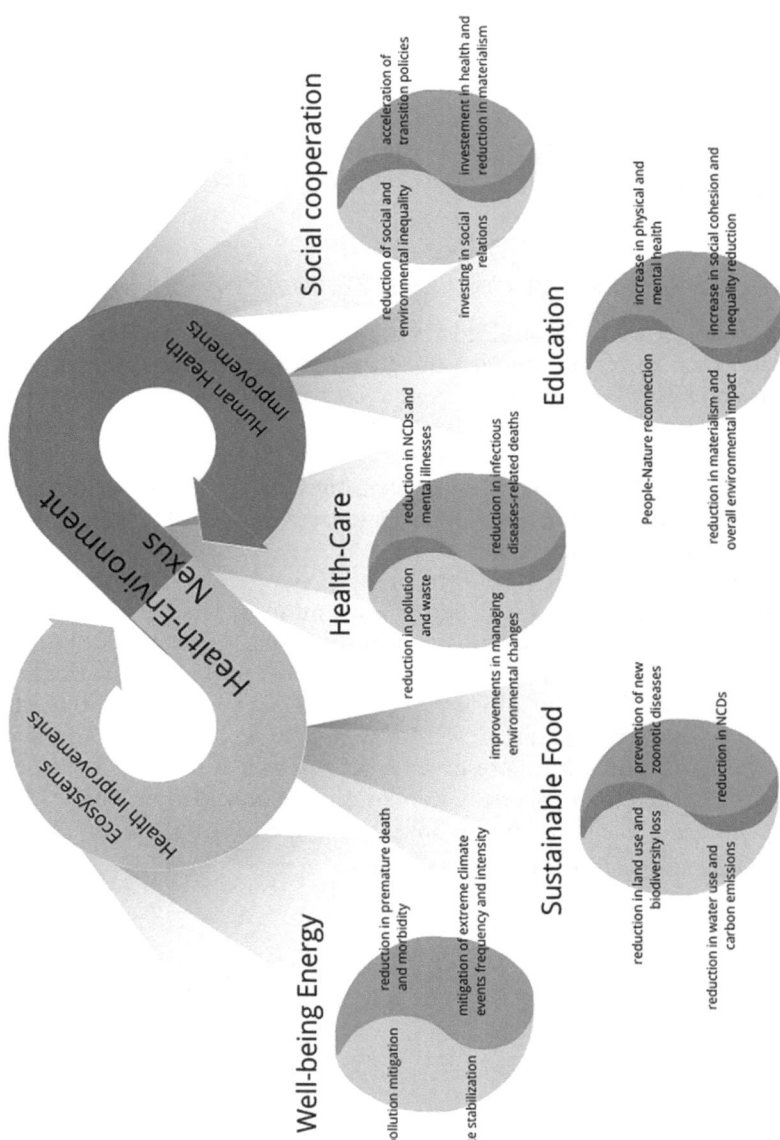

Fig. 5.1 The health-environment nexus

The Health-Environment Nexus: Five Co-benefits Key Policy Areas

As the world strives to navigate the global environmental and health crises, much of our failure to effectively respond comes from the perceived trade-off between health versus economy or economy versus nature. This is because our current economic system is inextricably linked with our health and environment and we cannot change one without influencing the other.

Our economies, particularly in the affluent world, drive systems of production and consumption that are exhausting our planet's resources (Wiedmann et al. 2020), destroying habitats and leading to humans being in much closer contact with animals who carry diseases such as COVID-19. As a Living Planet Report (LPR) 2020 report recently outlined (WWF 2020), "nearly half of all new emerging infectious diseases from animals are linked to land-use change, agricultural intensification and the food industry". Furthermore, the industrialization, urbanization and air pollution that can come from our current economic system has increased the severity of pandemics' impact on human health (Conticini et al. 2020; Setti et al. 2020).

Our collective hesitation to truly heal our society and the environment comes from a fear of the negative impact this would have on the "the economy". However, the economy is ultimately just a word for the way that we produce and provide for one another. Every good we produce ultimately comes first and foremost from the earth, and every service we provide is valuable insofar as it contributes to our well-being. Our economy is not something given. It is *us*, our interaction with one another and our natural environment, to produce and provide the things we need for a happy and healthy life. And, it is only a facet of the true force behind our prosperity: social cooperation. We must not forget that the economy and the wealth it generates is a means and that the ultimate measure of its success will be its contribution to our well-being.

In an effort to move beyond viewing the economy as a barrier for effective response to the crises of our time, we illustrate how transformations in key economic sectors can improve health and the environment. In the following section we outline five intervention areas for policy-makers in the economy and illustrate how reforms to our healthcare, food, energy, social cooperation and education systems can lead to substantial improvement and co-benefits for the health of our people and planet.

Area 1: Healthcare—Prevention and Mitigation

In the last two centuries, the pattern of diseases worldwide has changed drastically. On one side, we can celebrate achievements such as the increase in life expectancy (in general terms) and the decrease in maternal mortality. On the other, however, we must recognize that our way of living, especially in the Western countries, is threatening our health directly in many different ways, from the release of toxic substances in the environment to working routines causing many mental illnesses (Carson 1962; Watts et al. 2019; Wong et al. 2019). Therefore, it becomes fundamental to recognize the importance of healthcare prevention, on one side, and mitigation, on the other.

Prevention is a word often used, but rarely too little is put into practice. An Italian saying reads "preventing is better than curing". By now, for example, it is known that people who do not smoke are less likely to develop certain diseases, such as cancer (Walser et al. 2008). Collectively, when policy puts prevention into practice, great results can be achieved. For instance, in 2019, the city of London introduced Ultra Low Emission Zones (ULEZ). A few months later, those areas registered a 29% decrease of NO_2 concentration compared to no ULEZ.[14] In the 1990s, bans on (1) asbestos in most EU countries (Directive 76/769/EEC) and (2) the use of chlorofluorocarbons (CFCs) worldwide were put in place (Montreal protocol, 1990). Asbestos was proven to be highly carcinogenic and CFCs were found to cause the depletion of the ozone layer. These preventive measures have improved human and environmental health while reducing the cost and need for healthcare. Recently, for instance, NASA has reported that the ozone hole above Antarctica is at its smallest since its discovery in 1982.

However, prevention might no longer be possible in some cases, since we have already crossed three of the planetary boundaries and we now have to deal with the consequences (Steffen et al. 2015). For instance, heat waves due to climate change and the burst of new infectious diseases, such as COVID-19, are putting health systems under unprecedented pressure. The current pandemic highlighted the importance of being prepared

---

[14] Central London ultra low emission zone—six-month report.

to mitigate dramatic changes as well as the feasibility of major behavioral changes in a short period of time. Healthcare will need to be prioritized in the public spending with the goal of ensuring people's well-being. Therefore, privatization of the health system, where profit has priority over patients' and staff's health, is a dangerous move that should be avoided. A clear example of two conflicting approaches is the United States and South Korea. The United States has one of the highest spending in healthcare, but it remains, among the high-income countries, the place with the highest maternal mortality. One doctor when facing the US Congress said, "In all my work, I had one primary duty and that was to use my medical expertise for the financial benefit of the organization [insurance company] for which I worked".[15] Conversely, SARS and MERS outbreaks in South Korea in 2002–2003 and 2015, respectively, led to better preparedness in the government. These efforts culminated in a massive revamping of the Korean Centre for Disease Control, with new clinics and testing facilities, equipment and medical emergency tests (Oh et al. 2020; Kim et al. 2020). Previous outbreaks also led to a greater citizens' willingness to comply with personal restrictions.

For healthcare prevention and mitigation to function properly, public engagement is a fundamental component. The current pandemic has shown us the lack of knowledge among the public in how to deal with the virus, both in terms of protecting oneself and, most importantly, others. Public health education is not part of most school curricula (Paakkari and Okan 2019), unless it is a university degree, and it definitely is not incorporated in most workplaces training. However, making health knowledge accessible in everyday life will mean society as a whole will act to protect our health, and the environment our health depends on.

AREA 2: FOOD SYSTEMS

In the last decades, the agricultural sector has seen a remarkable increase in productivity, strongly driven by an increased use of fertilizers, pesticides and agricultural machinery. However, while these gains have allowed providing food for a greater share of a growing human population, aggressive agricultural practices are now taking a toll on the environment and on human health. The agriculture sector is a significant contributor to climate change, causing 37% of total global greenhouse gas (GHG) emissions

---

[15] The Dirty War On The NHS, documentary by John Pilger, 2010.

(Smith et al. 2014), as well as deforestation and resultant biodiversity loss, water and air pollution and soil degradation, and increased risk of pathogen spillover, to name a few. To top it off, the recent improvements in aggregate productivity have not been uniform either—millions of people still lack access to proper nutrition—and productivity gains are expected to slow down in the coming two decades (Ray et al. 2013).

It is imperative that new practices that minimize the use of non-renewable inputs, that integrate biological and ecological processes and that make efficient use of people's individual and collective capacities are implemented (McIntyre et al. 2009; Pretty 2007). The re-evaluation of current agricultural production practices and the integration of strategies that account for the climate crisis as well as food inequalities is a great well-being opportunity.

It is widely accepted that the animal industry is one of the most destructive components of agriculture, with cattle causing the most environmental damage than any other non-human species (e.g. GHG emissions, overgrazing, soil erosion, desertification, tropical deforestation, see Goodland 1997). Numerous studies have indicated that a reduction in meat consumption could deliver environmental, economic and health benefits (e.g. Galli et al. 2017; Kim et al. 2019), including a decrease in agricultural GHG release, in land clearing and the resultant species extinction, as well as reduction in the incidence of diet-related chronic non-communicable diseases (NCDs). And yet, no country has yet implemented any campaigns to significantly decrease animal product consumption.

No country currently penalizes animal product consumption, but other tax programs aimed at changing the public's behavior are already in place. Over the last decade, several countries including Brazil, France and Hungary have imposed consumption taxes on food as well as stimulants such as alcohol and tobacco in order to promote a healthier lifestyle. In 2010, the Danish government introduced a tax on saturated fat products—a strategy that led to a 10–15% reduction in the consumption of these products, as well as generated substantial tax revenue. According to recent models (8, 9, 10), a meat tax is a feasible strategy, likely to simultaneously lead to a reduction in pollutants as well as improve population health and provide monetary benefits.

In addition to the dysfunctionalities seen in the food production systems, there are flaws in the other phases of the food cycle: specifically in the distribution, consumption and disposal phase. The COVID-19 crisis has served as a harsh reminder of the fragilities of the global food systems (e.g. Garnett et al. 2020), as closed borders and disruptions in the food-supply chain have led to devastating food waste and loss on one end, and shortages on the other.

A large problem concerning food systems worldwide is the widespread wastage and loss at all phases of the food cycle. Currently, one-third of the food that is produced for human consumption does not make it on the plate, as it is either wasted, predominantly at the consumption stage in high-income countries, or lost during the production stage in low-income countries (El-Hage Scialabba 2019). The wasted food is a sink for natural resources such as agricultural land, as well as water, energy and fertilizer, as well as a source of emissions, specifically 6% of global GHG emissions or three times the amount of global emissions from aviation (Poore and Nemecek 2018). Cutting food crop losses by half, for instance, would reduce the environmental impact of human dietary choices, while also allowing 1 billion additional people to be fed at current food production levels (Kummu et al. 2012), thus highlighting the health-environment co-benefits associated with fixing the food wastage issue.

Another example of the dysfunctionality of the current food-supply chain is the imbalance in dietary patterns, with nearly 11% of the world population enduring malnourishment and about 2 billion suffering from obesity in 2016 (BCFN 2016). Urbanization, globalization of food systems and the homogenization of food behaviors are causing a shift toward more ultra-processed, protein- and sugar-rich foods (Kearney 2010), a trend which has been fueling obesity and non-communicable diseases, as well as putting pressure on the planet's ecological assets. In addition, as of today, more than 55% of the world's population live in cities and consume 79% of the global food supply (FAO 2019).

Only an approximate 30% of the world's population manage to source crop-based foods from within 100 km (Kinnunen et al. 2020). Most food systems in Europe are highly dependent on food resources from abroad, an interconnectedness characterized by trade-shock-related fragilities and lack of resilience, as well as energy inefficiency (Galli et al. 2020).

To sum up, global food systems are characterized by many anomalies and dysfunctionalities that often reinforce each other to the detriment of human and planetary health. Still, several well-being opportunities are connected with the way in which food is consumed—as dietary choices are among the leading global causes of mortality and environmental degradation (Clark et al. 2019), and they too can reinforce each other: opting for healthy food (e.g. fruit, vegetables, beans and whole grains) more often than not contributes to increasing our planet's health by protecting climate (Springmann et al. 2016) and water resources, thus helping us meet global sustainability targets (Willett et al. 2019). In other words, foods known to be associated with improved human health have among the lowest environmental impacts (Clune et al. 2017; Kim et al. 2019), while resource-intensive and environmentally harmful foods are often associated with the largest increases in disease risk (Bechthold et al. 2019; González-García et al. 2018), thus reinforcing the health-environment co-benefits of the food sector.

Moreover, further health-environment co-benefits could be realized through a shift toward healthier dietary choices as such shift would substantially lower the rising costs incurred by the healthcare systems of EU member states that are due to cardiovascular diseases (almost €111 billion in 2015) and diabetes ($181 billion in 2017) as well as the non-healthcare costs due to decreased labor supply and productivity, lower tax revenues and lower returns on human capital investments (EU Science Hub 2019).

AREA 3: TOWARD WELL-BEING ENERGY

To put it simply, the current global energy system does not make sense from a well-being point of view. While the Sun provides 8000 times what we need to power and operate our economies, they still massively rely on fossil fuels (representing 80% of today's global energy supply "mix"), which aggravate climate change that increasingly destroys human well-being.

Even more puzzling is the fact that this 80% proportion has barely changed in the last 50 years, all the while the destructive power of climate change on humans' lives was visibly intensifying and renewable energy competitiveness was increasing to the point of becoming cheaper than fossil fuels. According to IRENA, while solar photovoltaic was still more than twice more costly in 2010 than fossil fuels in electricity generation, it is now more than twice cheaper. The transition of energy systems away from fossil fuels is a huge well-being opportunity.

When the lens is enlarged and indicators other than monetary cost and competitiveness are considered, the magnitude of this opportunity becomes even more obvious. When all health co-benefits are taken into account (as they should), the transition to renewable energies leads to saving 15 times the cost of their deployment (according to IRENA). What is more, global and national energy transition strategies linking health, employment, sustainability and safety co-benefits offer compelling and robust evidence of immediate and long-term gains.

Mark Jacobson (Stanford University) and his co-authors have developed a roadmap for the transition to 100% of renewable energies by 2050 for 139 countries in the world and 50 US states, showing that it would lead to the elimination of 4–7 million premature deaths related to air pollution, the mitigation of the main sources of climate change while creating almost 25 million net new jobs and stabilizing energy prices. Health gains in particular are immediate and massive: the transition to low-carbon energy could save 4.6 million lives from premature ending.

Fully developed and detailed national plans also exist, such as the French 2017–2050 négaWatt scenario modeling, aiming for a halving of final energy consumption by 2050, driven by sufficiency (60%) and efficiency (40%) with the contribution of renewable sources to the energy supply multiplied by 3.4, allowing to cover 99.7% of the primary energy demand by 2050. Especially interesting in this case study is the purpose of this feasible national energy transition to do away with all non-renewable energy, including nuclear.

AREA 4: INVESTING IN EQUALITY AND SOCIAL RELATIONS

Investing in equality focuses on the co-benefits resulting from the mitigation of social and environmental inequality. Investing in social relations focuses on the health-environment benefits of a better allocation of time in favor of social relations and the co-benefits resulting from mitigating social isolation.

Regarding the first policy strategy, there is growing evidence of a sustainability-justice nexus that essentially means that it makes environmental sense to mitigate our social crisis (by reducing inequality) and social sense to mitigate our environmental crises (by reducing human pressure on ecosystems).

While the inequality triggered by environmental crises is painfully obvious around the world, the transmission channels from justice to sustainability need to be outlined.

First, equality reduces the need for environmentally harmful and socially unnecessary economic growth that destroys biodiversity and ecosystems (the most equal nations on the planet such as the Nordic countries are also the ones that have the most ambitious national environmental regulations). Second, equality reduces the ecological irresponsibility of the richest, within each country and among nations. Third, equality, which positively affects the health of individuals and groups, increases the social-ecological resilience of communities and societies and strengthens their collective ability to adapt to accelerating environmental change. Fourth, equality fosters collective action aimed at preserving natural resources. Finally, equality increases the political acceptability of environmental pre-occupations and the ability to offset the potential socially regressive effects of environmental policies (such as carbon taxation).

When it comes to co-benefits of investment in social relations, it should be said that the link between the quality and density of social life and physical and physiological health is of remarkable robustness.

Increasing family and social time, for instance, can be achieved by promoting a shorter working week, which—recent research has found—could have a series of co-benefits for both people and the planet. A reduced working week could in fact contribute to human health by improving employee satisfaction and ameliorating their quality of life; meanwhile, it can also boost productivity while decreasing the scale of human production and consumption activities thus curbing CO_2 emissions.

Addressing social isolation is an important part of such a policy strategy. Understood not as a choice of life, but as an insufficient connection to social networks, or even a total disconnection from sociability, social isolation is growing in strength in a number of developed countries (such as the US, the UK and France) with strong health-environment consequences. It is, for instance, a risk factor in case of heat waves.

AREA 5: EDUCATION

Education is likely to play a critical role in favoring transitioning to a sustainable future as it helps expand basic sustainability literacy, narrow social gaps (Abdullah et al. 2013), reduce inequality (De Gregorio and Lee 2003) and favor a decent quality of life. Moreover, educational attainments are the single strongest predictor of climate change awareness (Lee et al. 2015).

Education and Health are fundamental enabling factors of individuals' well-being. They should be at the center of well-being economies. Mutual relationships exist between them. On one side, education has important social impacts on health and its determinants as people with more years of schooling tend to have healthier lifestyles (thus reducing the need for healthcare), nurturing human development and favoring better personal, family and community well-being (Desjardins and Schuller 2006). On the other, although health is usually considered a co-product of education in mainstream public policy debates and further research might be needed (Behrman 1996), evidence exists of child and adolescent health (and nutrition for that matter) being a factor enabling educational achievements (Suhrcke and de Paz Nieves 2011).

Education is thus an important starting point for change, a position reinforced by it being named one of the six key transformations (Sachs et al. 2019) for achieving the SDGs. And modifying current education systems (e.g. via making issues such as climate change, resource use/over-use, limits-aware and system thinking mandatory at all levels of public education) represents a social tipping intervention (Otto et al. 2020) to catalyze a social shift toward sustainability (especially when current students will enter the job market and/or decision-making bodies). In fact, education should not be just accumulation of knowledge, but it should provide the tools to question how that knowledge can and should, or should not, be used. It should create the physical and mental space to practice critical thinking and explore the concept of responsibility as individuals and society. Through reformed education (R-Education), sustainability should not be imposed by educators but rather realized by students. Education has the power to shape the priorities of our society. The philosopher Deborah Osberg says that education should be the place where we experiment "with the possibility of the impossible" (Osberg 2010).

Unfortunately, most of the current Western education systems have so far failed in providing this space and a disconnect is seen between environmental education and personal responsibility. Outside classrooms, students fail to link their individual actions with environmental issues (Blumstein and Saylan 2007). In fact, the aim of the current system is to prepare people for the job market, which means to serve the current economic model, the backbone of the climate crisis and social inequalities (Fioramonti 2017). As David Orr pointed out in 1990, "today's high school or college graduate is poorly prepared for any but a fossil fuel-powered, urban existence" (Orr 1994). The dominant way that children are taught thus ends up fueling the very unsustainable roots of our way of living. Instead, education can and should encompass trans- and multidisciplinarity, evidence-based approaches and experiential learning (e.g. schools as living laboratories). The recognition that we are living through a global crisis of values, ideas, perspectives and knowledge—which makes it also a crisis of education—is the first step toward needed changes in the education system.

Since the 1972 United Nations (UN) Stockholm Conference, the education system has gained a central role in easing the transition to a sustainable world (Collins et al. 2018), with a particular call for reorienting education toward sustainability, first by Article 36 of the Agenda 21 (UNCED 1992), and then by the Global Action Program on Education for Sustainable Development (UNESCO 2014).

More recently, in the United Nations Sustainable Development Goals (SDGs), education has been linked with 16 out of the 17 SDGs and "education for all" is highlighted as one of the main achievements to be reached. However, the economist Helen Kopnina, in an article published this year, asks what kind of education we are trying to achieve since the SDGs are still perpetuating the growth economic model (literally, goal 8) (Kopnina 2020). Western education has been already exported to other parts of the world with detrimental effects on the local social fabric (Black 2010). Local valuable knowledge has been lost for the sake of progress. Little time is spent outside the classroom in experiential learning and teaching activities allowing both students and educators to connect with, and learn from, nature despite several studies reporting the positive effects of nature in incrementing learning and reducing stress, both in children and in adults (Kuo et al. 2019).

Even in universities where critical thinking should be promoted, the growth narrative is embedded in the structure. Classic economic theory is still taught as a dogma, and no alternatives are presented as valuable (Raworth 2017). Even in health research, economic competitiveness seems to be the main drive. High proportions of grants are allocated in developing new products and services, which can be commercialized, rather than toward health policy and system change (Pratt and Loff 2012). All of this jeopardizes the critical thinking process necessary to find solutions to complex issues such as the climate crisis we are facing.

Rethinking and truly prioritizing education will mean to focus on the health of communities in the short-term, through interaction with nature and local knowledge, as well as in the long-term, by increasing environmental awareness and collaborations between different fields. Many young people are already making steps by themselves questioning the purpose of education as it stands now and its use in a system where the goal is still economic growth.

Conclusion: Toward Well-being Policy

The interventions we have highlighted in the five key co-benefits areas we have identified may seem bold, but such transformations are actually already taking place in communities and countries around the globe.

The major shift that is required for these initiatives to multiply is to combine the shift in measuring economic success from its ability to generate wealth to its contribution to the health and well-being of our people and planet with a shift to democratic design of well-being policies. Democracy is much a dimension of well-being than the method through which it should be valued.

References

Abdullah, A., et al. (2013). Does education reduce income inequality? A meta-regression analysis. *Journal of Economic Surveys, 29*(2), 301–316.

Barilla Center for Food & Nutrition (BCFN). (2016). *Eating Planet—Cibo e sostenibilità: costruire il nostro futuro*. Edizioni Ambiente (In Italian).

Bechthold, A., et al. (2019). Food groups and risk of coronary heart disease, stroke and heart failure: A systematic review and dose-response meta-analysis of prospective studies. *Critical Reviews in Food Science and Nutrition, 59*, 1071–1090.

Behrman, J. R. (1996). The Impact of Health and Nutrition on Education. *The World Bank Observer, 11*(1), 23–27. Retrieved from https://academic.oup.com/wbro/article-abstract/11/1/23/1675050.

Black, C. (2010). Schooling the world documentary.

Blumstein, D. T., & Saylan, C. (2007). The failure of environmental education (and how we can fix it). *PLoS Biology, 5*(5), e120. https://doi.org/10.1371/journal.pbio.0050120.

Bowler, D. E., et al. (2010). A systematic review of evidence for the added benefits to health of exposure to natural environments. *BMC Public Health, 10*, 456–466.

Carson, R. (1962). *The silent spring*. Houghton Mifflin.

Clark, M. A., Springmann, M., Hill, J., & Tilman, D. (2019). Multiple health and environmental impacts of foods. *PNAS, 116*(46), 23357–23362. https://doi.org/10.1073/pnas.1906908116.

Clune, S., Crossin, E., & Verghese, K. (2017). Systematic review of greenhouse gas emissions for different fresh food categories. *Journal of Cleaner Production, 140*, 766–783.

Collins, A., et al. (2018). Learning and teaching sustainability: The contribution of Ecological Footprint calculators. *Journal of Cleaner Production, 174*, 1000–1010.

Conticini, E., Frediani, B., & Caro, D. (2020). Can atmospheric pollution be considered a co-factor in extremely high level of SARS-CoV-2 lethality in Northern Italy? *Environmental Pollution, 261,* 114465.

De Gregorio, J., & Lee, J.-W. (2003). Education and income inequality: New evidence from cross country data. *The Review of Income and Wealth, 48*(3), 395–416. https://doi.org/10.1111/1475-4991.00060.

Desjardins, R., & Schuller, T. (Eds.). (2006). *Measuring the effects of education on health and civic engagement.* OECD. Retrieved from https://escholarship.org/content/qt6h84705f/qt6h84705f.pdf?t=o24hvg.

El-Hage Scialabba, N. (2019). The food wastage challenge. *Encyclopedia of Food Security and Sustainability, 1,* 178–186.

EU Science Hub. (2019). Cost of non-communicable diseases in the EU. Retrieved from https://ec.europa.eu/jrc/en/health-knowledge-gateway/societal-impacts/costs.

Food and Agriculture Organization of the United Nations (FAO). (2019). *FAO framework for the urban food agenda. Leveraging sub-national and local government action to ensure sustainable food systems and improved nutrition.* FAO. Retrieved from http://www.fao.org/3/ca3151en/CA3151EN.pdf.

Fioramonti, L. (2017). *Well-being economy: Success in a world without growth.* First published by Pan Macmillan South Africa.

Frumkin, H., et al. (2017). Nature contact and human health: A research agenda. *Environmental Health Perspectives, 125*(7).

Galli, A., et al. (2017). Mediterranean countries' food consumption and sourcing patterns: An ecological footprint viewpoint. *Science of the Total Environment, 578,* 383–391.

Galli, A., Moreno Pires, S., Iha, K., Alves, A. A., Lin, D., Mancini, M. S., & Teles, F. (2020). Sustainable food transition in Portugal: Assessing the footprint of dietary choices and gaps in national and local food policies. *Science of the Total Environment, 749,* 141307.

Garnett, P., Doherty, B., & Heron, T. (2020). Vulnerability of the United Kingdom's food supply chains exposed by COVID-19. *Nature Food, 1,* 315–318.

González-García, S., Esteve-Llorens, X., Moreira, M. T., & Feijoo, G. (2018). Carbon footprint and nutritional quality of different human dietary choices. *Science of the Total Environment, 644,* 77–94.

Goodland, R. (1997). Environmental sustainability in agriculture: Diet matters. *Ecological Economics, 23*(3), 189–200.

Hartig, T., et al. (2014). Nature and health. *Annual Review of Public Health, 35,* 207–228.

ILO. (2018). *World employment and social outlook 2018: Greening with jobs.* Geneva: ILO. ISBN: 978-92-2-131646-6.

Kearney, J. (2010). Food consumption trends and drivers. *Philosophical Transactions of the Royal Society of London. Series B, Biological Sciences,* *365*(1554), 2793–2807. https://doi.org/10.1098/rstb.2010.0149.

Keniger, L. C., et al. (2013). What are the benefits of interacting with nature? *International Journal of Environmental Research and Public Health,* *10*, 913–935.

Kim, B. F., et al. (2019). Country-specific dietary shifts to mitigate climate and water crises. *Global Environmental Change*, 101926. https://doi.org/10.1016/j.gloenvcha.2019.05.010.

Kim, Y. J., et al. (2020). Preparedness for COVID-19 infection prevention in Korea: A single-centre experience. *The Journal of Hospital Infection,* *105*(2), 370–372.

Kinnunen, P., Guillaume, J. H. A., Taka, M., D'Odorico, P., Siebert, S., Puma, M. J., Jalava, M., & Kummu, M. (2020). Local food crop production can fulfil demand for less than one third of the population. *Nature Food, 1*, 229–237.

Kopnina, H. (2020). Education for the future? Critical evaluation of education for sustainable development goals. *The Journal of Environmental Education.*

Kummu, M., de Moel, H., Porkka, M., Siebert, S., Varis, O., & Ward, P. J. (2012). Lost food, wasted resources: Global food supply chain losses and their impacts on freshwater, cropland, and fertiliser use. *Science of the Total Environment,* *438*, 477–489.

Kuo, M., Barnes, M., & Jordan, C. (2019). Do experiences with nature promote learning? Converging evidence of a cause-and-effect relationship. *Frontiers of Psychology.*

Lee, T. M., Markowitz, E. M., Howe, P. D., Ko, C.-Y., & Leiserowitz, A. A. (2015). Predictors of public climate change awareness and risk perception around the world. *Nature Climate Change, 5*, 1014–1020.

McIntyre, B. D., Herren, H. R., Wakhungu, R., & Watson, R. T. (Eds.). (2009). *International assessment of agricultural knowledge, science and technology for development (IAASTD): Global report.* Washington, DC: Island Press.

Nordhaus, W. D. (2017). Revisiting the social cost of carbon. *Proceedings of the National Academy of Sciences, 114*(7), 1518–1523.

Oh, J., et al. (2020). National response to COVID-19 in the Republic of Korea and lessons learned for other countries. *Health Systems & Reform, 6*(1), e1753464. https://doi.org/10.1080/23288604.2020.1753464.

Orr, D. W. (1994). The effective shape of our future. *Conservation Biology,* *8*(3), 622–624.

Osberg, D. (2010). Taking care of the future?: The complex responsibility of education & politics. In Complexity theory and the politics of education.

Otto, M., et al. (2020). Social tipping dynamics for stabilizing Earth's climate by 2050. *PNAS, 117*(5), 2354–2365.

Paakkari, L., & Okan, O. (2019). Health literacy—Talking the language of (school) education. *Health Literacy Research and Practice, 3*(3), e161–e164.

Poore, J., & Nemecek, T. (2018). Reducing food's environmental impacts through producers and consumers. *Science, 360*(6392), 987–992. https://doi.org/10.1126/science.aaq0216.

Pratt, B., & Loff, B. (2012). *Health research systems: Promoting health equity or economic competitiveness?* Bulletin of the WHO.

Pretty, J. (2007). Agricultural sustainability: Concepts, principles and evidence. *Philosophical Transactions of the Royal Society, B: Biological Sciences, 363*(1491), 447–465.

Raworth, K. (2017). *Doughnut economics: Seven ways to think like a 21st-century economist.* Random House Business Books.

Ray, D., et al. (2013). Yield trends are insufficient to double global crop production by 2050. *PLoS One, 8*(6), e66428. https://doi.org/10.1371/journal.pone.0066428.

Sachs, J. D., et al. (2019). Six transformations to achieve the sustainable development goals. *Nature Sustainability, 2*, 805–814.

Sandifer, P. A., et al. (2015). Exploring connections among nature, biodiversity, ecosystem services, and human health and well-being: Opportunities to enhance health and biodiversity conservation. *Ecosystem Services, 12*, 1–15.

Setti, L., Passarini, F., De Gennaro, G., et al. (2020). Potential role of particulate matter in the spreading of COVID-19 in Northern Italy: First observational study based on initial epidemic diffusion. *BMJ Open, 10*, e039338. https://doi.org/10.1136/bmjopen-2020-039338.

Smith, P., Bustamante, M., Ahammad, H., et al. (2014). Agriculture, Forestry and Other Land Use (AFOLU). In O. Edenhofer, R. Pichs-Madruga, Y. Sokona, E. Farahani, S. Kadner, K. Seyboth, A. Adler, I. Baum, S. Brunner, P. Eickemeier, B. Kriemann, J. Savolainen, S. Schlömer, C. von Stechow, T. Zwickel, & J. C. Minx (Eds.), *Climate change 2014: Mitigation of climate change. Contribution of Working Group III to the Fifth Assessment Report of the Intergovernmental Panel on Climate Change.* Cambridge: Cambridge University Press.

Springmann, M., Godfray, H. C. J., Rayner, M., & Scarborough, P. (2016). Analysis and valuation of the health and climate change cobenefits of dietary change. *PNAS, 113*, 4146–4151.

Steffen, W., et al. (2015). Planetary boundaries: Guiding human development on a changing planet. *Science, 347*(6223).

Steffen, W., et al. (2018). Trajectories of the earth system in the anthropocene. *PNAS, 115*(33), 8252–8259.

Suhrcke, M., & de Paz Nieves, C. (2011). *The impact of health and health behaviours on educational outcomes in high-income countries: A review of the evidence.* WHO Regional Office for Europe: Copenhagen.

Tzoulas, K., et al. (2007). Promoting ecosystem and human health in urban areas using Green Infrastructure: A literature review. *Landscape and Urban Planning, 81*, 167–178.

Ulrich, R. S. (1984). View through a window may influence recovery from surgery. *Science, 224*(4647), 420–421.

United Nations Conference on Environment and Development (UNCED). (1992). *Agenda 21: Programme of action for sustainable development/Rio Declaration on Environment and Development/statement of forests principles.* The final text of agreements negotiated by Governments at UNCED, United Nations, Rio de Janeiro, June 3e14.

United Nations Educational, Scientific and Cultural Organization (UNESCO). (2014). *Roadmap for implementing the global action programme on education for sustainable development.* Paris: UNESCO.

Walser, T., et al. (2008). Smoking and lung cancer: The role of inflammation. *Proceedings of the American Thoracic Society.*

Wang, H., & Horton, R. (2015). Tackling climate change: The greatest opportunity for global health. *The Lancet, 386*(10006), 1798–1799.

Watts, N., et al. (2019). The 2019 report of The Lancet Countdown on health and climate change: ensuring that the health of a child born today is not defined by a changing climate. *The Lancet, 394*(10211), 1836–1878.

WHO. (1992). *Our planet, our health. Report of the WHO Commission on health and environment.* Geneva: World Health Organization.

WHO. (1994). *Environmental health. Action plan for Europe.* Copenhagen: World Health Organization Regional Office for Europe.

Wiedmann, T., Lenzen, M., Keyßer, L. T., & Steinberger, J. K. (2020). Scientists' warning on affluence. *Nature Communications, 11*, 3107. https://doi.org/10.1038/s41467-020-16941-y.

Willett, W., et al. (2019). Food in the Anthropocene: The EAT–Lancet Commission on healthy diets from sustainable food systems. *Lancet.* https://doi.org/10.1016/S0140-6736(18)31788-4.

Wong, K., et al. (2019). The effect of long working hours and overtime on occupational health: A meta-analysis of evidence from 1998 to 2018. *International Journal of Environmental Research and Public Health, 16*(12), 2102.

WWF. (2020). *Living planet report 2020—Bending the curve of biodiversity loss.* Ed. R. E. A. Almond, M. Grooten, & T. Petersen. Gland, Switzerland: WWF.

CHAPTER 6

Operationalizing the Health-Environment Nexus: Measuring Environmental Health Inequalities to Inform Policy

Julien Caudeville

INTRODUCTION: THE ENVIRONMENT AS A KEY DETERMINANT OF HUMAN HEALTH AND WELL-BEING

Economic systems have never extracted and exploited as many natural resources as they do today. This trend is driven by the growth in global population and the associated rise in production and consumption (Bringezu et al. 2017). The different phases of resource production and consumption generate a variety of environmental impacts—land clearance, destruction of fertile land or forests, damage to natural habitats, biodiversity losses, ecosystem service degradation, landscape degradation, emissions of pollutants into the environment and production of waste. These directly or indirectly affect human health and thus well-being.

The World Health Organization (WHO) first addressed the issue of environmental health in 1994 and defined this new concept as follows:

J. Caudeville (✉)
INERIS, Verneuil-en-Halatte, France
e-mail: Julien.CAUDEVILLE@ineris.fr

95

É. Laurent (ed.), *The Well-being Transition*,
https://doi.org/10.1007/978-3-030-67860-9_6

"Environmental health comprises those aspects of human health, including quality of life, that are determined by physical, chemical, biological, social, psychosocial and aesthetic factors in the environment." Over the last half century, there has been a dramatic shift in the health burden of Western populations from infectious diseases to chronic diseases such as cancer, birth defects and asthma, many of which may be associated with environmental exposures. Environmental conditions are a central foundation for health and well-being and account for at least 15% of mortality in the World Health Organization (WHO) European Region (WHO Regional Office for Europe 2018).

The adverse health consequences of exposure to environmental contamination are major and present a growing problem, but they receive insufficient attention. Pressures may be exerted on the environment, causing development sectors to generate various types of outputs (e.g. in the form of pollutant emissions). These result in the 'state' (i.e. quality) of the environment being degraded through the dispersal and accumulation of pollutants in various environmental vectors, such as air, soil, water and food. People may be 'exposed' to potential hazards in the environment when they come into direct contact with these media, through breathing, drinking or eating. A variety of health effects may subsequently occur, ranging from minor, subclinical effects (i.e. effects that have not yet manifested in overt symptoms) to illness and death, depending on the intrinsic harmfulness of the pollutant, the severity and intensity of exposure and the susceptibility of the individuals exposed.

The full costs of environmental health impacts (including burdens on healthcare services, reduced economic productivity and lost utility associated with premature death, pain and suffering) are not factored into the global and national markets and price systems. This absence of internalization is a source of environmental inequalities between those who create damage to others and degrade their well-being, and those who suffer the consequences. The many different market failures create a compelling economic rationale for institutional intervention in mitigating health inequality and protecting the environment, as a way of improving social welfare. Any public policy aiming at fairness that fails to take account of environmental issues is bound to fall short in an important dimension. The relation to social policy is also simple since it is mediated by health issues and, more generally, by the impact of environmental conditions on the well-being of individuals. Environmental inequalities refer to an environmental impact that is disproportionately or unfairly distributed among the most vulnerable social groups or territories, which are generally the most discriminated against, poorer populations and minorities affected by environmental risks.

Such Environmental Health Inequalities (EHI) occur in all countries in the WHO European Region, posing a triple challenge: reduction of social inequalities, mitigation of EHI and prevention of health inequalities. However, the interrelations of these challenges offer opportunities to achieve multiple benefits through environmental or social interventions (WHO Regional Office for Europe 2019). WHO assessment findings since 2012 indicate that:

- EHI occur in all countries, irrespective of the national level of development and the environmental preservation or economic activities;
- the occurrence of EHI has tended to persist or even increase over time, despite the improvements in environmental conditions observed in most countries in the WHO European Region;
- inequalities can often be significant, with the exposure to and impact of certain pollutions being five times higher in some population subgroups compared to others (WHO Regional Office for Europe 2012, 2019).

The goal of this chapter is to contribute to the development of policy-relevant environmental health inequality indicators. I first present the scientific contexts in which EHI characterization operates and the need for indicators to inform decision-making. Examples of existing indicators are then briefly examined to present concise measurement frameworks and issues in data processing. Finally, I offer some recommendations as to the type of indicators needed and their possible integration in public policies.

THE NEED FOR INDICATORS TO INFORM DECISION-MAKING

The aim when constructing or analysing indicators is to produce a simplified representation of one or more phenomena on a relative scale, using quantified information, in accordance with one or more assessment criteria.

An indicator is a set of statistics, characteristics or other measurable factors that provides the information required to perform two types of function:

- a representation of reality function (description, simplification, aggregation, prediction, evaluation, etc.). This representation function is characterized by the answers to the following three questions: What do we want to represent? What are the objectives? And how should this be assessed? It is then necessary to verify whether the tool truly represents the phenomenon to be characterized, whether there are biases in the data used and whether the tool can be applied to the conditions studied.
- a decision-support function, for use in the context of decision-making. This function covers various aspects, such as decision support, information on an aspect of the problem studied or the monitoring and evaluation of an action. Indicators can be chosen to support development policy decision-making and clarify the needs and interests of different stakeholders.

Indicators can be defined as scientifically based operational simplifications of complex realities: they convey data through parameters in ways that are more readily interpretable than the data themselves might be, particularly for policy and stakeholder audiences (Kyle et al. 2006). They can be used to assess trends or compare territorial performances, pilot global or sectorial policies or as decision-support tools. Indicators are practical means of communicating scientific and technical information to different groups of users, enriching public debate in real time and transforming information into action.

At a different scale, environmental health indicators provide information to determine and mitigate contamination impacts and inflect negative trends, recognize disease clusters and outbreaks, identify the populations and geographic areas most affected, assess the effectiveness of public health interventions and better understand the link between environment and health (WHO 1999).

The aim of environmental injustice is to identify, estimate and correct environmental inequality caused by laws, regulations, governmental programmes, enforcement and policies. The identification of vulnerable individuals and at-risk communities in order to target public health interventions relies on environmental health inequality indicators based on exposure assessment processes. The indicator framework should be able to investigate the processes taking place at the interface between the environment and the populations, and to characterize the principal environmental impact factors.

WHAT DO WE WANT TO MEASURE?

Environmental contamination and exposures affect health and contribute to chronic disease morbidity and significant mortality. The diseases identified as priorities are respiratory diseases including asthma, birth defects, cancers and neurological disorders (Litt et al. 2004).

The definition of a conceptual approach for environmental health indicators includes three elements: hazards, exposures and diseases. This model reuses the hazard surveillance concept, defined as "assessment of the occurrence of, distribution of, and secular trends in levels of hazards (toxic chemical agents, physical agents, as well as biological agents) responsible for disease" (McGeehin et al. 2004).

Experimental research in the laboratory has provided firm evidence that various pollutants can cause a specific effect (such as carcinogenicity). The 'concentration-response function' or 'dose-response relationship' describes the size of the effect of a burden (e.g. a pollutant) on an individual or population after exposure to a certain concentration or dose (respectively). Furthermore, a risk can be calculated by linking exposure to pollutants with specific health effects. For example, exposure to lead, measured in the blood, has been conclusively associated with a reduction in cognitive abilities in children (Needleman et al. 1990). In such cases, it is often necessary to rely on epidemiological research that assesses statistical evidence for an 'association' between an agent and an effect (such as development of a specific cancer). The most studied compartment is the atmosphere, in particular in environmental epidemiology. However, there are limits to what can be tested in the laboratory, particularly as concerns the numerous chemical substances and 'cocktail effects' from simultaneous exposure to several chemicals, under realistic conditions and for more or less vulnerable populations (Organisation for Economic Co-operation and Development 2018).

Ascribing a monetary value to pollution-related health outcomes (e.g. to death or disutility) helps to frame the market costs in the same way as non-market factors. This facilitates cost-effectiveness or cost-benefit analysis, which must be understood as two very different approaches. Yet, such values suffer from serious methodological weaknesses and ethical blind spots. Through their careful use, the relative worth of different actions and policies can be partially evaluated, as can the trade-offs between the value of an economic activity and its associated health risks. The cost of doing nothing (the cost of inaction) can also be estimated for future scenarios (EC 2018). It is not easy to directly use mortality or morbidity statistics to estimate a symptom of an environment-attributable health impact. There are multiple relationships between environmental factors and health outcomes, since multiple environmental factors can contribute to a single health outcome. Moreover, environmental factors interact with genetic, behavioural and social factors to affect health (Saib et al. 2014). The Center of Disease Control (CDC) augmented the EHI model by proposing to link data on hazards, exposures and diseases and to look for possible associations as part of the surveillance system (McGeehin et al. 2004).

The addition of disaggregated exposure assessments using spatial approaches permits supplementary purposes, such as:

- characterizing and mapping environmental disparities;
- stratifying assessment results according to socio-demographic or socioeconomic status (gender, age, income, etc.);
- identifying vulnerable populations and determinants of exposure to manage and plan remedial actions;
- assessing spatial relationships across health, environmental and socioeconomic data, to identify factors that influence the variability of disease patterns.

This approach requires the data to be described at fine spatial resolutions, that is for small areas, and the definition of indicators appropriate to the scale of analysis. Location permit to be closed to closely and rapidly guide action. The local public authorities have varying degrees of authority and capacity in terms of assessments and actions related to environment and health. The resident population also represents an important audience with regard to environmental issues at the local level. Stakeholders can influence policy-makers, especially elected officials. The needs of populations may best be met by blending technical aspects of environmental health sciences with health promotion (Kegler and Miner 2004).

The dissimilarities of the area-based measures across various geographic levels make it difficult to use them for comparisons. The understanding that environmental problems may impact certain locations and people more than others is a relatively new concept. It gained nationwide attention in the late 1980s with the emergence of the concept of environmental inequality. Environmental inequalities can be seen as a fourfold problem (Laurent 2011):

- Exposure and access inequalities: The unequal distribution of environmental quality between individuals and groups (defined in racial, ethnic or social terms), whether negatively (exposure to environmental risk and hazard) or positively (access to environmental amenities);
- Policy effect inequalities: The unequal effect of environmental policies, that is, not the unequal distribution of an environmental benefit or harm but of the effect on income of regulatory or tax policies, for instance, among individuals and groups;
- Impact inequalities: The unequal environmental impact for the different individuals and groups with regard to their income and/or lifestyles; some scholars point to the notion of 'ecological inequalities' to characterize this type of inequality;
- Policy-making inequalities: The unequal access to environmental policy-making, that is the unequal involvement and empowerment of individuals and groups in decisions regarding their immediate environment.

In order to construct environmental inequality indicators to provide diagnostics at a territorial level, all of these dimensions must be integrated. A wide range of data may potentially be mobilized for the integrated assessment.

WHAT DATA CAN WE USE?

The spatial data used to characterize environmental inequality were not always initially collected and collated to meet these objectives, which results in use bias. Data linkages could be accomplished by using common geographic and temporal identifiers to overlay or combine data over common areas and time frames.

The measurement frequencies or spatial densities of the sampling are not always sufficient. To partially overcome these problems, different techniques have been adopted to specifically address the different environmental, behavioural or population databases. The selection of a treatment method depends on the problem to be solved and the quality of the data available.

Environmental quality data are often available at a fine administrative or resolution level, making it possible to build environmental indicators on a regional or national scale. The processing of variables for the identification and characterization of environmental inequalities depends on the reuse of this type of data, which is very diverse by nature in terms of its initial intended objectives. Determining how representative these levels of contamination measured are of other locations or time frames is not always a simple task (Sarnat et al. 2006).

The development of databases in health and environment has been ongoing for several years now. They are still evolving and in full expansion. Different agencies, institutes or observatories have carried out projects to identify and monitor the quality of the environment, for soils, water and air.

The arrival of quality data and their integration into Geographic Information Systems (GIS) makes it possible to conduct territorial analysis work. These environmental data reflect the actual contamination of the environment and therefore the overall exposure of the populations. The monitoring of environmental factors is usually directed towards assessing compliance with regulatory mandates, rather than focusing on assessing health impacts.

A database must be set up in which the variables are associated with the modes of exposure (concentrations in the environmental and exposure media present, eating behaviour, space-time budget, etc.).

These variables must undergo several different processing stages in order to construct the indicators:

- the identification of data sources that make it possible to construct the different variables,
- the acquisition of these data in view of the access modalities and the financial, legal or human aspects,
- the analysis of the quality and representativeness of the databases regarding the objective of the study (choice of a database, validity and representativeness of the data) sometimes involving approximation or the application of simplifying assumptions,
- the pre-processing of databases: cleaning the databases, replacing missing data,
- the construction of ad-hoc data where the appropriate data sources are not available or are non-exhaustive in relation to the objectives of the study,
- data transformation (homogenization, aggregation or disaggregation of data).

Estimating exposure requires knowledge of the concentrations in environmental compartments to which an individual or a population is exposed. These concentrations can be measured or modelled. A wide range of data can potentially be mobilized for integrated assessment. The database selection and definition of the study design should be guided to reach the best compromise between data representativeness and method robustness, consistent with the objectives of the study.

What Indicator Can We Build?

United Nations Statistics Division (2015) sees an explicit need to structure the Sustainable Development Goal (SDG) indicators into a coherent framework that can be reused in the environmental health field. This framework would ensure that the indicator set is complete and emphasize linkages between the indicators thereby avoiding arbitrariness in the selection process. It sets several selection criteria for the indicators: they should be relevant, methodologically sound, measurable, easy to communicate and access, limited in number and outcome-focused. The first criterion—relevance—comprises three different aspects:

- Link to the target: the indicator should be clearly linked to one or more targets and provide robust measures of progress towards the target(s).
- Policy relevance: the indicator should be relevant to policy formulation and provide enough information for policy-making.
- Applicability at the appropriate level: for global monitoring, the indicator should be relevant to all countries; for national monitoring, the indicator should be relevant to national priorities.

The general absence of common methodological frameworks generates incompatible data, difficult-to-use information and the multiplication of sets of indicators that are impossible to calibrate. Indicators must therefore be developed in successive stages, and the different stages must be integrated. The reasoning may be that it is known that for some purposes, users may be willing to accept conceptual or methodological weaknesses in an indicator if it provides really important information (Kurtz et al. 2001). Operationalization is the justification of the global weaknesses but in practical use indicators are far from being ready to use.

Since environmental risk factors are very varied, many different EH indicators and indices have already been developed and new metrics are sure to appear in the future.

The D-P-S-S-E-A Framework

Decision-makers need not only better data on the linkages between the complex factors in the environment and development process affecting human health, but also an enhanced understanding of such linkages. In terms of sustainable development, a framework is needed in which the various environmental, economic and social factors and components can be considered in a balanced way. A framework for presenting the linkages between factors that affect health in the context of environment and development has been adapted from the "pressure-state-response" (P-S-R) model developed by OECD (Organisation for Economic Co-operation and Development 2003). The pressure-state-response (P-S-R) framework has been particularly useful in representing the way in which pollution affects the environment. For example, it can look into the various 'pressures' exerted on the environment which affect its 'state' (quality), and consequently call for a 'response' to deal with the situation. Other adaptations have been made to the pressure-state-response (P-S-R) framework to provide for the broader driving forces and their impacts. The result is the 'pressure-state-impact-response' (P-S-I-R) framework, which takes into account human health, ecosystem and social-economic impacts. Some themed frameworks exist which were specifically elaborated for certain risk factors (e.g. pesticide or noise). Some frameworks use an accounting approach or economic theory (mostly for atmospheric pollutants), while others are based on causality, such as D-P-S-S-E-A framework (driving forces, pressures, state, exposures, health effects and actions), to represent both the exposures and the potential resulting health effects (Corvalan et al. 1996). This is a descriptive representation of the way in which various driving forces generate pressures that affect the state of the environment and ultimately human health, through the various exposure pathways by which people come into contact with the environment. In the context of EHI mapping, the identification of vulnerable individuals and at-risk communities in order to target public health interventions relies on additional requirements in the exposure assessment processes in comparison to the traditional risk assessment methodology. The study design should be able to:

- investigate the processes taking place at the interface between the environmental contaminants of interest and the organisms,
- characterize the principal exposure pathways,
- build realistic scenarios that integrate past and present sources,
- describe the phenomena at a fine temporal and spatial resolution.

As an illustration, Ioannidou et al. (2018) built a Polycyclic Aromatic Hydrocarbon (PAH) exposure indicator at the national level in France, with a fine resolution (9 km²). The PAH congener benzo[a]pyrene (BaP) was used as a marker for PAHs since BaP constitutes a substantial proportion of the total carcinogenic potential of the total PAH burden (Delgado-Saborit et al. 2011).

Data from the different environmental compartments (water, air, soil, food) are available in France in different databases. In order to construct exposure maps from spatialized databases when assessing the EHIs, methods have been developed to process and harmonize the available data in the same resolution and geographic support (Ioannidou et al. 2018), with respect to their specificities (missing values, limited number of observations, etc.). These methods made it possible to construct the representative spatial database used to perform the integrated exposure assessment. This required the integration and combination of various levels of data from different environmental compartments and exposure media. To this end, the MODUL'ERS exposure model was employed (Bonnard and McKone 2010) to calculate the spatialized exposure indicators using georeferenced environmental databases from monitoring networks to estimate the contributions by ingestion and inhalation pathway. The final results of this work showed that the PAH exposure map results from the combination of contributions from inhalation and ingestion.

Dashboard Strategy

A set of indicators may be presented in dashboards and scoreboards to provide information about a population's health status, their environment and other factors. The goal here is to make it possible to monitor trends, compare situations and better understand the link between environment and health. Niemeijer and De Groot (2008) insist on the need for a transparent selection of the best available indicators based on a conceptual framework. They show that the indicators should be based on reliable statistics, should hold their value over time and should be of relevance to medium and long-term policy issues.

Each EH indicator comprises one or more items, characteristics or other elements, assessed through direct and indirect measures (e.g. levels of a pollutant in the environment as a measure of possible exposure), that describe health or a factor associated with health (i.e. environmental hazard, age) in a specified population.

The US Environmental Public Health Tracking Program proposes different sets of Nationally Consistent Data and Measures (NCDMs), with the first set being adopted in 2008. Since then, the Tracking Program's Content Workgroup has continued to develop new NCDMs and improve about 200 existing NCDMs covering 10 key themes, and aggregated at the national level: acute myocardial infarction, air quality, asthma, birth defects, cancer, carbon dioxide poisoning, childhood lead poisoning, drinking water, heat, reproductive health outcomes (Wilson and Charleston 2017). The recommendations cover indicators and measures and include how-to guides that describe the methods for extracting the necessary data and generating the measures.

The most prominent examples of EHI can be found in the WHO Europe indicators. The assessment considers various environmental settings and presents 19 EHI indicators aggregated at the country scale in the WHO European Region, categorized into five domains: housing-related inequalities, basic service inequalities, urban environment and transport inequalities, work-related inequalities, injury-related inequalities. The latest evidence confirms that socially disadvantaged population subgroups are those most affected by environmental hazards, causing avoidable health effects and contributing to health inequalities (WHO 2019).

Composite Indicator

The need to consider the impact of multiple exposures requires an integrated response for the different types of risk factors. It is considerably more complex methodologically and computationally to assess multiple different risk factors and their associated multiple impacts than it is to assess aggregate risks or single-effect cumulative risks. Different approaches could be considered for the screening-level analysis of spatialized cumulative risks, based either on toxicology data or on a multivariate approach to combine exposure variables at population level. The approaches and methods that can potentially be applied to developing indicator frameworks can be classified into two categories: policy-based approaches and conceptual approaches.

The first type of approach uses deliberative processes and stakeholders' judgement as a means of linking two or more separate scales of risks adapted to policy objectives. Whereas the latter relies on knowledge to combine the multiple risk factors (based on toxicological models and environmental processes and/or chemical interactions, etc.) (Caudeville et al. 2017).

One of the recognized methods to simplify a complex research problem and follow the evolution of a given phenomenon is based on the creation of composite indices. A composite index is a mathematical combination of variables reflecting one or more selected dimensions that are usually evaluated separately. A composite indicator should ideally measure multidimensional concepts that cannot be captured by a single indicator. Such indicators often seek to measure highly aggregated but also diffuse and non-reliable concepts that are rich in value judgements and not always grounded in hard science.

It often seems easier for the general public to interpret composite indicators than to identify common trends across many separate indicators, and they have also proven useful in benchmarking country performance (Saltelli 2007). Such composite indicators provide simple comparisons of countries that can be used to illustrate complex and sometimes elusive issues in wide-ranging fields such as environment, economy, society or technological development. For example, three dimensions are defined in the United Nations Development Programme's (UNPD's) Human Development Index (United Nations Development Programme 1990): a long and healthy life, knowledge and a decent standard of living. Within the knowledge dimension, the component indicators are arithmetically averaged. The dimensions themselves are then geometrically averaged to produce the final index.

The Handbook on Constructing Composite Indicators, made available by the OECD (2008), provides guidelines for building environmental composite indices, mainly in terms of the overall uncertainties linked to each step of the methodology. In particular, the Handbook discusses the following steps in the construction of composite indicators: theoretical framework, data selection, imputation of missing data, multivariate analysis, normalization, weighting and aggregating methods, uncertainty and sensitivity analysis.

Many articles have focused on weighting and/or aggregation (Becker et al. 2017; Gan et al. 2017; Caudeville et al. 2017) to highlight the complexity of including weighting in composite indices and have presented tools to help developers investigate the effects of weights (Habran et al. 2019).

An important example to illustrate how an environmental health composite indicator can reflect the cumulative impacts of environmental exposures and population vulnerabilities is the California Communities Environmental Health Screening Tool version 3.0 (CalEnviroScreen). CalEnviroScreen is a screening methodology that can be used to help identify Californian communities that are disproportionately burdened by multiple sources of pollution (Office of Environmental Health Hazard Assessment 2018). CalEnviroScreen generates a numeric score, ranging from 0 to 100. The score is based on 20 indicators: 12 measures of environmental exposure, 5 of socioeconomic vulnerability and 3 of health outcomes (asthma, low birth weight and cardiovascular disease) (Fig. 6.1).

The tool employs a model that can be adapted to different uses, such as highlighting contaminated areas or guiding state resource allocation.

All of these indicators hold the same amount of weight, except for the Environmental Effects indicators which feature in the Pollution Burden score. The Environmental Effects indicators include five items: Cleanup Sites, Groundwater Threats, Hazardous Waste Generators and Facilities, Impaired Water Bodies and Solid Waste Sites and Facilities. These indicators hold a half weight within the formula that determines the CalEnviroScreen Score.

The composite indicator built by French Lorraine region is another illustration of combining multiple publicly available data sources, where regional stakeholders were involved in the overall procedures for data collection and organization. Various different indicators have been developed by combining technical approaches to assessing and characterizing human health exposure associated with chemical substances (in soil, air and water) and noise risk factors, using environmental monitoring networks. Using a limited data set, a sensitivity analysis demonstrated the impact of data transformation in identifying the more impacted areas. This approach permits the combination of quantitative and qualitative assessments of risks to health by integrating stakeholders in the decision-making process. This makes it possible to define a subjective conceptual analysis framework or make assumptions when there is uncertainty or a knowledge gap. Other approaches have been developed

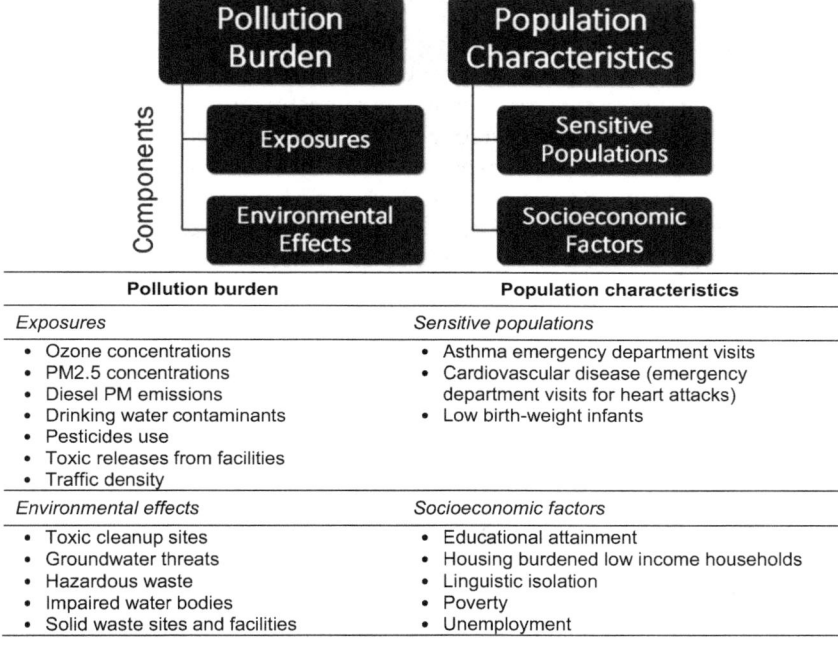

Pollution burden	Population characteristics
Exposures	*Sensitive populations*
• Ozone concentrations • PM2.5 concentrations • Diesel PM emissions • Drinking water contaminants • Pesticides use • Toxic releases from facilities • Traffic density	• Asthma emergency department visits • Cardiovascular disease (emergency department visits for heart attacks) • Low birth-weight infants
Environmental effects	*Socioeconomic factors*
• Toxic cleanup sites • Groundwater threats • Hazardous waste • Impaired water bodies • Solid waste sites and facilities	• Educational attainment • Housing burdened low income households • Linguistic isolation • Poverty • Unemployment

Fig. 6.1 List of indicators included in the four components of the CalEnviroScreen tool. (Source: Faust et al. 2017)

for assessing spatial relationships across health, environmental and socioeconomic indicators and identifying factors that influence the variability of disease patterns (Saib et al. 2014).

Composite indicators however can send misleading policy messages if they are poorly constructed or misinterpreted. Their 'big picture' results may invite users (especially policy-makers) to draw simplistic analytical or policy conclusions. In fact, composite indicators must be seen as a means of initiating discussion and stimulating public interest. Their relevance should be gauged with respect to the constituencies affected by the composite index (OECD, 2008).

Other Possible Approaches

Other approaches can be used to combine several risk factors in a single metric. For example, cumulative risk assessment (CRA) is defined as a science-policy tool for organizing and analysing relevant scientific information to examine, characterize and quantify the combined adverse effects on human health from exposure to a combination of environmental stressors (Callahan and Sexton 2007). The ultimate goal of CRA is to provide answers to decision-relevant questions based on organized scientific analysis, even if the answers, at least for the time being, are inexact and uncertain (Sexton 2012). CRA therefore involves the quantitative or qualitative assessment of risks to health and/or the environment from multiple exposures, sources and routes, while considering the differential susceptibility and vulnerability of population subgroups (United States Environmental Protection Agency 2003).

A measure has also been developed that captures both mortality and impacts on health (morbidity): the quality-adjusted life year (QALY). This measure is used for economic evaluation in some countries, for example, the Netherlands, Sweden and the United Kingdom (Torbica et al. 2018). A QALY is defined as a year of life spent in perfect health. A disability-adjusted life year (DALY) associated with a disease or condition takes into account the years of life lost from premature death (mortality) and the years of healthy life lost due to disability (morbidity). One DALY can be thought of as one lost year of 'healthy' life (EC 2018). Unfortunately, there are very few dose-responses available for environmental stressors permitting estimations of QALY and DALY.

To characterize the health of a general population, the most frequently observed health variable is life expectancy at birth, at 60 or at 65 years of age. Since life expectancy reflects interactions between environmental, genetic, behavioural, social and economic factors, it is not easy to use this indicator to directly estimate environmental risk factors. However, it could be a good candidate to aggregate all dimensions that may characterize human well-being (Laurent 2020).

Conclusion: Towards a Better Policy Integration of Environmental Health Indicators

The existing indicators and data are limited in their ability to properly reflect combined health impacts. There is a need for risk assessors to identify at-risk populations in the context of substantial data deficiencies that hinder the evaluation of EHIs. This places the operation of the exposome concept on a territorial scale. The characterization of the territorialized (eco)exposome (Caudeville 2021) should make it possible to combine multiple risks through the development of dynamic, multidimensional and temporal approaches and information systems. These require the adoption of transdisciplinary methods of data analysis. Integrated approaches could bring together all the information required to assess the source-to-dose continuum using GIS, and to establish an integrated exposure assessment framework.

The Covid-19 crisis has further highlighted the need to broaden the WHO definition of health from 1946 ("a state of complete physical, mental and social well-being") to include the health of ecosystems which underpin that of populations (Laurent 2020). Environmental degradation has a direct impact on human health but also on the ecosystem functions necessary to ensure the sustainability of economies and the well-being of populations. Fairly assessing human well-being with respect to ecosystem-based management requires an assessment of the trade-offs, not only between ecological integrity and human well-being, but also between the well-being of different groups of people (Breslow et al. 2017).

The One Health concept goes beyond a simple observation of the close interdependence between human health and ecosystems by seeking to develop integrated approaches to characterize these interrelationships. These include integration across the impacts of environmental stressors, integration of the effects in humans and in ecosystems, integration across scientific disciplines and integration of various stakeholders' perspectives in the assessment process.

The coronavirus crises have led to a re-examination of the links between environmental degradation, health and human well-being. The majority of COVID-19 victims were chronically ill (obesity, diabetes, hypertension and cardiovascular disease). Chronic health impacts linked to environmental exposure increase territorial health vulnerability, corresponding to the decreased ability for a population to respond or recover following an additional aggression. Indicators that fail to integrate the largest dimensions of human well-being are extremely limited in their ability to assess social equity and justice. The notion of territorial and environmental health inequality therefore depends on two aspects:

- vulnerability (exposure and sensitivity) in a logic of a territorialized exposome;
- resilience of the territories (population capability and territorial reactivity).

It is ever more pressing today, when studying the link between health and environment, to consider social factors as variables that are related to environmental exposure and play an important role in health inequalities.

Environmental Public Health Tracking information systems must be routinely developed to provide access to data or databases and integrate them at different administrative levels, promote the interoperability of systems, improve the quality of the indicators produced and better incorporate the environmental dimension in all policies. The approach should include the systematic collection, integration, analysis, interpretation and dissemination of data relative to environmental exposure and socioeconomic and health effects within the network, in order to identify the areas and populations likely to be the most impacted. Organized by researchers, stakeholders and decision-makers, this dynamic also has to address data gap issues and produce recommendations to increase the efficiency of the statistical information systems.

Environmental health inequality indicators must become coherent measures to characterize contemporary well-being and sustainability. The current indicators present pictures that allow spatial and temporal comparisons and should be oriented towards the future (forecast model) to ensure that future living conditions will be comparable to those of today. Modelled on the SDG indicators, the new indicators should be able to support the different stages of a policy cycle: policy formulation (identifying issues, setting goals and objectives reflecting ideas and visions and formulating issues in such a way as to facilitate successful operationalization), policy legitimization, policy implementation, policy evaluation and policy change. The contemporary representation of the world underlies the current accounting and conventions, but this could be changed to make it a tool in the service of sustainable public policies. Hence, these indicators could participate in orienting and renewing public policy at every administrative scale, from global to local.

REFERENCES

Becker, W., Saisana, M., Paruolo, P., et al. (2017). Weights and importance in composite indicators: Closing the gap. *Ecological Indicators, 80,* 12–22.

Bonnard, R., & McKone, T. E. (2010). Integration of the predictions of two models with dose measurements in a case study of children exposed to the emissions of a lead smelter. *Human and Ecological Risk Assessment, 15*(6), 1203–1226.

Breslow, S. J., Allen, M., Holstein, D., et al. (2017). Evaluating indicators of human well-being for ecosystem-based management. *Ecosystem Health and Sustainability, 3*(12), 1–18.

Bringezu, S., Ramaswami, A., Schandl, H., et al. (2017). *Assessing global resource use: A systems approach to resource efficiency and pollution reduction.* A Report of the International Resource Panel, United Nations Environment Programme, Kenya.

Callahan, M. A., & Sexton, K. (2007). If cumulative risk assessment is the answer, what is the question? *Environmental Health Perspectives, 115,* 799–806.

Caudeville, J. (2021). Diagnostics and policy tools to measure and mitigate environmental health inequalities. In É. Laurent & K. Zwickl (Eds.), *The Routledge handbook of the political economy of the environment.* Routledge. (In press).

Caudeville, J., Ioannidou, D., Boulvert, E., et al. (2017). Cumulative risk assessment in the Lorraine region: A framework to characterize environmental health inequalities. *International Journal of Environmental Research and Public Health, 14*(3), 291.

Corvalan, C., Briggs, D., & Kjellstrom, T. (1996). Development of environmental health indicators. In D. Briggs, C. Corvalan, & M. Nurminen (Eds.), *Linkage methods for environment and health analysis* (pp. 19–54). Geneva: World Health Organization.

Delgado-Saborit, J. M., Stark, C., & Harrison, R. M. (2011). Carcinogenic potential, levels and sources of polycyclic aromatic hydrocarbon mixtures in indoor and outdoor environments and their implications for air quality standards. *Environment International, 37,* 383–392.

Faust, J., August, L., & Bangia, K., et al. (2017). *CalEnviroScreen 3.0: Update to the California communities environmental health screening tool.* Office of Environmental Health Hazard Assessment, California Environmental Protection Agency, Sacramento.

Gan, X., Fernandez, I. C., Guo, J., et al. (2017). When to use what: Methods for weighting and aggregating sustainability indicators. *Ecological Indicators, 81,* 491–502.

Habran, S., Crespin, P., Veschkens, M., et al. (2019). Development of a spatial web tool to identify hotspots of environmental burdens in Wallonia (Belgium). *Environmental Science and Pollution Research International, 27,* 5681–5692.

Ioannidou, D., Malherbe, L., Beauchamp, M., et al. (2018). Characterization of environmental health inequalities due to Polyaromatic Hydrocarbons exposure in France. *International Journal of Environmental Research and Public Health, 15*, 2680.

Kegler, M. C., & Miner, K. (2004). Environmental health promotion interventions: Considerations for preparation and practice. *Health Education & Behavior, 31*(4), 510–525.

Kurtz, J. C., Jackson, L. E., & Fisher, W. S. (2001). Strategies for evaluating indicators based on guidelines from the environmental protection agency's office of research and development. *Ecological Indicators, 1*, 49–60.

Kyle, A. D., Balmes, J. R., Buffler, P. A., et al. (2006). Integrating research, surveillance, and practice in environmental public health tracking. *Environmental Health Perspectives, 114*(7), 980–984.

Laurent, E. (2011). Issues in environmental justice within the European Union. *Ecological Economics, 70*(11), 1846–1853.

Laurent, E. (2020). *Et si la santé guidait le monde—L'espérance de vie vaut mieux que la croissance*. Paris: Les Liens qui liberent.

Litt, J., Tran, N., Malecki, K. C., et al. (2004). Identifying priority health conditions, environmental data, and infrastructure needs: A synopsis of the Pew environmental health tracking project. *Environmental Health Perspectives, 112*, 1414–1418.

McGeehin, M. A., Qualters, J. R., & Niskar, A. S. (2004). National environmental public health tracking program: Bridging the information gap. *Environmental Health Perspectives, 112*(14), 1409–1413.

Nardo, M., Saisana, M., Saltelli, A., et al. (2008). *Handbook on constructing composite indicators. Methodology and user guide*. OECD Statistics Working Paper.

Needleman, H. L., Schell, A., Bellinger, D. A., et al. (1990). The long-term effects of exposure to low doses of lead in childhood: An 11-year follow-up report. *New England Journal of Medicine, 322*, 83–88.

Niemeijer, D., & De Groot, R. S. (2008). A conceptual framework for selecting environmental indicator sets. *Ecological Indicators, 8*(1), 14–25.

Office of Environmental Health Hazard Assessment. (2018). *CalEnviroScreen version 3.0. California Environmental Protection Agency*. Office of Environmental Health Hazard Assessment. Retrieved November 11, 2020, from https://oehha.ca.gov/calenviroscreen/report/calenviroscreen-30.

Organisation for Economic Co-operation and Development. (2003). *OECD environmental indicators: Development, measurement and use*. OECD Environmental Performance and Information Division.

Organisation for Economic Co-operation and Development. (2018). *Considerations for assessing the risks of combined exposure to multiple chemicals*. Series on Testing and Assessment No. 296, OECD Environment, Health and Safety Division, Environment Directorate.

Saib, M. S., Caudeville, J., Carre, F., et al. (2014). Spatial relationship quantification between environmental, socioeconomic and health data at different geographic levels. *International Journal of Environmental Research and Public Health, 11*(4), 3765–3786.

Saltelli, A. (2007). Composite indicators between analysis and advocacy. *Social Indicators Research, 81*, 65–77.

Sarnat, S. E., Klein, M., Peel, J. L., et al. (2006). Spatial considerations in a study of ambient air pollution and cardiorespiratory emergency department visits. *Epidemiology, 17*(6), S242–S243.

Science for Environment Policy. (2018). *What are the health costs of environmental pollution?* Future Brief 21, Brief Produced for the European Commission DG Environment by the Science Communication Unit, Bristol.

Sexton, K. (2012). Cumulative risk assessment: An overview of methodological approaches for evaluating combined health effects from exposure to multiple environmental stressors. *International Journal of Environmental Research and Public Health, 9*, 370–390.

Torbica, A., Tarricone, R., & Drummond, M. (2018). Does the approach to economic evaluation in health care depend on culture, values, and institutional context? *The European Journal of Health Economics, 19*, 769–774.

United Nations Development Programme. (1990). *Human development report 1990.* New York: Oxford University Press.

United Nations Statistics Division. (2015). *Discussion paper on principles of using quantification to operationalize the SDGs and criteria for indicator selection.* New York: United Nations Statistics Division.

United States Environmental Protection Agency. (2003). *Framework for cumulative risk assessment.* Washington: United States Environmental Protection Agency, Office of Research and Development, National Center for Environmental Assessment.

Wilson, H., & Charleston, A. (2017). Environmental Public Health Tracking Program advances and successes: Highlights from the first 15 years. *Journal of Public Health Management and Practice, 23*, S4–S8.

World Health Organization. (1999). *Environmental health indicators: Framework and methodologies.* Geneva: World Health Organization.

World Health Organization Regional Office for Europe. (2012). *Environmental health inequalities in Europe: assessment report.* Copenhagen: WHO Regional Office for Europe.

World Health Organization Regional Office for Europe. (2018). *Healthy environments for healthier people.* Copenhagen: WHO Regional Office for Europe.

World Health Organization Regional Office for Europe. (2019). *Environmental health inequalities in Europe. Second assessment report.* Copenhagen: World Health Organization Regional Office for Europe.

PART III

From Well-being Metrics to Well-being Policies: Building a Well-being Policy

From Fantasy to Transformation: Steps in the Policy Use of "Beyond-GDP" Indicators

Anders Hayden

INTRODUCTION

Many supporters of alternative indicators of well-being, prosperity, or societal success—that is, "beyond-GDP" metrics—have been motivated by hopes of considerable policy change and, indeed, wider social change. For many supporters of the beyond-GDP movement, new indicators are linked to a broader goal of *transformation*—that is, changing core features of society, notably a shift from the prioritization of growth in production and consumption to an emphasis on well-being, equity, and sustainability. Among those with transformative goals, different emphases are possible, including challenging the growth paradigm and a consumerist vision of well-being, or significantly redistributing resources and power within society. For others, including many mainstream political actors, the goal is limited to *reform*, that is, using more comprehensive and direct measures

A. Hayden (✉)
Dalhousie University, Halifax, NS, Canada
e-mail: Anders.Hayden@dal.ca

É. Laurent (ed.), *The Well-being Transition*, https://doi.org/10.1007/978-3-030-67860-9_7

of well-being to inform policy choices and produce better policies—without questioning the growth paradigm or other core features of the economic and social system (Hayden et al. Forthcoming; Hayden and Wilson 2017). That said, the boundaries between transformative and reformist perspectives can be somewhat blurred within the nuanced spectrum of steps beyond GDP that is evident in recent national and local experiences.

This chapter integrates findings from recent research that I have conducted on beyond-GDP initiatives in Canada, Britain, Bhutan, and the US states of Maryland and Vermont (Dasilva and Hayden Forthcoming; Hayden 2015; Hayden and Wilson 2016, 2017, 2018) and lessons from other case studies including New Zealand. It also draws on the existing literature on indicator uses. It examines various steps in the use of beyond-GDP metrics in policy, starting at one end of the spectrum with the "indicators fantasy"—which assumes that it is enough to produce new indicators and policy impacts will follow—and genuine transformative change at the other. Intermediate steps in the direction of greater policy impacts are also discussed, including political use of indicators in policy debates, conceptual use that is contributing to changing understandings of well-being and prosperity, and actions to embed indicators into the policy process (enabling "instrumental use"). Such steps have expanded the possibilities for policy reform. While there is still a considerable way to go to achieve transformative goals, the transitional objective of downplaying the centrality of GDP and economic growth, without abandoning either, may now be within reach.

THE INDICATORS FANTASY

While alternative well-being indicators have considerable value in making visible key issues that conventional measurements ignore, producing them is only a first step, and provides no guarantee of policy impact. Beyond-GDP initiatives have often been based on what one can call the "indicators fantasy,"[1] that is, the assumption that simply producing new measurements will, on its own, lead governments to take notice, resulting in policy change—perhaps even transformative change. This expectation is based on a rationalist-positivist perspective in which indicators are assumed to feed directly into evidence-based policymaking and influence decisions

---

[1] I first encountered this idea in an interview with Charles Seaford, New Economics Foundation (NEF), in July 2014.

(Scott 2012; Rinne et al. 2013; Lehtonen et al. 2016). However, the influence of indicators on decisions is rarely so direct and mechanical. Influences on policymakers include ideology, interests, information, and institutional constraints—and information is frequently not the most important of these four "I's" (Bell and Morse 2011). Meanwhile, Durand and Exton (2019, p. 142) point out that "it is not sufficient to rely on the adage 'what gets measured gets done' since in several cases, national efforts to measure well-being remain largely disconnected from policy practice."

Some supporters of beyond-GDP measurement, including this author, confess to having been guilty of the indicators fantasy to some degree in the past (see, e.g., Dasilva and Hayden Forthcoming). As Ronald Colman (Forthcoming), who has made important contributions since the 1990s to efforts to move beyond GDP in Canada, New Zealand, and Bhutan, puts it:

> [W]hat brought many of us to this work was our belief that governments were making such bad decisions on environmental, social, health, education and other key constituents of wellbeing largely because they weren't getting the full story. They were being deceived by the dominant GDP-based measures that equate how well we are doing as a society with economic growth. ... All we had to do, my colleagues and I naively believed, was tell the whole truth and governments would see the necessity of urgent action to improve societal wellbeing and—without being overly dramatic—to save humanity.
>
> Twenty-five years later ... I have to conclude that our new progress measures have failed to make a significant dent in the policy arena or to shift policy in any fundamentally transformative or meaningful way. ... On the contrary, the economic growth imperative at huge (and now well-documented) ecological and social costs, is more dominant and powerful than ever.

Three points stand out in response to Colman's assessment. First, there are many measurement initiatives without significant policy impacts (Bleys and Thiry Forthcoming; Whitby et al. 2014; Bleys and Whitby 2015; Hayden and Wilson 2016, 2018; Durand and Exton 2019, p. 142), which support the idea that is insufficient to provide more accurate information through beyond-GDP metrics and expect results. Second, whether or not new progress measures have made a "significant dent" in the policy arena is partly a matter of subjective interpretation; some recent developments, discussed below, can be interpreted more positively in terms of the degree of impact and increasing opportunities for policy reform. Third, despite such advances, transformative goals have not yet been achieved and the obstacles hindering their achievement remain substantial, a point returned to below.

POLITICAL AND CONCEPTUAL USE, AND AN EMERGING NARRATIVE OF SUSTAINABLE WELL-BEING

One step beyond simply producing new indicators is "political use" (Hezri 2004; Rinne et al. 2013)—that is, political actors' use of well-being and sustainability indicators as "ammunition" to defend policy positions and attempt to persuade others. Even where direct policy impacts are not evident, political use is common, such as referring to beyond-GDP metrics and well-being evidence to urge action to reduce income inequality and poverty, cut greenhouse gases (GHGs), expand public provision of psychological therapies, or reduce working hours—or, more generally, critique the limits of neoliberal economics (e.g., APPGWE 2014; Hayden and Wilson 2018). Such political use is obviously not guaranteed to determine policy outcomes—and it will often encounter opponents wielding their own indicator evidence—but it is one avenue through which impact may occur. It also draws our attention to the political nature of indicators, which, behind an appearance of objective, neutral data, reflect normative understandings of what matters most and what we ought to focus our attention on (McGregor 2015).

The possibility also exists that, aside from any direct policy impacts, indicators may have indirect impacts over time through "conceptual use," that is, introducing new ideas, reshaping frameworks of thought, and enabling people to see the world differently (Hezri 2004; Rinne et al. 2013). Participants in indicator initiatives often express considerable hope for longer-term conceptual use, even when immediate policy impacts are disappointing. For example, in Canada, interviewees pointed to the spread of the idea that "well-being is not exclusively about the scale or scope of the Canadian economy" as a development that "opens up a possibility for the future" (Hayden and Wilson 2016), while participants in Maryland's Genuine Progress Indicator (GPI) initiative spoke of "changing the thinking" that will ultimately result in changes in policy (Hayden and Wilson 2018).

More than a hope for the future, there are indications that decades of work questioning the primacy of GDP and developing alternative measurements have resulted in shifts in thinking, with growing acceptance that GDP is not an adequate measure of well-being or national success. This is evident from the international level—the work of the Organisation for Economic Co-operation and Development (OECD) in this area (e.g., Stiglitz et al. 2018)—down to more localized contexts. According to a senior public official in the Canadian province of Nova Scotia, across a range of policy issues, "we're all having conversations where our measure of success is not more jobs created, or GDP contribution made. There's a greater level of layering and complexity of what people understand successes in policy to be." He added that, at the senior management levels within government, "it's almost now the orthodoxy that GDP is not the way to measure progress and success—it is one of many indicators."[2]

New well-being and sustainability indicators have challenged existing understandings of the success of the United States, for example. Although critics have long pointed to specific failings of the US social model—such as deep-seated racial inequalities, millions without health insurance, high incarceration rates, and high GHG emissions—the size of US GDP (and its related military capacities) was long sufficient to maintain the idea that the country was "number one." While some observers undoubtedly still believe that to be the case, this claim can increasingly be questioned in light of many indices and indicators showing middling or poor outcomes in the United States compared to other nations. For instance, the United States ranks number 15 in the world according to the Human Development Index (28 when adjusted for inequality),[3] 28 on the Social Progress Index,[4] 18 on the Legatum Prosperity Index,[5] 10 on the OECD Better Life Index (with equal weightings), 31 on the Sustainable Development Goal Index,[6] and 18 on *World Happiness Report* life evaluations.[7] The fact that all of these metrics have a Nordic country in the number one spot—and a number of them have multiple Nordic countries at or near the top—reinforces

[2] Interview, July 2020. See Dasilva and Hayden et al. (Forthcoming).
[3] 2018 data from UNDP (2019, pp. 300, 308).
[4] 2020 rankings: https://www.socialprogress.org/index/global/results.
[5] 2019 rankings: https://www.prosperity.com/rankings.
[6] 2020 rankings: https://sdgindex.org/reports/sustainable-development-report-2020/.
[7] 2020 rankings from Helliwell et al. (2020b, p. 19).

the impression that US "free market" capitalism is failing to serve the well-being of its people as well as Scandinavian social democracy.[8]

Of course, none of the above-mentioned indices offers the final word on well-being or prosperity. One can raise legitimate questions about what each of them shows or does not show, how they are constructed, and weightings of different factors incorporated into them. Meanwhile, there are other indicators and indices that emphasize the dependence of human development and well-being on ecological sustainability—and highlight the overall environmental impacts linked to a nation's resource consumption and GHG emissions, including those beyond its borders—on which neither the United States nor Nordic countries fare particularly well, such as the ecological footprint or Sustainable Development Index. The latter (not to be confused with the SDG Index) aims to measure the "ecological efficiency of human development."[9] It concludes that Cuba, Costa Rica, and Sri Lanka are the three top performing nations in delivering high human development while respecting planetary boundaries. Of course, as noted above, each metric reflects different normative and political stances about what matters most (McGregor 2015). For our purposes here, the key point is that beyond-GDP indicators have made a considerable conceptual contribution in challenging GDP as the dominant measure of national success—and the related idea that well-being is equivalent to income and the capacity to consume. Although debate continues over which alternative metrics ought to be prioritized, there is at least increasing pluralism in understandings of prosperity and success.

One important illustration of changing understandings of national success is the emergence of the Well-being Economy Governments (WEGo), which include New Zealand, Iceland, Scotland, and Wales. According to First Minister Nicola Sturgeon (2020), Scotland is "redefining" what it means to be a "successful country" and "putting well-being at the heart of what we are doing." Although not abandoning GDP growth as a goal, Sturgeon stated that GDP "cannot be … the only measure of national progress"—indeed, the country has a dashboard of multiple indicators,

[8] For an analysis of factors behind the Nordic countries high happiness levels, see Martela et al. (2020).

[9] It divides each nation's HDI score by the extent to which consumption-based CO_2 emissions and material footprint exceed "per-capita shares of planetary boundaries." See https://www.sustainabledevelopmentindex.org.

the National Performance Framework.[10] Meanwhile, Icelandic Prime Minister Katrín Jakobsdóttir (2020) has written that "well-being is the measure of our success," and—hinting at more transformative possibilities—referred to the "attempt to develop a new economic model, which is centred on well-being rather than on production and consumption." Time will tell to what degree such statements are followed by substantive policy changes, but there are initial signs that these changing understandings of national success are beginning to impact policy through "well-being budgets," discussed below.

Conceptual use is linked to the storytelling role that indicators can play. Corlet Walker and Jackson (2019) distinguish between indicators that act mainly as narrative or storytelling devices and those that primarily act as decision aids for policy (although many indicators have been created with aspirations to do both). A key aspect of indicators in their storytelling role is that they reflect a new vision of societal progress. For example, the Happy Planet Index shows that nations with high per-capita GDP are frequently far less efficient than others in converting resource consumption into longer, happier lives (Jeffrey et al. 2016). The GPI typically tells a story of "genuine progress" trailing behind GDP growth (Kubiszewski et al. 2013), while specific national versions have their own stories, such as the New Zealand GPI's illustration of a sharp decline in well-being during the neoliberal reform and austerity of the 1980s and 1990s (Patterson et al. 2020). Meanwhile, measurement of subjective well-being and analysis of the variables associated with it can tell a variety of stories, including the importance of trust and social connections in improving life evaluations (Helliwell et al. 2020a), and the greater potential of such non-material factors to enhance well-being compared to increases in material consumption (Barrington-Leigh and Galbraith 2019). Such stories not only help to challenge the narrative that GDP growth is the key to social progress, they may also provide some hints about the types of policies that would be helpful or harmful (or at least point toward policy areas needing attention). However, further steps are needed to integrate alternative indicators into the policy process to ensure they are taken into account in decision-making.

---

[10] Some proponents of a well-being economy have argued that Scotland's government needs to go further in its economic recovery strategy by moving beyond "strong economic growth" as a core goal and reducing dependence on growth as a means to generate well-being (WEAll Scotland 2020).

INSTRUMENTAL USE: EMBEDDING INDICATORS INTO THE POLICY PROCESS

"Instrumental use" involves a direct link between indicators and decisions (Hezri 2004). This fundamental step has often been elusive, as noted above. In response, there is growing recognition of the need to go beyond merely producing new metrics to taking active steps to integrate them into the stages of the policy process (Stiglitz et al. 2018; Durand and Exton 2019)—as emphasized at the OECD's October 2019 conference on "Putting Well-being Metrics Into Policy Action." Many options are available, such as integrating indicators into national development strategies, creating new institutions with responsibility to monitor well-being indicators, further expanding the evidence base on the determinants of well-being and the policies that can enhance it, and capacity building and guidance for public servants in the use of well-being metrics (Durand and Exton 2019). This section focuses on a sub-set of available options: using new tools for cost-benefit analysis and policy assessment, using alternative indicators in "well-being budgeting," and requiring use of new indicators through legislation or mandates issued to public bodies.

New Cost-Benefit Analysis and Policy Assessment Tools

One challenge with alternative indicators is that "it's not always immediately obvious how to take the information … and apply it to decision making," according to a state official in Maryland (Hayden and Wilson 2018). Fortunately, there has been progress in developing tools that allow policymakers to do so. In Maryland, the state took preliminary steps, on a pilot basis, to bring the spirit of the GPI into cost-benefit analysis (CBA) through Net Present Value Plus (NPV+) analysis, which counts previously uncounted social and environmental considerations.[11]

Other approaches to beyond-GDP measurement have seen their own cost-benefit analysis innovations. Advances in subjective well-being measurement have led to techniques using life satisfaction as a benefit measure in cost-benefit analysis (Layard and O'Donnell 2015), which have seen

---

[11] Such analysis showed, for example, that it made more economic sense for the state to purchase and protect wetlands and forests, and continue to enjoy ecological services such as water treatment, than to allow revenue-generating but environmentally damaging suburban development (GFN 2015).

some initial application in Britain and Canada, resulting in quite different rankings of policy options and understandings of the return on investment compared to conventional CBA (Helliwell et al. Forthcoming; Shi et al. 2019). Meanwhile, use of indicator dashboards can benefit from tools such as New Zealand's CBAx, which allow conversion of various non-monetary impacts into monetary units for use in cost-benefit analysis (Ng Forthcoming; see also Durand and Exton 2019).

While such policy tools frequently involve debatable monetization techniques to estimate the full range of costs and benefits in comparable units, Bhutan developed an instrument for non-monetized, multi-criteria analysis of policy options. Decision-makers use the Gross National Happiness (GNH) Policy Screening Tool to assess proposed policies' impacts on some two dozen variables, which are related to GNH's nine domains[12] (Centre for Bhutan and GNH Studies n.d.). A proposal's likely impact on each variable is given a score out of four; proposals with total scores below a minimum threshold need revision before they can be approved. The GNH Policy Screening Tool is noteworthy for its role in arguably the most significant decision ever made using beyond-GDP metrics and related tools. In 2008, application of the screening tool led most of Bhutan's policy planners to reverse their previous support for joining the World Trade Organization (WTO) and reject membership (Hayden 2015, p. 168). Applying new approaches to policy analysis can clearly lead to substantially different choices; however, such examples are still far from the norm when it comes to beyond-GDP approaches.[13]

Well-being Budgeting

Another important step is integration of well-being and sustainability indicators into government budgeting. Use of alternative indicators to inform budget decisions has been an aspiration of many supporters of

---

[12] The domains are health, education, living standards, ecological diversity and resilience, good governance, psychological well-being, time use, community vitality, and cultural diversity and resilience.

[13] Colman, who highlights a lack of policy impact from beyond-GDP metrics, acknowledges the significance of Bhutan's WTO decision, but sees little discernible influence of GNH on recent policies.

beyond-GDP initiatives.[14] Indeed, there have been a growing number of efforts to do so—albeit with varying "shades of sincerity" (Laurent Forthcoming).

A prominent example is New Zealand's 2019 "well-being budget" (NZ Government 2019). It builds on the country's Living Standards Framework (LSF), which draws heavily on the OECD's well-being approach. The LSF includes a multidimensional dashboard of economic, social, and environmental indicators to assess "intergenerational well-being." The LSF dashboard includes indicators in 12 domains[15] of current well-being, as well as indicators for four forms of capital—natural, human, social, and financial and physical. In addition to national-level data to measure the state of "our country," individual-level data allows comparisons across social groups, that is, "our people," while data on the four capitals help to assess the ability to sustain well-being in "our future" (Treasury 2018a).

The New Zealand Treasury used the LSF and related tools for diagnostic and proposal assessment purposes in the 2019 budget process, that is, helping to identify important issues requiring the government's attention and assessing how intervention options would affect well-being domains and capitals. Information from the LSF dashboard was used—along with evidence from sectoral experts and input from government agencies—to determine the budget's five priorities: mental health, child well-being, supporting indigenous (Māori and Pasifika) people, supporting a thriving nation in the digital age through innovation, and the transition to a sustainable, low-emissions economy (Ng Forthcoming; Treasury 2018b). The five priorities were included in guidance to public agencies about the budget process and criteria for assessing proposed spending initiatives. In their budget bids, agencies had to show how proposed expenditures aligned with the five priorities and refer, where applicable, to the well-being impacts of their initiatives. Agencies also had to describe how they collaborated with others in developing their initiatives—with the aim of transcending agency boundaries. The LSF was then used as part of the process to assess and rank spending proposals for decisions about budget

---

[14] Such hopes have not always been fulfilled, as in the case of Maryland's GPI (Hayden and Wilson 2018).

[15] The domains are civic engagement and governance, cultural identity, environment, health, housing, income and consumption, jobs and earnings, knowledge and skills, safety, social connections, subjective well-being, and time use.

allocations (Ng Forthcoming; Treasury 2018b; NZ Government 2019). The budget ultimately included record levels of spending on mental health along with significant investments in efforts to address family and sexual violence, venture capital to help start-ups expand, low-carbon innovation, railways, and fixing hospitals, among other items.

How different is a well-being budget from a conventional budget? The answer will become clearer over time, as examples proliferate. New Zealand's initial experience shows both continuity and change. While some spending decisions, such as substantial investment in mental health, reflect a well-being orientation and the growing evidence base about contributors to well-being, some observers have noted that, on the whole, the priorities are not so different from previous budgets (Schumacher 2019). While transforming the economy toward sustainability was a major budget theme, it is not clear that such intentions are backed by sufficiently large shifts in spending to accelerate GHG reduction (McLachlan 2019; Baisden 2019). Meanwhile, as discussed in more detail below, dependence on economic growth to generate revenues for spending on well-being-enhancing programs and ensure high employment levels meant that GDP remained an important consideration.

That said, there are important innovations. The budget document's inclusion of an overall well-being outlook for New Zealand—alongside a conventional economic and fiscal outlook—is one indication that a genuinely new approach is at play (NZ Government 2019). A commonly expressed goal of supporters of beyond-GDP measurements is to use new overarching goals such as well-being to break down silos and create more cohesive, "joined up" policies (APPGWE 2014, pp. 15–16; Hayden and Wilson 2017, 2018; Durand and Exton 2019). New Zealand has shown a way to do so by using well-being as a common "language" across departments, while requiring ministries and agencies to collaborate in developing well-being-enhancing initiatives (Ng Forthcoming; NZ Government 2019, pp. 3, 5, 7). The budget also advanced the idea of treating public spending as investment (e.g., early intervention to address mental health) that generates positive social returns and reduces future costs (Mintrom 2019)—an approach buttressed by the LSF's emphasis on maintaining key forms of capital needed to generate future well-being.

Most fundamental is the explicit shift away from GDP as the primary indicator of prosperity toward a multidimensional understanding of well-being. While New Zealand is not abandoning pursuit of GDP growth, economic growth is now seen as one means among others to achieve the ultimate objective of well-being (Ng Forthcoming; NZ Government 2019, pp. 2, 5). While not transformative in the sense of aiming to move beyond growth or changing other core elements of the socio-economic system and the distribution of power within it,[16] New Zealand's approach could be seen as a significant reformist step—one that is potentially "transitional" in helping to "loosen the grip of GDP on the minds of decision makers" (Hall 2019) and open up "space in which more transformational possibilities can be cultivated" (Clarke 2014, p. 9).

The need to focus on the COVID-19 response temporarily set back further exploration of well-being budgeting in New Zealand and elsewhere.[17] Nevertheless, it is one of the most promising methods to date to integrate alternative indicators into policymaking.

Mandating Indicator Use

An additional option is simply to require decision-makers to use alternative indicators and broader well-being approaches through legislation or other types of mandates. Durand and Exton (2019) point to various examples of legislation, such as France's Sas Law, which requires the government to regularly report on a set of well-being indicators. In Wales, where 46 National Indicators are used to measure progress, the Well-being of Future Generations Act requires ministers and other public bodies to work to achieve seven well-being goals[18]—in effect establishing a "legally binding common purpose, overseen by the Future Generations Commissioner for Wales" (Durand and Exton 2019, p. 145). Analysis of the effectiveness of these specific laws is beyond this chapter's scope; indeed, questions exist about how much difference they have made in practice so far.[19] The key point is that legislation represents an increasingly

[16] Some observers may consider well-being budgeting to be "transformative" in the way it changes the process of allocating public resources, although it is not transformative in the way that I am using the term in this chapter, as outlined in the introduction.

[17] New Zealand had intended to deliver a second well-being budget in 2020. In January 2020, Icelandic Prime Minister Katrín Jakobsdóttir (2020) stated that a "well-being budget is in the works," while Canada's government was tentatively exploring the idea before COVID-19.

[18] These goals are as follows: a Wales that is prosperous, resilient, healthier, more equal, globally responsible, a Wales of cohesive communities, and a Wales of vibrant culture and thriving Welsh language.

[19] Laurent (Forthcoming) argues that although France's Sas Law is useful, the government's response has involved manipulation, as it selected indicators that put its record in a favorable light. Stewart (2020) raises questions about the Welsh approach's impact.

common option to embed alternative indicators in the policymaking process—and further variations are undoubtedly forthcoming.

Beyond legislation, government leaders can mandate use of alternative indicators by ministers, their departments, senior bureaucratic officials, and their agencies, although procedures and possibilities differ depending on each country's institutional context. In Canada, ministers receive mandate letters from the prime minister (or provincial premier) outlining the core policy objectives they are to pursue. An initial, exploratory step toward integrating alternative indicators into the policy process took place when Prime Minister Trudeau's (2019) mandate letter to the Minister of Middle Class Prosperity directed her to lead work to "better incorporate quality of life measurements into government decision-making and budgeting, drawing on lessons from other jurisdictions such as New Zealand and Scotland."

An example of a stronger mandate requiring monitoring and action to improve indicators—albeit with an important qualification—comes from Nova Scotia. The Canadian province has been the site of a non-governmental Quality of Life Initiative, which has included publication of a Nova Scotia Quality of Life Index, a related dashboard of well-being and sustainability indicators, and a large-scale Nova Scotia Quality of Life Survey (Dasilva and Hayden Forthcoming; Engage and CIW 2018). The Initiative's leaders have been conscious of the need to go beyond simply producing new indicators and hoping that change will result. One step has been the establishment of local teams to analyze quality-of-life data from the survey and develop priorities for actions that respond to it. Another hope has been that action to monitor and improve a core set of quality-of-life indicators could be embedded in the mandates of top-level bodies within the province's public service.

Nova Scotia already offers a relevant example: the mandate of its Office of Strategic Management, which works across departments to ensure implementation of the government's policy priorities, includes responsibility to "manage, measure, and publicly report" on progress toward a set of core goals tracked through an indicator dashboard (Nova Scotia 2019, pp. 2, 4). Unfortunately for those seeking a greater emphasis on well-being and sustainability, the indicators prioritized in the Office's mandate are not the Quality of Life Initiative's beyond-GDP metrics, but the

conventional growth-oriented OneNS dashboard[20] that grew out of the
Nova Scotia Commission on Building Our New Economy (Ivany et al.
2014). That Commission emphasized urgency in uniting around the drive
for economic growth and outlined a mostly neoliberal agenda to do so.
Similar integration of quality-of-life and sustainability indicators into the
Office's mandate or ministers' mandate letters would signal a new well-
being orientation, but for now more conventional economic goals reign
supreme in the province.

Beyond Reformism to Post-growth Transformation

The Nova Scotia example brings us back to the reality that despite growing questioning of GDP as an indicator of national success and efforts to
integrate alternative indicators into policy, established economic priorities
are indeed deeply rooted. While some policy impacts are becoming evident, beyond-GDP measurement and the related emphasis on well-being
has not yet been the transformative force that many proponents have
hoped for (e.g., Quick 2019). One interviewee expressed disappointment
that rather than broad changes in economic and social policy such as
income redistribution justified by well-being evidence, the agenda risked
being reduced to "let's do things a bit better."[21] Meanwhile, for those
who believe that the "GDP-led development model that compels bound-
less growth on a planet with limited resources no longer makes economic
sense" (Thinley 2012), and that alternative indicators can be a key part of
the creation of a "new economy suited to the reality of a finite planet"
(e.g., Zencey 2018, p. 8), there remains a long way to go.

Even in countries that have declared themselves "well-being economies," GDP growth is still pursued as an important means to achieve the
overriding goal of well-being (NZ Government 2019, pp. 2, 5; Sturgeon
2020) and the perceived political imperative of economic growth remains
strong (Richters and Simoneit 2019; Wiedmann et al. 2020). Choosing
another indicator or end goal to prioritize does not, in itself, reduce governments' reliance on growth to generate the revenues needed for public

---

[20] The dashboard includes indicators that can all be seen as related to the overriding goal
of economic growth, such as inter-provincial migration, international immigration, business
start-ups, export value, labor-force participation, venture capital, tourism expansion, net
debt to GDP, among others. See Dasilva and Hayden et al. (Forthcoming) and https://
www.onens.ca/.
[21] Interview, Juliet Michaelson, NEF, July 6, 2015.

spending and to ensure high employment levels, both of which are important for well-being. Nor does changing indicators affect the pursuit of profit by business in capitalist economies, which is a fundamental driver of economic growth and a source of pressure on governments to maintain an economic climate conducive to expansion.

While adopting new indicators and integrating them into the policy process are important, a post-growth transformation will require many other steps, some of which will confront very substantial obstacles. These include a new narrative of sustainable and equitable well-being—"the sustainability–justice nexus" (Laurent Forthcoming)—supported by beyond-GDP indicators in their storytelling role. Continued advances in post-growth economics will be essential (Bleys and Thiry Forthcoming) to develop strategies for how to manage and prosper without growth (e.g., Jackson 2017; Lange 2018; Victor 2019), and achieve goals such as employment creation and economic security that currently depend on growth. Possibilities include policies such as work-time reduction, a job guarantee, and variations on a basic income, and more fundamental shifts to economic institutions to ensure more widely shared asset ownership and more equitable taxation so that a greater share of production can be devoted to meeting core needs. Meanwhile, researchers have questioned the need for economic growth to finance social policy and sketched outlines of a post-growth welfare state (Hirvilammi 2020; Laurent 2020). While advocates of beyond-GDP measurement have often sidestepped the issue of political conflict—focusing on the information in alternative indicators to convince governments of the need for change—overcoming resistance to change from vested interests and building support for a shift in priorities will require a key contribution from social movements. Particularly important are the efforts of the climate justice movement to build public and political support to address the climate emergency and crisis of inequality. Stronger connections between beyond-GDP researchers and such movements are needed (Colman Forthcoming)—as part of a broader effort to build the political coalition necessary for post-growth transformation.

CONCLUSION

The belief that simply producing alternative indicators will inevitably lead to policy reform, and perhaps even transformation, is clearly flawed. Fortunately, this "indicators fantasy" is not the end of the story. Political use of indicators to defend policy positions and attempt to persuade others is one step toward policy impacts, although it is far from guaranteed to succeed. Also uncertain in its impact, but potentially quite significant, is conceptual use that results in new understandings and frameworks of thought. Such conceptual use is evident in the changing understandings—and emerging new narratives—of prosperity and national success. As for instrumental use in which indicators are directly linked to policy decisions, there is growing awareness of the need to take active steps to integrate alternative indicators into the policymaking process, and a growing number of possibilities to do so, such as the use of new cost-benefit analysis and policy assessment tools, well-being budgeting, and legislating or mandating indicator use.

These steps forward have generated considerable optimism within the beyond-GDP community about the possibilities for further advances and policy reform, yet there is also disappointment among some researchers and practitioners over the fact that the transformative goals that originally motivated many contributors to the field have remained elusive. If transformation is seen not only in terms of moving beyond GDP as the dominant indicator of national success, but beyond growth as a policy priority, then the requirements for such a transformation amount to a very tall agenda, one that will not be achieved overnight. Nor is it an agenda shared by all supporters of beyond-GDP measurement, some of whom insist that beyond-GDP thinking should not be seen as "anti-growth" (Stiglitz et al. 2018, p. 14).

In the interim, a transitional step with potential appeal both to those seeking post-growth transformation and more limited reform is to downplay the centrality of GDP and downgrade economic growth from an overarching goal to one means, among others, to achieve more important ends. That is, the step taken by the Well-being Economy Governments, and a similar message appears in a recent report to the OECD by the Secretary General's Advisory Group on a New Growth Narrative (2019).[22] This appears to be the "next iteration of what's possible"[23]—another step toward an economy focused not on ever-expanding production and consumption, but on sustainable and equitable well-being.

---

[22] This "Beyond Growth" report does not reject growth as an objective, but no longer sees it as the primary goal, highlighting four paramount objectives for economic policy: environmental sustainability, rising well-being, falling inequality, and system resilience.

[23] Interview, Danny Graham, Engage Nova Scotia, June 2020.

References

APPGWE. (2014). *Wellbeing in four policy areas: Report by the All-Party Parliamentary Group on Wellbeing Economics.* London: All-Party Parliamentary Group on Wellbeing Economics.

Baisden, T. (2019). *How New Zealand's well-being budget delivers for the environment.* The Conversation.

Barrington-Leigh, C., & Galbraith, E. (2019). Feasible future global scenarios for human life evaluations. *Nature Communications, 10,* 161. https://doi.org/10.1038/s41467-018-08002-2.

Bell, S., & Morse, S. (2011). An analysis of the factors influencing the use of indicators in the European Union. *Local Environment, 16,* 281–302. https://doi.org/10.1080/13549839.2011.566851.

Bleys, B., & Thiry, G. (Forthcoming). Beyond "Beyond GDP" in the EU: What's next? In A. Hayden, C. Gaudet, & J. Wilson (Eds.), *Towards sustainable wellbeing: Moving beyond GDP in Canada and the world.* Toronto: University of Toronto Press.

Bleys, B., & Whitby, A. (2015). Barriers and opportunities for alternative measures of economic welfare. *Ecological Economics, 117,* 162–172. https://doi.org/10.1016/j.ecolecon.2015.06.021.

Centre for Bhutan & GNH Studies. (n.d.). GNH policy & project screening tools. Retrieved June 22, 2020, from http://www.grossnationalhappiness.com/gnh-policy-and-project-screening-tools/.

Clarke, S. (2014). *Town Creek Foundation stakeholder meeting.* Easton, MD: Town Creek Foundation.

Colman, R. (Forthcoming). Time for a reality check: Lessons from Bhutan, Canada and New Zealand. In A. Hayden, C. Gaudet, & J. Wilson (Eds.), *Towards sustainable wellbeing: Moving beyond GDP in Canada and the world.* Toronto: University of Toronto Press.

Corlet Walker, C., & Jackson, T. (2019). *Measuring prosperity—Navigating the options.* Guildford, UK: Centre for the Understanding of Sustainable Prosperity.

Dasilva, C., & Hayden, A. (Forthcoming). Beyond dollars and cents: The Canadian index of wellbeing and Nova Scotia quality of life initiative. In A. Hayden, C. Gaudet, & J. Wilson (Eds.), *Towards sustainable wellbeing: Moving beyond GDP in Canada and the world.* Toronto: University of Toronto Press.

Durand, M., & Exton, C. (2019). Adopting a well-being approach in central government: Policy mechanisms and practical tools. In Global Council for Happiness and Wellbeing (Ed.), *Global happiness and wellbeing policy report 2019* (pp. 140–162). New York: Sustainable Development Solutions Network.

Engage, CIW. (2018). *Nova Scotia quality of life index: 1994–2014.* Halifax, NS: Engage Nova Scotia / Canadian Index of Wellbeing.

GFN. (2015). Making the economic case for sustainable investments in Maryland.

Hall, D. (2019). *NZ has dethroned GDP as a measure of success, but will Ardern's government be transformational?* The Conversation.

Hayden, A. (2015). Bhutan: Blazing a trail to a postgrowth future? Or stepping on the treadmill of production? *The Journal of Environment Development, 24,* 161–186. https://doi.org/10.1177/1070496515579199.

Hayden, A., & Wilson, J. (2016). Is it what you measure that really matters? The struggle to move beyond GDP in Canada. *Sustainability, 8,* 623.

Hayden, A., & Wilson, J. (2017). "Beyond GDP" indicators: Changing the economic narrative for a post-consumerist society? In M. J. Cohen, H. S. Brown, & P. J. Vergragt (Eds.), *Social change and the coming of post-consumer society: Theoretical advances and policy implications* (pp. 170–191). New York: Routledge.

Hayden, A., & Wilson, J. (2018). Taking the first steps beyond GDP: Maryland's experience in measuring "genuine progress". *Sustainability, 10,* 462. https://doi.org/10.3390/su10020462.

Hayden, A., Gaudet, C., & Wilson, J. (Eds.). (Forthcoming). *Towards sustainable wellbeing: Moving beyond GDP in Canada and the world.* Toronto: University of Toronto Press.

Helliwell, J. F., Huang, H., Wang, S., & Norton, M. (2020a). Social environments for world happiness. In J. F. Helliwell, R. Layard, J. Sachs, & J.-E. De Neve (Eds.), *World happiness report 2020* (pp. 13–46). New York: Sustainable Development Solutions Network.

Helliwell, J. F., Layard, R., Sachs, J., & De Neve, J.-E. (Eds.). (2020b). *World happiness report 2020.* New York: Sustainable Development Solutions Network.

Helliwell, J. F., Gyarmati, D., Joyce, C., & Orpana, H. (Forthcoming). Building an epidemiology of happiness. In A. Hayden, C. Gaudet, & J. Wilson (Eds.), *Towards sustainable wellbeing: Moving beyond GDP in Canada and the world.* Toronto: University of Toronto Press.

Hezri, A. A. (2004). Sustainability indicator system and policy processes in Malaysia: A framework for utilisation and learning. *Journal of Environmental Management, 73,* 357–371. https://doi.org/10.1016/j.jenvman.2004.07.010.

Hirvilammi, T. (2020). The virtuous circle of sustainable welfare as a transformative policy idea. *Sustainability, 12,* 391. https://doi.org/10.3390/su12010391.

Ivany, R., D'Entremont, I., Christmas, D., et al. (2014). *Now or never: An urgent call to action for all Nova Scotians: The report of the Nova Scotia Commission on building our new economy.* Nova Scotia: Halifax.

Jackson, T. (2017). *Prosperity without growth: Foundations for the economy of tomorrow* (2nd ed.). Abingdon, UK: Routledge.

Jakobsdóttir, K. (2020). *In Iceland, well-being is the measure of our success.* Evening Standard.

Jeffrey, K., Wheatley, H., & Abdallah, S. (2016). *The happy planet index 2016*. London: New Economics Foundation.

Kubiszewski, I., Costanza, R., Franco, C., et al. (2013). Beyond GDP: Measuring and achieving global genuine progress. *Ecological Economics, 93*, 57–68. https://doi.org/10.1016/j.ecolecon.2013.04.019.

Lange, S. (2018). *Macroeconomics without growth: Sustainable economies in neo-classical*. Keynesian and Marxian Theories, Metropolis-Verlag, Marburg, Germany.

Laurent, É. (2020). Comment construire un État social-écologique libéré de la croissance? *Les Notes de la FEP*, 1–6.

Laurent, É. (Forthcoming). Integrating well-being indicators in budgetary procedures: Four shades of sincerity. In A. Hayden, C. Gaudet, & J. Wilson (Eds.), *Towards sustainable wellbeing: Moving beyond GDP in Canada and the world*. Toronto: University of Toronto Press.

Layard, R., & O'Donnell, G. (2015). How to make policy when happiness is the goal. In J. Helliwell, R. Layard, & J. Sachs (Eds.), *World happiness report* (pp. 76–87). New York: Sustainable Development Solutions Network.

Lehtonen, M., Sébastien, L., & Bauler, T. (2016). The multiple roles of sustainability indicators in informational governance: Between intended use and unanticipated influence. *Current Opinion in Environmental Sustainability, 18*, 1–9. https://doi.org/10.1016/j.cosust.2015.05.009.

Martela, F., Greve, B., Rothstein, B., & Saari, J. (2020). The Nordic exceptionalism: What explains why the Nordic countries are constantly among the happiest in the world. In J. Helliwell, R. Layard, J. Sachs, & J.-E. De Neve (Eds.), *World happiness report 2020* (pp. 129–146). New York: Sustainable Development Solutions Network.

McGregor, J. A. (2015). *Global initiatives in measuring human wellbeing: Convergence and divergence*. Sheffield, UK: Centre for Wellbeing in Public Policy, University of Sheffield.

McLachlan, R. (2019). *NZ budget 2019: Support for lower-emission business, transport, land use*. The Conversation.

Mintrom, M. (2019). New Zealand's Wellbeing budget invests in population health. *The Milbank Quarterly, 97*, 893–896. https://doi.org/10.1111/1468-0009.12409.

Ng, T. (Forthcoming). Measuring what matters: Policy applications in New Zealand. In A. Hayden, C. Gaudet, & J. Wilson (Eds.), *Towards sustainable wellbeing: Moving beyond GDP in Canada and the world*. Toronto: University of Toronto Press.

Nova Scotia. (2019). *Business plan 2019–20: Department of Business*. Halifax, NS: Province of Nova Scotia.

NZ Government. (2019). *The wellbeing budget*. Wellington, NZ: New Zealand Government.

Patterson, M., McDonald, G., Forgie, V., et al. (2020). *Beyond gross domestic product: The New Zealand genuine progress indicator to measure the economic, social and environmental dimensions of well-being from 1970 to 2016*. Palmerston North, NZ: Massey University.

Quick, A. (2019). *Does new economics need wellbeing?* New Economics Foundation. Retrieved March 23, 2019, from https://neweconomics.org/2019/03/does-new-economics-need-wellbeing?mc_cid=c5a6dde7e7&mc_eid=863939ed46.

Richters, O., & Simoneit, A. (2019). Growth imperatives: Substantiating a contested concept. *Structural Change and Economic Dynamics, 51*, 126–137. https://doi.org/10.1016/j.strueco.2019.07.012.

Rinne, J., Lyytimäki, J., & Kautto, P. (2013). From sustainability to well-being: Lessons learned from the use of sustainable development indicators at national and EU level. *Ecological Indicators, 35*, 35–42. https://doi.org/10.1016/j.ecolind.2012.09.023.

Schumacher, C. (2019). *New Zealand's "well-being budget": How it hopes to improve people's lives*. The Conversation.

Scott, K. (2012). *Measuring wellbeing: Towards sustainability?* London: Routledge.

Secretary General's Advisory Group on a New Growth Narrative. (2019). *Beyond growth: Towards a new economic approach*. Paris: Organisation for Economic Co-Operation and Development.

Shi, Y., Joyce, C., Wall, R., et al. (2019). A life satisfaction approach to valuing the impact of health behaviours on subjective well-being. *BMC Public Health, 19*, 1547. https://doi.org/10.1186/s12889-019-7896-5.

Stewart, C. (2020). *Will wellbeing be a gimmick or a policy that changes lives?* The Herald.

Stiglitz, J. E., Fitoussi, J.-P., & Durand, M. (2018). *Beyond GDP—Measuring what counts for economic and social performance*. Paris: Organisation for Economic Co-Operation and Development.

Sturgeon, N. (2020). Wellbeing economy alliance conference: First Minister's speech.

Thinley, J. (2012). Address by the Hon'ble Prime Minister on well being and happiness at the UN Head Quarters, New York.

Treasury. (2018a). *Our people, our country, our future: Living standards framework: Introducing the dashboard*. Wellington, NZ: New Zealand Government.

Treasury. (2018b). *Budget policy statement*. Wellington, NZ: New Zealand Government.

Trudeau, P. (2019). Minister of Middle Class Prosperity and Associate Minister of Finance mandate letter.

UNDP. (2019). *Human development report 2019*. New York: United Nations Development Programme.

Victor, P. A. (2019). *Managing without growth: Slower by design, not disaster* (2nd ed.). Cheltenham, UK: Edward Elgar.

WEAll Scotland. (2020). *WEAll Scotland's initial response to the Scottish Government's economic recovery report.* Wellbeing Economy Alliance. Retrieved November 25, 2020, from http://dev.wellbeingeconomy.org/weall-scotlands-initial-response-to-the-scottish-governments-economic-recovery-report.

Whitby, A., et al. (2014). *BRAINPOoL project final report: Beyond GDP—From measurement to politics and policy.* Hamburg: World Future Council.

Wiedmann, T., Lenzen, M., Keyßer, L. T., & Steinberger, J. K. (2020). Scientists' warning on affluence. *Nature Communications, 11*, 1–10. https://doi.org/10.1038/s41467-020-16941-y.

Zencey, E. (2018). *The 2018 Vermont genuine progress indicator report.* The Vermont Genuine Progress Indicator Project, University of Vermont, Burlington, VT.

CHAPTER 8

The Forum for Alternative Indicators of Wealth: Beyond GDP, Democratically

Florence Jany-Catrice and Dominique Méda

INTRODUCTION[1]

The construction of alternative indicators of wealth is a battlefield, as the past two decades have shown. In this chapter, we focus on a particular moment in this conflict-ridden process of construction, namely the establishment in 2008 of a commission on the measurement of economic growth and social progress known as the "Stiglitz-Sen-Fitoussi Commission", and its significance and impact. Far from being an unremarkable event, the establishment of the Commission by then French

[1] This chapter was translated by Andrew Wilson.

Translator's note: This is a translation of the forum's French name, le Forum pour d'Autres Indicateurs de Richesse, from which the acronym FAIR is derived. The French acronym is retained throughout the chapter.

F. Jany-Catrice (✉)
University of Lille, Lille, France

Clersé, Villeneuve-d'Ascq, France

Institute for Advanced Study, Princeton, NJ, USA
e-mail: florence.jany-catrice@univ-lille.fr

© The Author(s), under exclusive license to Springer Nature Switzerland AG 2021
É. Laurent (ed.), *The Well-being Transition*,
https://doi.org/10.1007/978-3-030-67860-9_8

141

president, Nicolas Sarkozy, was underlaid by a series of paradoxical dynamics. Firstly, the unequivocal recognition in the Commission's final report of the unresolved contradictions—hitherto unacknowledged—in the measurement of GDP and economic growth was at odds with the appropriation of the report by the appointment to the Commission of international economists, the majority of whom were mainstream. Secondly, the Commission almost totally rejected the idea of a dialogue with civil society on the question of indicators of wealth even though, in the opinion of one of its most celebrated members, the Nobel laureate Amartya Sen, the Commission's purpose was to "think about the world we want". At the same moment, a movement challenging the use of economic growth and GDP as benchmarks had been gathering considerable strength since the end of the 1990s, and particularly so in France.

As soon as the gathering of this Commission was announced, a French collective called the Forum pour d'Autres Indicateurs de Richesse (FAIR) was set up. Its aim was to force its way into the debate and make itself heard in the public debate, in contrast to the Commission, which had decided to work *in camera* away from the public eye. The group's main demand was that a lively dialogue be opened up on these questions of general interest—since indicators are always frameworks for representing and interpreting the world. In this chapter, we look back at the birth of FAIR, investigate its heterogeneity and the alternatives in terms of both form and content that it was putting forward. Finally, the chapter examines the future of this type of movement, which seeks both to challenge mainstream economics and to reconstruct public dialogue on economic policies.

The Birth of a Movement: Putting New Indicators of Wealth in Motion

Scattered International Initiatives

Although criticism of GDP is as old as the concept itself (see Méda 2008, 2013), the end of the 1990s saw an upsurge of activity on the question. Crisis succeeded crisis and growth, although continually brandished as the

D. Méda
Institute for Interdisciplinary Research in Social Sciences, University of Paris Dauphine-PSL, Paris, France

Fondation Maison des Sciences de l'Homme (Collège d'études mondiales), Paris, France
e-mail: dominique.meda@dauphine.psl.eu

ultimate goal of any economy, had slowed down considerably in Western economies since the end of the 1970s. From the early 1990s onwards, the United Nations Development Programme (UNDP) had been constructing and disseminating several indicators of human development, including the HDI. These outputs provided the basis for extremely detailed "annual human development reports". This initiative initially constituted an all-out attack on the IMF's structural adjustment policies that at the time were rife in some developing countries. By responding with the HDI as its "weapon", the UNDP was seeking to destabilise the dominant way of representing the power of nations by using an indicator, albeit a fairly crude one, to promote the idea that, in order to be on a human development trajectory, the individuals in a society certainly have to be able to access economic resources but they also—and at the same time—need education and healthcare services. Around the same time, a network of academic and voluntary associations had been developing an initial version of the "environmental footprint" of humankind. The aim of this initiative was to spell out the unsustainability of our ways of life, and particularly those of the rich countries, and to develop the environmental footprint as an indicator to warn the world when it was approaching the threshold beyond which the planet's biocapacity, that is the available supply of renewable natural resources, was likely to be exceeded.

A French "Wealth School"?

At that time, a number of authors in France were reintroducing the critique of GDP into the national debate by attacking the practice of equating a society's wealth to its GDP and advocating an alternative conception of what constitutes wealth. They drew on the work of two categories of authors who had paved the way for, on the one hand, a historicised and socio-political approach to the compiling of national accounts (Alonso and Starr 1987; Fourquet 1980) and, on the other hand, a socio-history of quantification (Porter 1995; Espeland and Mitchell 2008; Desrosières 2008). Two scholars played a major part in making the critique of GDP a matter for public debate in France. In an internal critique, the economist Jean Gadrey explored the difficulties and uncertainties associated with the measurement of productivity in services and hence with the measurement of total economic output and thus with GDP (Gadrey 1996). For her part, the philosopher Dominique Méda, one of the authors expended considerable energy on reopening the question of how to define wealth. In her book *Qu'est-ce que la richesse?*, first published in 1999, the idea she puts forward is that national account systems are based on conventional definitions of wealth that are outdated and should be adapted: national accounts are constructs (Fourquet 1980; Coyle 2014; Gadrey and Jany-Catrice 2006; Jany-Catrice and Méda 2013) the underlying principles of which are based on both political considerations and a certain representation of the (existing and desirable) world (see also Méda 2020).

As head of the French Ministry of Labour's research department at the beginning of the 2000s, Dominique Méda commissioned Jean Gadrey and Florence Jany-Catrice to produce a report on the "new indicators of wealth" (Gadrey and Jany-Catrice 2006). At the same time, then Secretary of State for the Social and Solidarity Economy commissioned the philosopher Patrick Viveret to produce a report on "new wealth factors". Despite certain differences, these scholars found common ground around the idea that GDP should, as a matter of urgency, be replaced or supplemented by alternative indicators. This would both give force to a broader concept of what constitutes wealth and, at the same time, furnish public policies with collective reference points that would be less narrow than growth and more oriented towards social and environmental sustainability. It was also during this period that it started to become clear that questions about the appropriateness of alternative indicators of wealth were not primarily technical in nature; rather they were social and political in character and needed to be addressed in public debates. The theoretical or interpretative framework, the selection of indicators, the choice of format (aggregated or multidimensional) and the language to be adopted (monetary/non-monetary) all embodied representations of society and its sustainability based on conventions. These areas of convergence between these economists, sociologists, philosophers and so on were to lead some observers to put forward the idea of a "French wealth school" (Pouch 2005[2]), not simply because they were supporting an original idea but also because they were doing so through multiple exchanges within an (as yet informal) deliberative space.

The Role of International Organisations

Interestingly, certain international organisations also began to deliberate on the limitations of GDP. This might have seemed a paradoxical move at

[2] See also the article by Kail et al. (2005).

a time when the knowledge regime had conferred upon human capital and, above all, endogenous growth theories their privileged positions at the very summit of academicism. Why paradoxical? Because human capital theory asserts the importance of innovation for growth and at the same time sets out the intellectual conditions for envisaging the possibility of infinite growth, which in turn underlies the notion of "endogenous growth" (Romer 1994). And yet, against this background of brazen assurance with regard to growth, the OECD and the World Bank were both to add fuel to the critiques of GDP as a measure of wealth. This can be seen as a desire on the part of these international organisations to position themselves within this burgeoning field of inquiry. Thus in 2001–2002 the OECD published a report entitled *The Well-being of Nations: The Role of Human and Social Capital*, in which, having found fault with growth for its regrettable effects and negative externalities, the authors referred to the possibility of collective well-being. "They also supported the idea that there needed to be a shift from an indicator of flows to an indicator of stocks and that we needed to think in terms of "capital", and in particular of human and social capital" (Méda 2020). This positioning was a way of leaving this vast and multidisciplinary question of sustainability in the hands of economists. For its part, the World Bank focused on the question of the quality of growth and considered amending it in order to measure a form of social well-being (the same wording is found in the OECD report) that would include both environmental sustainability and human development.

Thus, two positions that may seem extremely close to each other were being set out at the same time; both challenged the ability of GDP and national accounts to provide a precise picture of wealth and proposed replacing an indicator of flows with an indicator of stock. In reality, however, they were to turn out to be diametrically opposed. In the first case, the whole of this stock is monetised and its various strands aggregated (which attests to a weak concept of sustainability). In the other, the crucial assets are considered separately, such that improvements in one are not liable to compensate for deteriorations in the other, and are expressed in physical or social language. These contradictions were to come to light particularly in the course of interactions with the Stiglitz-Sen-Fitoussi Commission.

In January 2008, at the first press conference, held just as the financial crisis had broken out, the French President, Nicolas Sarkozy, announced the establishment of the Commission on the measurement of economic performance and social progress. Dumbfounded by this announcement, and alerted by the economist Jean Gadrey, who asked them whether it would be appropriate to respond favourably to the invitation he had received to join the Commission, the members of the small, informal network set up at the beginning of the new millennium to fight the cause of the new wealth indicators decided to set up themselves up officially as an association by founding FAIR (Forum pour d'Autres Indicateurs de richesse).

Its initial aim was to support Jean Gadrey and to argue that this Commission (made up mainly of men and economists) should open up to civil society and discuss its proposals with its representatives. The network had as its patron Danielle Mitterrand (widow of former president François Mitterrand [1981–1995]), who at the time was director of a foundation called "France Libertés", a public figure very committed politically and particularly active in support of democracy in Latin American countries and the fight against poverty. The founder members were Jean Gadrey, Florence Jany-Catrice, Dominique Méda, Patrick Viveret and Hélène Combe. From the outset, the group had some thirty members from a variety of backgrounds.[3] This network was to meet very frequently throughout 2009.

A Diverse Movement for a Genuine Alternative

A Hybrid Collective

FAIR is neither an academic coterie, nor a learned society, nor a collective made up solely of academics, nor a purely campaigning organisation. Rather it is a hybrid collective that brings together a diverse set of

[3] The founding members included, notably, Jean Fabre, former assistant director of the United Nations Development Programme, Georges Menahem (CNRS researcher), Michel Veillard (chartered accountant), Celina Whitaker (Nouvelles richesses collective), Marc Humbert (academic, Pékéa network), Bernard Perret (Insee, former chair of the Scientific Council for the Evaluation of Public Policies), Jacques de Saint Front (chartered accountant), David Flacher (academic, member of Utopia), Jean-Marie Harribey (economist, member of Attac), Muttiah Yogananthan (chartered accountant), Pierre-Jean Lorens (Department of Economic Forecasting, Nord-Pas de Calais region), Pascal Petit (regulationist economist), Michel Renault (academic, member of Pekea), Rodrigue Olavarria (Fondation France Libertés), Grégory Marlier (Nord-Pas de Calais region) and Aurélien Boutaud (sustainable development consultant).

protagonists united by the conviction that a task as important as the construction of new indicators of wealth cannot be left to a few economists working in isolation but must involve collective deliberations. It was also set up with the aim of acting as an interlocutor for the Stiglitz-Sen-Fitoussi Commission. Thus it is a network set up to fight a cause. Ultimately, it is fairly similar to a think tank in terms of its composition and its mission to act as an advocate for a particular cause and to intervene in the public debate. However, it also has a stronger theoretical orientation, since it also seeks to refine the analyses of the new indicators of wealth and to advance and share knowledge on the subject. Besides a number of academics (more than ten, most of them affiliated to heterodox schools of thought, notably regulation and convention theory), many of the original members were directors or officials of networks such as the *Nouvelles richesses* collective, the *France Libertés* foundation, Utopia, Attac and so on; chartered accountants specialising in business accounting, which in their view was also in need of reform, were also fairly strongly represented. At a fairly early stage, strong links were also forged with the French regions and with Belgium, notably with the regulationist economist Isabelle Cassiers and her PhD student Géraldine Thiry, as well as with future members of the Walloon government, who were seeking to hasten the introduction of new indicators (see Cassiers et al. 2017). The Forum met at the premises of the *France Libertés* foundation in Paris and published its work on the IDIES (Institut pour le Développement de l'Information Economique et Sociale) website, where its main analyses were to be posted.[4] The collective met very regularly, prepared and discussed with Jean Gadrey the Commission's positions and took all its decisions democratically. Minutes were taken of all the meetings, which were then circulated and approved at the next meeting. The association appointed a chair, Jean Gadrey, a treasurer, Michel Veillard, and an honorary president, Danielle Mitterrand.

FAIR's Actions and Outputs

Throughout 2009, FAIR produced a number of proposals of a strategic nature in an attempt to influence the work of the Commission, whose meetings were all held in Paris, either by preparing positions to be defended by Jean Gadrey at its meetings, by meeting the Commission or by

[4] http://idies.org/index.php?category/FAIR. See also Jany-Catrice and Méda (2011).

publishing analyses. Three FAIR members[5] officially met the Commission at one of its meetings in Paris in order to explain the collective's position. Two main ideas were put forward at this meeting: indicators other than GDP were necessary and civil society had to be involved in selecting the new indicators. The members of the Commission tried to make the network one of the representatives of civil society (in the end it was the only one). The main outlet for FAIR's ideas was the IDIES website, where all its analyses were posted. These included analyses of the Commission's interim and final reports as well as of the various indicators that were to be proposed after its report had been published. FAIR was to be present at the major press conference at which the final report was launched, but its critical position went almost unheard. It was to organise a sort of counter-summit with the trade unions in particular, but it did not succeed in widening support for its cause. FAIR embarked on a series of meetings with the trade unions and questioned the various political parties, asking them to state their positions on the question of the predominance of GDP and their interest in the introduction of new indicators of wealth. Most of the parties responded at some length, noting their awareness of the limitations of GDP and the need for alternative indicators. The network was to continue expressing its views on a regular basis through regular forums, radio broadcasts and publications, notably in a special edition of the magazine *Alternatives économiques*[6] entitled "La Richesse autrement" that was published in 2011 and included a large number of analyses, both theoretical and empirical, penned by many of the members of FAIR.[7] The most critical moment was obviously the reception of the intermediate and final reports, which gave FAIR an opportunity to list all its disagreements.

FAIR's Analysis of the Stiglitz Report

The report gave the impression of being made up of a series of proposals derived from a multiplicity of schools of thought in economics, without any great coherence and with each one striving to assert the importance and relevance of its own position. They include Sen's capabilities theory,

---

[5] Florence Jany-Catrice, Dominique Méda and Celina Whitaker.

[6] Founded in 1980, the monthly *Alternatives économiques* aims to create the conditions for pluralism in economic thought by restoring the heterodox schools of thought to favour. It makes available to the broad public analytical tools that can be used to understand the world.

[7] https://fr.calameo.com/read/001191387db149e2121b6?authid=FuwqnKgA4zKd.

welfare economics and theories of happiness, the main protagonists of which were members of the Stiglitz Commission: Daniel Kahneman, Amartya Sen, Tony Atkinson, Marc Fleurbaey and so on (Méda and Jany-Catrice 2010).

Two schools of thought in particular played their game well in the report. The first was the economics of happiness, which is based on a subjectivist conception and measure of individual well-being in which people are considered to feel better when they are able to satisfy their preferences and desires. Wholly in keeping with utilitarian theory, its starting hypothesis is that individuals themselves are the best equipped to judge their own situation.

Secondly, Jean Gadrey identified, from his position within the Commission, a strong push by the economists, expanding on studies by the World Bank and particularly those on adjusted net savings, in favour of monetised indicators. By their very construction, these indicators are able to give expression only to a very weak version of sustainability because of the specific language and general equivalent that money represents. Incidentally, the economists on the Commission were not the only ones involved in this push for monetised indicators. The history of the production of reports over the period preceding the Stiglitz Commission attests to a strong preference on the part of international organisations for monetised indicators, which in turn encourages an approach in which economic growth and environmental concerns can be reconciled. Although the pressure exerted in particular by Jean Gadrey and the FAIR network in the (only) public critique of the Commission's interim report[8] helped to prevent adjusted net savings from being presented in the final report as one of the Commission's choices, this confrontation is a reminder that indicators are not neutral and that they embody not just a representation of the world but also sectional interests.

As for the debate with civil society, this was blocked straightaway by a Commission that worked in private and which was to make available to the public an interim report written entirely in English. The report's expert-led positioning created the impression of a technical citadel that excluded the broad public from discussion of these questions of general interest. Against this background, and despite the pressure exerted by many

---

[8] http://www.idies.org/index.php?post/Le-rapport-Stiglitz-%3A-un-diagnostic-lucide-une-methode-discutable-et-des-propositions-qui-ne-sont-pas-a-la-hauteur-des-enjeux2.

interested parties in an attempt to persuade the Commission to open up at some point to a debate with civil society, that debate was postponed until after the Commission had finished its work. It was never to take place.

The impact of the Stiglitz-Sen-Fitoussi Commission's report was mixed (Stiglitz et al. 2009; Stiglitz et al. 2010). On the one hand, it clearly acted as a release mechanism in the academic knowledge regime, giving scholarly legitimacy to all those who wished to address these issues and to all those who dived in opportunistically. On the other hand, the Commission's findings were to bring about little in the way of changes to official statistics.

Even the recommendation that publications of GDP statistics should be supplemented with income data divided into quartiles has never really been implemented.[9] There is a (four-page) issue produced by INSEE, the French national institute responsible for producing official statistics, entitled "Qualité de vie et bien être vont souvent de pair/Quality of life and well-being often go hand in hand".[10] This publication (Amiel et al. 2013) presents the results of an unpublished survey in which 10,000 French adults (contacted by post but answering online) were questioned about their feelings of well-being, defined as "their degree of satisfaction with life measured on a scale from 0 to 10". This evaluation of life satisfaction is now carried out annually in the statistical survey on resources and living conditions. Thus as far as the construction of new indicators was concerned, this was all something of an anti-climax; this is a view shared by other well-informed authors, who see the outcomes as nothing but "Old Wine in New Skins" (Noll 2011). On the other hand, awareness was growing, with FAIR playing its part in getting media coverage of the issues at stake, and the academic backing provided by the Commission also undeniably played a part in the questioning of the legitimacy of GDP and its ability to give an idea of wealth more in keeping with contemporary environmental and social concerns.

[9] See, for example, L. Aeberhardt, T. Laurent and J. Montornès 2020, "Les comptes de la Nation en 2019. Le PIB ralentit mais le pouvoir d'achat des ménages accélère" *Insee Première* no. 1802, May.

[10] This publication was to be challenged behind the scenes by INSEE administrators and statisticians.

FAIR Beyond the Stiglitz Commission

Activism Between Local and Global Transitions

During the years following the publication of the Commission's report, the FAIR movement continued to meet, to produce analyses and diagnoses, and to question politicians. During this period, the protagonists could be observed adopting different positions, depending on whether they were operating at regional or international level.

On the one hand, and without waiting for a universal indicator that would determine the direction of development, several of the French regions decided to turn the design of new indicators over to public debate and deliberation. In Nantes, the Pays de Loire, the Gironde, Nord-Pas de Calais, Rennes and then later in the Grenoble metropolitan area, citizens' networks set up to address these issues organised various deliberative exercises on "what counts" and put forward concrete proposals for new indicators. Members of FAIR were called on to assist. Thus the Nord-Pas de Calais region commissioned Florence Jany-Catrice and her team to construct an index of social health, which was to be developed as part of a broader public consultation exercise (Jany-Catrice 2009). For their part, researchers, politicians and citizens brought these questions about wealth indicators on to the Walloon government's agenda. In November 2012, that same government decided to calculate five flagship indicators as a matter of priority and commissioned the Institut Wallon de l'Évaluation, de la Prospective et de la Statistique (IWEPS) to develop them.

On the other hand, the international environment is characterised by "ferocious international competition" (Méda 2020) between international organisations intent on producing the new reference indicator likely to rival GDP and thus to determine the new vision of sustainable wealth. So much effort was being put into the construction of new indicators in the 2010s that it was enough to make one's head spin, whether we think of the OECD's Better Life Index or the World Bank's Inclusive Wealth Index (which had many similarities with that same organisation's ANS, particularly the use of monetisation). Mention must also be made in this international overview of the Social Progress Index, which originated in the USA, where it was first developed under the technical guidance of Michael Porter[11] in collaboration with a group of scholars and business

---

[11] Professor at Harvard Business School.

leaders. It was to be taken up in 2016 by the European Commission. Members of FAIR were to produce critical assessments of these indicators, all of which originated in the English-speaking world. They included the article by Roman and Thiry on the IWI (Roman and Thiry 2016), the studies by Jany-Catrice (2009, 2016) and Jany-Catrice and Marlier (2013), which dissected these indicators' inadequacies and particularly their failure to take adequate account of environmental considerations, and those by Gadrey and Lalucq (2015) and Renault (2017), which highlighted the unresolved contradictions of the reliance on monetisation. At the same time as these critical studies were being published, others sought to further substantiate the characteristics of an epistemology of participatory indicators (e.g. Renault et al. 2017; Jany-Catrice and Pinaud 2017; Le Roy and Ottaviani 2017).

The differences in the principles underlying the approaches adopted at regional and international level can be interpreted as follows. At the regional level, the public authorities were won over by indicators that took account of the variety of their regions' *specific* assets. The indicators had to "speak to the people"; they had to tell a story, the story of their region. Some of them even went so far as to think they had to decentre (in the spatial sense of the term) the big picture (Cunningham and Williams 1993). Furthermore, these actors were intuitively aware of the need for the plans for change to be socially acceptable. From this point of view, the experiments in deliberative democracy that contributed to the construction of the regional indicators played their part in developing that acceptability. The international organisations, in contrast, claimed a sort of monopoly over the universal (Bourdieu 2005) and they were unstinting in emphasising the power of their universalising indicators, treating them as so many arguments in favour of subjecting the social and natural worlds to economic discipline.

The Sas Law and Its Aftermath

Just as the cause of the new indicators of wealth appeared to have sunk into oblivion, it re-emerged from 2012 onwards in a working group set up by the socialist deputy Serge Bardy within the National Assembly's Commission on Sustainable Development and Regional Development and in studies by environmentalist deputy Eva Sas, which were to lead to a draft organic or institutional bill. Several members of FAIR gave evidence in both cases and provided analyses and assistance. The draft organic bill, which sought the incorporation of new wealth indicators into the finance acts, stipulated that the evolution of these new indicators of wealth, and particularly the indicator of social health and the environmental footprint, should be debated each year when the finance bill was being debated, in the same way as GDP.

The government rejected the draft bill for technical (and undoubtedly also political) reasons but undertook to include it in an ordinary act and to trial new indicators in the 2015 budget. The new bill, which contains just one article, was passed on 2 April 2015. The article is drafted as follows: "The Government shall each year on the first Tuesday in October present to Parliament a report setting forth the evolution over the past years of new indicators of wealth, such as indicators of inequalities, of quality of life and of sustainable development, as well as a qualitative or quantitative evaluation of the impact of the main reforms introduced in the previous year and those planned for the coming year, particularly those to be included in the finance acts, in respect of these indicators and the evolution of the gross domestic product. This report may the object of a debate in Parliament".

However, the path was a treacherous one, strewn with pitfalls: after all, the task now was to define which indicators should be the ones to be tracked. While the first draft bill of January 2014 contained some concrete proposals for indicators, the second delegated the choice to other bodies. The work was entrusted to a consultative committee chaired jointly by the Economic, Social and Environmental Council and France Stratégie, which was to produce indicators far removed from the draft bill's initial intentions. Several members of FAIR were to be involved, battling within the committee to get the indicators stipulated in the first draft bill adopted. The ten indicators finally proposed were less an alternative to growth and GDP than a refinement of the method for calculating them, under the banner of the "quality of growth". The report was to be published for the first time in 2015 under the aegis of the government information service and no longer had anything to do with an alternative measure of wealth. The subsequent reports, published late, were not debated.

Conclusion: The Road Ahead

The battle for new indicators of wealth, pursued relentlessly since the end of the 1990s by a small but diverse group of actors, has up to now failed. The dominant position of GDP has scarcely been dented at all, even though a high share of high-school students in their final year understand the limitations of that indicator and those limitations have been pointed out on numerous occasions, including in the Stiglitz-Sen-Fitoussi Commission's report. How is this to be explained? It might be thought that the champions of this cause did not have sufficiently powerful political connections or had not forged good alliances. In any event, the power relations were out of kilter, as the network enjoyed neither the material resources nor the symbolic connections nor the power of the international organisations that were putting forward rival proposals.

Although the proposals advanced by the Stiglitz Commission and the international organisations have not themselves borne fruit, the proliferation of plans for a "green new deal" or for "green growth" might be regarded as very close in spirit to the initiatives for monetised indicators (or very compatible with them). In both cases, after all, the aim is to encourage or interpret a form of business that is not constrained by environmental limits but which, on the contrary, has to open out in order to protect nature. Whether or not this alliance between the public authorities and the advocates of monetised indicators was intentional, it is certainly indicative of the fact that the construction of indicators requires intensive efforts of a social nature (Orléan 2004; Turnbull 1997), whether it encourages the stabilisation of new knowledge, marginalises even more the advocates of alternative indicators or conjures up the spectre of a natural world whose subjugation to economic interests is universal, institutionalised or even imperialist.

REFERENCES

Alonso W. Starr, P. (1987). The Politics of Numbers, Russell Sage Foundation.

Amiel, M. H., Godefroy, P., & Lollivier, S. (2013). "Qualité de la vie et bien être vont souvent de pair", Insee Première, n° 1428.

Bourdieu, P. (2005). *On the state: Lectures at the Collège de France, 1989–1992.* ed. Wiley.

Cassiers, I., Maréchal, K., & Méda, D. (Eds.). (2017). *Post-growth economics and society: Exploring the paths of a social and ecological transition.* Routledge.

Coyle, D. (2014). GDP A brief but affectionate history.

Cunningham, A., & Williams, P. (1993). De-centring the 'big picture': the origins of modern science and the modern origins of Science. *The British Journal for the History of Science, 26,* 407–432.

Desrosières, A. (2008). *L'argument statistique. Tome 1: Pour une sociologie histo-rique de la quantification. Tome 2: Gouverner par les nombres*. Paris: Éd. Mines ParisTech, coll. "Sciences sociales".

Espeland, W., & Mitchell, S. (2008). A sociology of quantification. *European Journal of Sociology, 49*(3), 401–436.

Fourquet, F. (1980). *Les comptes de la puissance*. Paris: ed. Recherches, coll "Encres".

Gadrey, J. (1996). *Services. La productivité en question*. Paris: ed. Desclée de Brouwer.

Gadrey, J., & Jany-Catrice, F. (2006). *The New Indicators of wellbeing and develop-ment*. Palgrave Macmillan.

Gadrey, J., & Lalucq, A. (2015). *Faut-il donner un prix à la nature?* Les petits matins/Institut Veblen.

Jany-Catrice, F. (2009). The French regions and their social health. *Social Indicators Research, 93*(2), 377–391.

Jany-Catrice, F. (2016). La mesure du bien-être territorial. Travailler sur ou avec les territoires? *Revue de l'OFCE, 145*, 63–91.

Jany-Catrice, F., & Marlier, G. (2013). Estimer la santé sociale des régions fran-çaises: enjeux économiques, épistémologiques et politiques. *Revue d'économie régionale et urbaine, 4*, 647–678.

Jany-Catrice, F., & Méda, D. (2011). Le rapport Stiglitz et les limites de l'expertise. *note de travail de l'IDIES*, no. 14.

Jany-Catrice, F., & Méda, D. (2013). Well-Being & the Wealth of Nations. How Are They To Be Defined? *Review of Political Economy, 25*(3), 444–460.

Jany-Catrice, F., & Pinaud, S. (2017). Entre ingénierie de la participation et ingé-nierie de la quantification. Quand les conventions de richesse sont mises en débat. *Participations, 2*(18), 39–67.

Kail, M., Lantz, P., & Sobel, R. (2005). Pour une économie politique de la richesse. *L'Homme & la Société, 2–3*(156–157), 21–25.

Le Roy, A., & Ottaviani, F. (2017). Quand la participation bouscule les fondamen-taux de l'économie. La construction participative d'indicateurs alternatifs locaux. *Participations, 2*(18), 69–92.

Méda, D. (2008). *Au-delà du PIB. Pour une autre mesure de la richesse*. Flammarion et Champs Actuel.

Méda, D. (2013). *La mystique de la croissance. Comment s'en libérer*. Flammarion.

Méda, D. (2020). Promouvoir de nouveaux indicateurs de richesse: histoire d'une "cause" inaboutie. FMSH-Working Paper-2020-145, juin.

Noll, H.-H. (2011). The Stiglitz-Sen-Fitoussi-report: Old wine in new skins? Views from a social indicators perspective. *Social Indicator Research, 102*, 111–116.

Orléan, A. (2004). *Analyse économique des conventions*. Presses Universitaires de France, coll. "Quadrige".

Porter, M. (1995). *Trust in numbers: The pursuit of objectivity in science and public life*. Princeton, NJ: Princeton University Press.

Pouch, T. (2005). Actualité de la richesse, oubli de l'économie politique? *L'Homme & la Société, 2–3*(156–157), 87–99.

Renault, M. (2017). Compter le gratuit, un enjeu moral? Un essai sur l'équivalence. *Entreprise & Société, 1*(2017-1), 97–126.

Renault, M., Meriot, P., & Gouzien, A. (2017). Élaborer des indicateurs avec les citoyens. Lecture pragmatiste d'une méthode d'enquête sur les valeurs. *Revue Française de Socio-Économie, 2*(19), 47.

Roman, P., & Thiry, G. (2016). The inclusive wealth index. A critical appraisal. *Ecological Economics, 124*(C), 185–192.

Romer, P. (1994). The Origins of Endogeneous Growth. *Journal of Economic Perspectives, 8*(1, Winter), 3–22.

Stiglitz, J., Sen, A., & Fitoussi, J.-P. (2009). Report by the commission on the measurement of economic performance and social progress. Paris. Retrieved from http://www.stiglitzsen-fitoussi.fr/en/index.htm.

Stiglitz, J., Sen, A., & Fitoussi, J.-P. (2010). *Mismeasuring our lives: Why GDP Doesn't add up*. New York: The New Press.

Turnbull, D. (1997). Reframing science and knowledge traditions. *Futures, 29*(6), 551–562.

CHAPTER 9

Building the Transition Together: WEAll's Perspective on Creating a Wellbeing Economy

Rabia Abrar

INTRODUCTION

At the time of writing, our economies and societies are undergoing unprecedented transformation as a result of the COVID-19 pandemic. At the same time, our world was already facing multiple crises: rising inequality, accelerating climate breakdown and rapid biodiversity loss. These issues are interconnected and stem from the same core problem: our economies are structured, governed, and measured to promote short-term gain over long-term stability. The global pandemic has made the injustice, unsustainability, and fragility of our current economic system clearer than ever—and exposed the urgency of transforming our economic system.

The Wellbeing Economy Alliance (WEAll) is a collaboration formed to catalyse a cooperative, harmonised, and effective approach to creating Wellbeing Economies. This chapter will explore the purpose for which

R. Abrar (✉)
Wellbeing Economy Alliance, Toronto, ON, Canada
e-mail: rabia@weall.org

© The Author(s), under exclusive license to Springer Nature Switzerland AG 2021
É. Laurent (ed.), *The Well-being Transition*,
https://doi.org/10.1007/978-3-030-67860-9_9

WEAll was created, its evolution over time, and examples of Wellbeing Economy policies being put into practice to shift the economic system towards a Wellbeing Economy. These examples can serve as inspiration for how policy makers can implement policies to make a Wellbeing Economy a reality.

The Need for WEAll

The Context: A Failing Economic System

Our current economic system is driven by the "growth at all costs" mentality, as measured by gross domestic product (GDP) (Costanza et al. 2017). There is an entrenched belief that GDP growth is synonymous with increasing wellbeing and prosperity and is universally beneficial, with the only concessions in recognition of its flaws coming in the form of qualifying adjectives such as 'inclusive', 'shared', or 'green'. While having delivered improvements to many, the current economic system is not supporting the flourishing of society *as a whole* and is now jeopardising progress achieved to date. Despite 'economic growth', we see widening economic inequalities, higher levels of insecurity, and indicators of despair and loneliness: rising rates of suicide, self-harm, and overdosing and the emergence of coping mechanisms that turn people inwards or against each other—all while trust in institutions withers away.

Trebeck (2020a) explains that much of the wealth that was created in the last few decades has gone to those at the very top. Meanwhile, living standards have stagnated for many worldwide. It is no surprise then, that Edelman global surveys (2020) found that in a majority of markets, 57 per cent of respondents believe that governments only serve the interests of a few, *less than half* of the population trust their institutions to 'do what is right', and 56 per cent believe that capitalism, in its current form, is doing more *harm* than good.

For those whose lives it has improved, a focus on 'growth' has done so by working against the planet. Our home is on the brink of the sixth mass extinction, with the prospect of catastrophic climate breakdown getting closer and closer (Ceballos et al. 2020). In the last 40 years, humanity as a whole has gone from using one planet's worth of natural resources each year, to using one and a half, and is on course to using three planets worth by 2050 (United Nations 2020).

The current economic system is, in short, unfair, unsustainable, unstable, and unhappy.

Trebeck and Williams (2019) explain that in our current economic system, growth in GDP is demanded as a means to pay for services that people need. But very often, these services are needed to *fix* the harm to people, communities, and the environment that is *created* by the excessive pursuit of growth. Much of our current policy efforts and a *substantive* part of what is counted in GDP is deployed for reactive amelioration measures, that could be *avoided*. In addition to being avoidable, this downstream intervention is also inadequate and expensive. According to the Joseph Rowntree Foundation, poverty alone costs Britain £78 billion every year (Bramley et al. 2016). IMF analysis demonstrated that effective 'subsidies' to fossil fuel companies cost $5.3 trillion a year, taking into consideration expenditure due to pollution, floods, droughts, and storms linked to climate change (Coady et al. 2015).

The good news is that the current economic system has been designed—and hence can be designed *differently* to prevent this avoidable demand for intervention and expenditure.

Building Back Better to a Wellbeing Economy

Recent dialogue around the COVID-19 pandemic has been dominated by the idea of 'Building Back Better', a phrase that captures simply and effectively, the need and urge to create a better system after the crisis. If we are to build back to an economic system that is truly 'better', it must be designed to deliver wellbeing for all, in harmony with nature. This shift in the purpose and functioning of the economy requires systems change.

The concept of 'collective wellbeing' is familiar the world over, even though different terms might be used to describe its key idea. A 'Wellbeing Economy' is a broad term designed to be inclusive of the diverse movement of ideas and actions striving towards this shared vision: an economy that delivers *social justice on a healthy planet*. At its core, a Wellbeing Economy is designed with a different *purpose*: it starts with the idea that the economy should serve people and communities, first and foremost. In a Wellbeing Economy, business, politics, and economic activity would exist *solely* to deliver collective wellbeing. GDP growth would not be the top priority. Instead, we would only pursue growth in those areas of the economy that *contribute* to collective wellbeing and shrink those areas of the economy that damage it.

A Wellbeing Economy would employ upstream prevention strategies that avoid the need for expensive downstream interventions. For instance, reactive measures such as in-work tax credits for those with insufficient wages would be less necessary in a Wellbeing Economy that 'pre-distributes' wealth much more fairly. Wellbeing Economy policies could also deliver benefits such as job creation in a growing renewables sector and Circular Economy.

A Wellbeing Economy recognises that the economy is embedded in society and nature. A system of economic governance aimed at promoting wellbeing will, therefore, account for *all* of the impacts of economic activity, both positive and negative. Economic success would be measured less in terms of the *rates* of growth; it would focus on the *direction* and *composition* of growth. WEAll's definition of a Wellbeing Economy, co-created by its members, is an economy that delivers on five universal human needs for a good life:

1. **Connection:** A sense of belonging and institutions that serve the common good.
2. **Dignity:** Everyone has enough to live in comfort, safety, and happiness.
3. **Fairness:** Justice, in all of its dimensions, at the heart of economic systems, and the gap between the richest and poorest greatly reduced.
4. **Participation:** Citizens are actively engaged in their communities and locally rooted economies.
5. **Nature:** A restored and safe natural world for all life.

These are the factors a Wellbeing Economy would grow, to be 'successful'. At the same time, a Wellbeing Economy approach would reduce activities which often increase GDP but that damage collective wellbeing.

There is not *one* blueprint for a Wellbeing Economy; the shape, institutions, and activities that get us there will look different in different contexts, both across countries and between different communities *within* countries. However, the high-level *goals* for a Wellbeing Economy are the same everywhere.

The Wellbeing Economy Movement

A global movement is coalescing among a large number of individuals and organisations around the need to shift economies to one broadly focused on 'sustainable wellbeing'. The Wellbeing Economy movement already has many of the answers, ideas, and examples that illustrate what 'better' can look like. 'What is needed' has been clear to many groups and academics and to large numbers of citizens for some time. 'How to make it happen' is the key issue.

How to Deliver a Wellbeing Economy: WEAll's Approach to Change

While many of the component parts of a new economic system already exist, they are fragmented, under-resourced, and fragile. Evidence from successful system change shows that individual policies and great exemplars are not enough. Cross-sectoral collaboration, on a long-term basis, is required. The challenge is to *connect* initiatives at all levels of society that are working towards a Wellbeing Economy, in order to shift policies and practices at a *meaningful scale*.

The Wellbeing Economy Alliance (WEAll)

The Wellbeing Economy Alliance (WEAll), a ten-year project, was created to serve this purpose: to catalyse systems change towards the realisation of a Wellbeing Economy, by creating unprecedented cooperation between actors working in their own areas and layers of the economic system. A crucial role for WEAll, as an organisation, is providing the connective tissue between the different elements of the Wellbeing Economy movement. Today, WEAll has become the leading global collaboration working together to transform the economic system. WEAll's ambition is to remain a small core team.

WEAll is a broad 'network of networks', with the aim of building a movement across society that has the confidence, knowledge, and connectivity needed to challenge the dominant economic paradigm. A key challenge in creating the critical mass needed is overcoming the disconnectedness of existing groups or singular focuses on *one* part of the systems change required. Currently, cross-sector coordination is poor.

WEAll approaches this challenge by acting as a supportive team of 'Amplifiers'. The 'Amp Team' acts as the *agents* (connectors and facilitators), rather than the *makers*, of change; its role is to create spaces and opportunities for members to connect and thrive together. WEAll can be described as the 'salespeople for Wellbeing Economy agenda'. WEAll's guiding principle is '*togetherness above agreement*'. The focus of this movement is on commonalities of shared values, goals, and principles, rather than on policy differences. The goal is to promote the Wellbeing Economy as the destination that all diverse efforts are working towards.

WEAll's *vision* is that within a decade, the WEAll project is no longer needed, as it has catalysed economic system change in multiple countries towards a Wellbeing Economy. In this future, policy would be framed in terms of human and ecological wellbeing, not simply economic growth; businesses would provide dignified lives for their employees and exist to meet social needs and contribute to the regeneration of nature, and the rules of the economy would be shaped by collaboration between government, business, and civil society. This vision and model of change was born out of a number of pioneering local and global movements.

The Genesis of WEAll

In July 2011, Bhutan (the small Himalayan country that gained prominence in 1972, when the fourth King of Bhutan, Jigme Singye Wangchuck, famously declared that "Gross National Happiness is more important than Gross National Product") proposed its first UN resolution, which was passed unanimously. Resolution 65/309, *Happiness: towards a holistic approach to development*, stated that "the pursuit of happiness is a fundamental human goal" and that "unsustainable patterns of production and consumption can impede sustainable development". To advance this effort, the government of Bhutan organised a meeting of more than 600 participants at the UN in New York in April 2012, to further discuss the creation of a new development paradigm based on happiness and wellbeing. One result of that meeting was the creation of a New Development Paradigm International Expert Working Group (IEWG) at the invitation of Bhutan's King and its Prime Minister, Jigme Thinley. In January 2013, the 60-member IEWG met in Thimphu, Bhutan, to draft a report to the UN on what this new development paradigm would look like and how to implement it. During the final preparation of the report, the government of Bhutan changed and enthusiasm for the report waivered. However, several of the participants in the IEWG decided to form a new group to carry the ideas forward: the Alliance for Sustainability and Prosperity (ASAP).

In May 2016, a parallel group with very similar ideas and agenda was formed in the US, called Leading for Wellbeing (L4WB); this group included many of the ASAP members. In May 2017, ASAP and L4WB committed to merging into a new organisation, to be called the Wellbeing Economy Alliance (WEAll). Meanwhile, the New Economy and Social Innovation (NESI) Forum, convened a global gathering in Europe in April 2017, around very similar ideas. NESI created a charter based on input from over 700 people. NESI became a vital element in the formation and development of WEAll.

In October 2017, a meeting in Glasgow, Scotland was initiated by members of what became the WEAll team, hosted by the Scottish Government's Office of the Chief Economist and welcomed by Nicola Sturgeon, first minister of Scotland. At this meeting, a group of governments, including Scotland, Costa Rica, Slovenia, and New Zealand committed to creating what became the Wellbeing Economy Governments (WEGo) partnership.

In June 2018, many of the founding members of WEAll met in Malaga, Spain, and debated key aspects of WEAll's operations. The WEAll website went 'live' in August 2018, and in September, WEAll held a formal launch event at Fordham University and led a viral campaign stunt for Free Money Day in New York City.

Since its inception, WEAll has successfully mainstreamed the ideas of the Wellbeing Economy and 'Build Back Better' agenda, growing demand for a Wellbeing Economy and building collaborations required to innovate, test, and scale solutions in order to meet this demand. The second stage of WEAll's theory of change is the deepening of connections and expanding WEAll's reach to over 20 territories, especially in the Global South; the third and final stage will focus on actively supporting governments, businesses, and citizens to prioritise Wellbeing as the primary goal of decision making. WEAll's mission has three pillars.

Creating New Powerbases

WEAll creates spaces to *convene and connect* stakeholders from different focus areas and geographies, to bring them into each other's work, thus catalysing new powerbases.

1. Active members: Build, connect, convene, and facilitate cooperation and collaboration between diverse meta movements through membership in WEAll. These meta movements include businesses, finance, faith and values groups, academia and think tanks, civil society organisations, governments, institutional innovators and practitioners such as cities, which are implementing Wellbeing Economy initiatives at scale. WEAll supports members' strategy, collaborations, dissemination, and replication. Today, WEAll has almost 200 organisational members from every continent. Regular meetings and open communications channels allow members to connect with one another, make requests for support, and collaborate.

2. Engaged citizens: Encourage a global citizen's movement, in which individuals contribute to change in their local communities and add their voice globally. To date, almost 2000 individual changemakers from around the world participate and collaborate on WEAll's Citizens online platform. WEAll Youth, a collaboration of changemakers under 30 which participate as WEAll members, has grown to 75 members. WEAll Youth was one of 50 organisations selected from over 4300+ organisations from 170+ countries to be featured in the UN Youth Solutions Report 2019 as a top 50 global solution to deliver the Sustainable Development Goals (SDGs). It has created place-based hubs globally, including in Melbourne, Warwick, Scotland, Uganda, and the US.

3. Cross-disciplinary, place-based hubs: Support the creation of hubs, which are microcosms of the global Wellbeing Economy movement in a specific geography. These hubs formulate, implement, test, and lobby for change strategies relevant to their locality's need and potential, in partnership with relevant local, regional, and national partners. WEAll has launched hubs in California, Canada, Costa Rica, Iceland, New Zealand, Scotland, Trinidad and Tobago, and Wales, with interest to create new hubs in Australia, Barcelona, Ireland, the Netherlands, and Vermont. The WEAll Scotland hub, set up in 2018, is the most established place-based hub to date. It is registered for charitable status; has a board of trustees and a core team; hosted sold-out events with a significant number of leaders from government, business, civil society, academia, and community groups; established funding partnerships; cultivated influential relationships with key government officials; and achieved significant media coverage including on the BBC and major daily newspapers. The accomplishments of the hub, run entirely by a team of volunteers, are a testament not only to the energy driving the team, but also a wider demand for guidance on building a Wellbeing Economy.

4. Influencing arenas: Influence existing movements and alliances to adopt a Wellbeing Economy approach, bring Wellbeing Economy ideas and knowledge into spaces where change can happen, establish strategic partnerships with some of these groups, and instigate groupings in sectors where none exist. This includes groupings like WEGo, Capitals Coalition, UN Global Compact, Global Commons Alliance, and the Global Alliance for Banking on Values. To support this agenda promotion work, WEAll has recruited 20 high-profile leaders in the movement as WEAll Ambassadors, as well as over 90 eminent Research Fellows and academics. After instigating the WEGo partnership, WEAll continues to support and influence WEGo by providing encouragement, promotion and profile, connections, and knowledge and evidence from its Knowledge and Policy working group.

Building a Coherent Knowledge and Policy Evidence Base

The Wellbeing Economy vision spans far beyond traditional economics and embraces an understanding of the economy as embedded within the cultural, political, environmental, and spiritual dimensions of life. Currently, the Wellbeing Economy theoretical base is disparate and relatively hard to access; while much is already known about how a Wellbeing Economy might work and how to get there, this knowledge is scattered across different types of knowledge and different sectors, including academia and think tanks. In addition, knowledge gaps remain. There is a need to produce knowledge content that clearly expresses the Wellbeing Economy vision and that presents the various existing debates, proposed solutions, ideas, policies, and examples that can make this vision a reality.

WEAll works to synthesise and disseminate the existing knowledge and evidence base on what a Wellbeing Economy looks like and how to get there, in a more coherent, solutions-oriented, and accessible format. This is urgently needed to help audiences understand and feel that it is achievable. WEAll has developed and published a range of knowledge outputs to support this goal.

1. Business guide: In collaboration with its members, WEAll published a guide to "Alternatives for Business as Usual", aimed at businesses and launched a "Build Business Back Better" Pledge.

2. Briefing papers: A series that synthesises various existing academic and grey literature that informs Wellbeing Economy analysis and propositions, in an accessible and inspiring manner.

3. Policy papers: A series that presents concrete, evidence-based Wellbeing Economy policy proposals to tackle complex issues, that can support leaders in various spaces and levels to build Wellbeing Economies.

4. Policy design guidebook: A guidebook that explains how relevant stakeholders can advance the creation and implementation of Wellbeing Economy policies and explores case studies of successful Wellbeing Economy policy design and implementation from around the world.

5. Fiscal benefits analysis: An analysis to clarify the fiscal impact of the current economic model; that is, quantifying how much of current budgets is currently spent to fix and *respond* to the collateral damage to people, communities, and the environment of the current growth-focused economy.

Sharing New Positive and Empowering Narratives

Changing the purpose of the economy is one of the highest order leverage points to make systemic change. A big part of this change is *believing* that a different system is possible and that we collectively have the power to make it a reality. At present, the current economy is seen as the *only* kind of economy that we can have. Much of the discussion in the Wellbeing Economy movement is focused on the failures of the current system. Furthermore, the destination of a different economy can feel abstract or irrelevant, to most audiences. As a result, there is a dearth of positive visions of a Wellbeing Economy in the media. This is a problem, as humans make sense of the world through stories—and these stories shape how they behave in it.

A shift in the narratives in public discourse can shift culture and produce tangible impact through behaviour change, activism, advocacy, and policy change. With this in mind, we urgently need Wellbeing Economy narratives, which summarise the *vision* towards which policies work, make the concept of a new economic system *accessible* to all, and help *galvanise* widespread support of the policies required to make this new economic system a reality. The ultimate goal is to make a Wellbeing Economy *common sense*, the way the free-market economy is now. Increasingly, work is being done to create positive Wellbeing Economy narratives, but little of this has been trialled in practice and is not yet making a significant difference. WEAll works to shift the narrative beyond criticisms of the current system, towards one that establishes a Wellbeing Economy as a desirable and viable goal, thus inspiring action towards achieving this vision.

1. Storytelling: WEAll works with a diverse network of partners around the world to co-create and communicate new common narratives. Spokespeople regularly make high-profile appearances and deliver talks in six continents. WEAll's website, newsletter, and social media channels generate consistently high levels of engagement. WEAll's work has been featured regularly in books, blogs, articles, videos, and podcasts, and has generated high-profile media coverage in at least ten countries. Wellbeing Economy narratives work has been launched in the UK, the US, Africa, and Australia. WEAll's storytelling involves using practical examples of what 'flourishing' looks like for various stakeholders, as a result of Wellbeing Economy policies and practices.

2. Amplification: WEAll amplifies Wellbeing Economy ideas and relevant work from the WEAll network, across different specialisms, sectors, demographics and geographies. WEAll curates existing ideas and solutions in forms that accelerate their influence and adoption by decision makers in government at all levels, business, and civil society across the globe.

3. Narratives Playbook: The 'Playbook' will support media partners, including journalists, musicians and TV content producers, to frame elements of a new economic narrative, design creative and cultural interventions, and media products, and disseminate them to bring the Wellbeing Economy agenda into the mainstream.

THE WAY FORWARD: WELLBEING ECONOMIC POLICY

Building a Wellbeing Economy requires changing 'the rules of the game' and redesigning institutions, infrastructure, and laws to incentivise a boost in activities and behaviours that support the wellbeing of people and planet, and disincentivise those that undermine it.

Two main types of barriers can hinder the Wellbeing Economic policy making. Firstly, the concentration of political and financial power creates a *power imbalance* between policy makers, business and civil society (McKay 2018). Secondly, economists, constant media attention and geopolitical power competition around growth, short-term political agendas and associated governance processes create a *political value system* that prioritises short-term economic impacts of policies, rather than long-term environmental and social impacts (Hirschman and Berman 2014). This makes it difficult for policy makers to break away from growth as a policy objective and to argue in favour of a wider set of objectives (Philipsen 2015).

To tackle power imbalances, policy makers must not only put limits on the power of influential actors, but also increase the power of less powerful groups. One way to achieve this is to create new forms of collaboration between policy, the private sector, and civil society (Mortensen and

Petersen 2017). Governance is needed to steer these collaborations to achieve shared goals: finding new ways of generating employment, promoting equality and reducing debt, and investing where the economy creates real public use-value: health care, education, nursing care, public parks and clean energy, transport and infrastructure (Jackson 2017). The state of the world's governance—both within and between states—must be enhanced. The Wellbeing Economy Governments (WEGo) partnership was designed to address this issue.

The Wellbeing Economy Governments (WEGo) Partnership

The Wellbeing Economy Governments (WEGo) partnership is a collaboration of national and regional governments, promoting sharing of expertise, best practice and transferable policy practices to advance a common ambition of building a Wellbeing Economy. WEGo currently comprises Iceland, New Zealand, Scotland, Finland, and Wales, with the Scottish Government's Office of the Chief Economist providing secretariat support. WEGo's annual Policy Labs create the space for civil servants and ministers to learn from, collaborate and challenge each other to implement and continuously improve on innovative, upstream, preventative economic policy making approaches to create Wellbeing Economies. This includes sharing what works and what doesn't; progressing the SDGs through partnership and cooperation, in line with Goal 17; and addressing the pressing economic, social, and environmental challenges of our time.

Dr Katherine Trebeck, WEAll's Advocacy and Influencing Lead, had been working with the Scottish Government for many years to promote the merits of a Wellbeing Economy and to build the appetite of officials and ministers to be at the forefront of this agenda. In April 2016, Lorenzo Fioramonti, then an academic in South Africa, shared with Trebeck an idea for an alternative to the G7: a "WE7" (Wellbeing Economy 7). Trebeck took this concept back to her colleagues in Oxfam GB and undertook substantial research and consultation to deepen the proposal in terms of theory of change, likely membership, and internal operations of the group. At Oxfam and then more recently at WEAll, Trebeck has undertaken extensive work in spurring the Scottish Government to embrace taking a leadership role in forming WEGo, recruiting possible members, and supporting the Secretariat to work to the WEGo launch.

The first meeting of interested governments and the OECD, together with members of (what became) the WEAll Knowledge and Policy working group, took place at Scotland's Inclusive Growth Conference in 2017. WEGo was officially launched at the OECD's (2018) sixth Global Wellbeing Forum in South Korea, hosted by the OECD's statistics unit, which has been at the forefront of measuring quality of life for over a decade. The conference, during which the launch took place, was attended by 3000 senior OECD officials, academics and statisticians, Nobel laureates, royalty, heads of international agencies, civil servants, and activists from around the world. The fact that the OECD (2020) hosted this event is significant. It is an influential agency and a key enabler to the Wellbeing Economy movement that provides wellbeing statistics and measurements, shares frameworks to turn thinking into actions, and reinforces the importance of a broad-based understanding of wellbeing. At the launch, the Chief Economist for the Scottish government, Dr Gary Gillespie, described WEGo as "bringing the economic lens back" to the wellbeing agenda. Nobel Laureate Joseph Stiglitz spoke of the importance of persisting—and this has been the story of getting WEGo to where it is now.

The development of the WEGo partnership has been a bumpy and often uphill road, as political changes altered governmental priorities and personnel. There is the task of identifying the best official in a certain government: it must be someone who both appreciates how the economy needs to be transformed and has sufficient influence within their administration to gain traction towards prioritising Wellbeing Economic approaches. There is also the challenge of when officials get promoted or governments change, and new administrations are not willing to carry on the projects of their predecessors. New connections must be made, and the case presented and championed again from the beginning, often with adjustments, so as to maintain a realistic scope for engagement. And government officials are busy; so, it is a challenge to catch their attention and gain buy-in. In order to do this, it is important to communicate that a Wellbeing Economy will ultimately make the job of *all* government officials easier, as it will reduce avoidable demands on the state that arise from an economy misaligned with the needs of people and planet. Hence, it will allow governments to focus on *un*avoidable challenges, like an ageing population.

WEGo's first policy lab took place in Edinburgh in May 2019. It was attended by the First Minister of Scotland, Nicola Sturgeon; the Prime Minister of Iceland, Katrín Jakobsdóttir; and senior officials from New Zealand and the OECD. The discussions included areas of mutual concern to members, ranging from specific subject areas such as sustainable tourism and tackling child poverty to policy mechanisms, that is, shaping Wellbeing Economy frameworks and targets, Wellbeing Economy budgeting, using predictive analytics, and natural capital accounting. In April 2020, representatives from Wales, Finland, the OECD, and the founding WEGo members participated in a virtual Policy Lab; after this, Wales announced its membership. Finland joined WEGo in January 2021.

It is hoped that future WEGo membership will grow in terms of diversity of political unit (nation states and regional governments), geography (every major continent represented), and income level (members from GDP-rich and low-income entities). This diversity will demonstrate that a Wellbeing Economy is relevant for all countries and can take different forms. As the WEGo partnership expands, the longer-term governance structure could evolve, including an Advisory Board, professional Secretariat, topic-specific working groups, and inputs from values-led, non-state actors, such as civil society organisations and for-benefit enterprises.

Today, WEGo is the only living laboratory at scale in the world that is implementing Wellbeing Economy policies. The existence of the WEGo partnership is a subtle challenge to dominant economic policy making. For now, WEGo sits in the 'end of the bell curve' territory, where innovation happens most readily amongst smaller actors unencumbered by strong path dependencies and where players have the courage to experiment. But if it remains here, its impact will be inadequate. Current relations of power between actors in global-level institutions cannot be swept aside overnight and it will take more than WEGo, as currently configured, to begin the task (hence why the wider Wellbeing Economy Alliance was created). As more governments join WEGo and as its profile rises, the collaborative potential will increase—and the will to move towards a Wellbeing Economy will be bolstered. It is promising that rather than being deprioritised during the global pandemic, WEGo has proved itself to be a valuable space for policy makers as they work on their responses.

Iceland's Wellbeing Framework

Boyes (2009) and Tan (2018) describe that when the financial crisis hit in 2008, Iceland's banking sector, which accounted for 96 per cent of GDP, collapsed, and nearly every business in the country fell into bankruptcy. Relative to the size of its economy, Iceland's financial crisis was the largest in the world. While many other countries deemed their banks 'too big to fail', Iceland decided their banks were 'too big to save'. After a bailout by the International Monetary Fund (IMF), Iceland embarked on a path of financial consolidation and reforms, including nationalising Iceland's banks, implementing a programme of widespread debt forgiveness for citizens, increasing taxes, and allowing the currency to devalue by almost 60 per cent to increase demand for local products on the international market. Importantly, however, social benefits were safeguarded, and Iceland became the only country who prosecuted bankers as criminals for the damage they had caused to the economy and society. The country's recognition of the need for a new approach to economic governance is what allowed it to stage one of the speediest recoveries on record, returning to growth only two years later, in 2011.

Tan (2018) highlighted, "What makes the story behind Iceland's recovery important is not simply that it recovered. Iceland's recovery is important because of its *priorities*—the decisions made about who to protect, and who to shoulder the cost of recovery". Iceland's experience encouraged the Government to re-write its constitution based on a participatory process on people's values and priorities. While it did not pass through Parliament, its priorities informed many of Iceland's policy reforms and initiatives since the crisis.

Icelandic prime minister, Katrín Jakobsdóttir (2019), described that a public "*campaign for women's equality in Iceland*" informed the government's decision to set gender equality as a primary economic goal. The Government instigated a gender mainstreaming and budgeting initiative, which allowed Iceland to lead the world in gender equality (Marinósdóttir and Erlingsdóttir 2017) and to join WEGo in 2018.

At a Beyond COVID (2020) event, Benedikt Arnason, Director General for Policy Coordination and Economic Affairs in Iceland, explained that following on from its experience with gender budgeting, the Government of Iceland (2019) decided to explore more holistic, multi-dimensional methods for assessing and selecting policies to improve quality of life. As a first step, the Government conducted a survey to determine the general public's top priority areas, which found that health was the most significant factor in quality of life, followed by relationships, housing, and making a living. Iceland introduced a framework of 39 wellbeing indicators in 2019, a balanced set of financial, social and environmental metrics which are considered equally significant measures of the country's success. The process of developing and securing consensus on the wellbeing indicators spanned two years and involved various stakeholders, including the public, political opposition, and public service. The outcomes of the process are six wellbeing priorities, mental health, secure housing, better work-life balance, zero carbon emissions, innovation growth, and better communication with the public, which will guide the country's Five Year Fiscal Strategic Plan. While the framework and priority list have been approved by the Government, they could be improved upon as collaboration with stakeholders continues. Iceland has committed to conducting regular surveys on the nation's wellbeing due to COVID-19; the first is underway.

This framework of indicators informed not only Iceland's Five Year Fiscal Strategic Plan, but also global efforts to reach a *common* understanding of which factors improve quality of life. While many states and international organisations rely on a single composite indicator, which factors in various aspects of wellbeing, Iceland's framework is able to inform more specific policy formulation, as it produces insights at the indicator level.

Multiple important takeaways from this process were shared with WEGo counterparts. Lack of information on the environmental factors, and a lack of measurements directed at social capital and the work-life balance, made it difficult to choose indicators for prosperity and quality of life. This highlights the need for governments to support the systematic collection and dissemination of statistical data on environmental issues and social capital. This includes increasing the frequency of measurements for indicators that have limited prior data, in order to assess trends. Finally, when comparing indicators, it is important to note that measurements for indicators are often done in different time periods.

Statistics Iceland is tasked with gathering, monitoring, analysing, and disseminating data on wellbeing indicators on a regular basis, as well as further developing these indicators in collaboration with key stakeholders. This was done because measurements are largely based on Statistics Iceland's data and this work complements the agency's existing work on measurements for the SDGs.

Wales' Wellbeing of Future Generations Act

In 2015, the Welsh Government launched the Wellbeing of Future Generations Act, with the aim to "improve the way in which decisions are made across specified public bodies in Wales" towards the achievement of the seven wellbeing goals. The Act is embedded in the Welsh Constitution.

Public bodies are mandated to consider the long-term impact of their policy decisions and work with communities and with each other, to ensure their actions are complementary, and that the people and communities involved are reflecting the diversity of the population that the particular bodies serve.

After the country's biggest National Conversation on 'The Wales We Want', the Welsh Government (2015) identified a wellbeing framework, organised into seven core wellbeing goals: a prosperous Wales, a more equal Wales, a globally responsible Wales, a resilient Wales, a healthier Wales, a Wales of cohesive communities, as well as a Wales of vibrant culture and thriving Welsh language. It is also mandated that all public bodies design and publish 'wellbeing objectives' that maximise their contribution to achieving all seven of the defined wellbeing goals, publish statements about their set objectives, and report annually on their progress in a Wellbeing Report. In order to measure progress against these goals, a range of 46 national indicators have been identified. The emphasis was placed on identifying indicators that could be easily communicated to the general public and that reflect public priorities. Public bodies are called to set 'milestones' to present their expectations for performance on the indicators in the future, in accordance with principles for "measuring the right thing" and "measuring the right way" (Welsh Government 2015). Both quantitative and qualitative, for example, survey-based data is gathered and published annually.

To normalise a preventative policy making approach, the Welsh Government (2015) introduced guidance on five ways of working: employing *long-term* thinking; taking an *integrated* approach so that public bodies look at all the wellbeing goals when deciding on their wellbeing objectives; *involving* a diversity of the population in decisions that affect them; working *collaboratively* to find solutions; and understanding the root causes of issues to *prevent* them from occurring. As the legislation has a particular focus on sustainability, a 'Sustainable Development Principle' has been defined, highlighting that the wellbeing of future generations should not be compromised by decisions which aim only to meet current needs. In order to ensure that the 'Sustainable Development Principle' is being promoted, the role of a Future Generations Commissioner has been introduced. The Commissioner acts as a guardian of future generations, supports and encourages public bodies to consider the long-term impact of their decisions, provides advice and assistance in relation to wellbeing objectives, and has the power to conduct a review into the extent to which public bodies are safeguarding future generations' needs.

Scotland's National (Wellbeing) Performance Framework

The Government of Scotland used a participatory approach to develop a way of measuring and managing national wellbeing. The National Performance Framework (NPF), Scotland's wellbeing framework, sets out a holistic assessment of progress on wellbeing. Financial, social and environmental measures are all given equal weighting in the assessment of the country's performance. The framework was put into law in 2015 and calls for collaboration between national and local government, businesses, civil society and communities, in order to inform policy planning decisions. To ensure that the NPF reflected the wellbeing priorities of people in Scotland, the Scottish government organised a *two-phased consultation*, including both public and expert engagement:

Phase 1: Public engagement. During this phase, public views and opinions were collected through consultations via the government's website, social media platforms, email and freepost, and 200 open events. Seven thousand people took part in public events and 17,500 visited social media platforms. Responses were then summarised into five core categories: working and living standards; homes and communities; early years, education and health; community participation and public services; respect and dignity. These categories relate to some of the National Performance Framework themes.

Phase 2: Expert consultation. During this phase, a lead Committee was formed, comprised of the Local Government and Communities Committee, and various stakeholders, to share feedback on the revised National Outcomes and National Indicators. The Scottish Government also organised conversations with stakeholders via an online survey and a series of discussions, to explore whether the National Performance Framework reflected the set vision.

After this large-scale consultation, the Scottish Government's National Performance Framework Team, a part of the Data, Statistics and Outcomes Division, collated the data into thematic areas and then into 11 National (Wellbeing) Outcomes, which include areas like culture, poverty, communities, human rights, fair work and business, and the environment. Each of the 11 National Outcomes has a set of indicators, which measure the country's performance in terms of both financial and broader wellbeing;

there are 81 National Indicators in total. Assessments are made by the Government's senior analysts and decisions on performance are made independently of Scottish Government's Ministers.

In 2018, the National Performance Framework was reviewed and updated, with the aim to publish a new set of National Outcomes, while incorporating the SDGs and Scotland's Action Plan for Human Rights. In 2019, the Scottish Government issued a Wellbeing Report presenting data and analysis on key issues, trends, and features of Scotland's performance, which should be considered in decision making around policy, services, and spending. In February 2020, the Scottish Government presented the Scottish Budget 2020–2021, which prioritises investment for driving well-being and sustainable and inclusive growth.

Scotland is further down the path than many other economies, where the conversation about new priorities is *not even happening*. The beginnings of mechanisms conducive to building a Wellbeing Economy include the creation of the Citizens' Assembly of Scotland (2020), the cross-party support for payment of Living Wages (Living Wage Scotland 2020); the encouragement of pro-social businesses via Scottish Enterprise, by making job-related grants contingent on fair work practices; the Business Pledge; Scotland's leadership of the WEGo partnership; the Scottish Government's (2020a) world-leading climate change legislation, which sets a target date for net-zero emissions of all greenhouse gases by 2045; the creation of the Just Transition Commission to advise the Scottish Government (2020c) on how to support communities, while powering down industries incompatible with a low carbon economy; the Sustainable Procurement duty; and the work of Zero Waste Scotland (2020) to build a Circular Economy. Other mechanisms with potential for driving forward the Wellbeing Economy agenda, were they undertaken with more vigour, include the Community Empowerment Act, and community wealth building efforts. These are the glimmers of existing practice to build on.

While Scotland's attention to the Wellbeing Economy agenda is growing, this is offset by a very real possibility to disappoint, considering the 17.6 per cent drop in GDP in mid-2020 from when COVID-19 lockdown measures were put into place in February 2020 (Scottish Government 2020b). Now is the time to scale up Scotland's nascent Wellbeing Economy policies.

New Zealand's Wellbeing Budget

New Zealand's Government launched the country's first Wellbeing Budget in May 2019, committing to putting people's wellbeing and the environment at the heart of its policies. In doing so, New Zealand became the first developed country to base its budget on priorities related to the wellbeing of its inhabitants.

The Wellbeing Budget is designed to use social and environmental indicators, along with economic and fiscal ones, to guide the Government's investment and funding decisions. The official Wellbeing Budget document describes the design principles behind this novel approach to economic policy: it breaks down agency silos and works across Government to assess, develop, and implement policies that improve wellbeing; it focuses on outcomes that meet the needs of present generations at the same time as thinking about the long-term impacts for future generations; and it tracks the Government's progress with broader measures of success, including the health of the country's finances, natural resources, people, and communities.

The Budget cycle began with the Cabinet selecting a small number of Wellbeing Budget priorities, gathering statistical evidence on wellbeing and its distribution among the population, from the Treasury's Living Standards Framework (LSF), and soliciting advice from sector experts and the Government's Chief Science Advisors. The LSF is divided in two sections: current wellbeing (income, housing, security, education, health, etc.) and future wellbeing (land use, skills and knowledge, health, natural and social environment). Some measures are taken annually, some quarterly, and some more often. The aim is to take into account both the quality of economic activity and the long-term impact of current policies.

After this period of research, the New Zealand Government (2020) set five wellbeing priority areas for the 2019 Wellbeing Budget: aiding the transition to a sustainable and low-emissions economy, supporting a thriving nation in the digital age, lifting Māori and Pacific incomes, skills and opportunities, reducing child poverty, and supporting mental health for all New Zealanders.

Ministers and agencies then developed initiatives targeting international wellbeing outcomes, analysed using the LSF. For each outcome, the Government has selected a set of statistical indicators for monitoring trends over time. Government Ministries and Departments collaborated in bids for new funds, to show how proposals would contribute to the priority areas. The Cabinet then agreed on an integrated programme of policies to meet its prioritised wellbeing outcomes. The standard Budget documentation was redesigned to communicate the links between the integrated policies and the wellbeing outcomes; this practice is spreading throughout the public service. The Treasury, for example, has begun to evaluate and communicate how the government's balance sheet and asset management contribute to improving wellbeing. The Government of New Zealand has embedded this wellbeing approach into legislation through the Public Finance (Wellbeing) Amendment Act 2020.

Child poverty was an area that created the impetus for the creation of this Wellbeing Budget. Following years of pressure from social movements and expert advice to address the issue, it became a national scandal that 30 years of GDP growth had not improved the measure of child poverty, not even in absolute terms. This issue was a widely accepted illustration of the need to look beyond GDP growth. Per the Child Poverty Reduction Act 2018, the New Zealand Government presented the country's first Child Poverty Report within the Wellbeing Budget of May 2019. The Report presented baseline data for the primary measures of child poverty, defined targets for the measures that the government aimed to achieve in three years and in ten years, and presented modelling work by the Treasury explaining how the whole-of-government policies in the Budget would contribute to achieving those targets. Following this, the New Zealand Government also created a Child and Youth Wellbeing Strategy, which it published in August 2019, to work towards the targets set.

Barriers to change include New Zealand's short election cycle, and the need for further clarification on how to compare policy proposals that have different impacts on wellbeing. However, with the recent re-election of Prime Minister Jacinda Ardern in October 2020, there is a positive outlook for the continuation of Wellbeing Economy policies in New Zealand, in accordance with the Wellbeing Budget.

CONCLUSION

We know what a Wellbeing Economy looks like, because we see it in microcosm across the world. The strength of the ever-growing WEAll membership and network is also indicative of the catalysation of the Wellbeing Economy movement. Scotland, New Zealand, Wales and Iceland are already implementing Wellbeing Economics principles, through their participation in the WEGo partnership and their individual initiatives: New Zealand's wellbeing budget, Scotland's ambitious climate change legislation and National Performance Framework, Wales' world-leading Future Generations Act, and Iceland's framework of wellbeing indicators. These examples demonstrate the feasibility and desirability of implementing Wellbeing Economic policy, as they show that traditional economic metrics, and moving towards greater wellbeing, can go hand in hand. In these difficult times, when conventional approaches are being discredited, these countries embody the possibility of doing things differently. The focus should now be on cohering and scaling these approaches and realigning policy regimes to be supportive of these approaches, rather than destructive.

As it builds its profile and reach, WEGo will spread best practice in policy making in the pursuit of collective wellbeing. If the WEGo partnership can live up to its potential, Benedikt Arnason suggests that, "*maybe the small, like-minded economies of the world can change the world*" (Beyond COVID 2020). These are reasons for hope of taking the concept of a Wellbeing Economy from theory into practice, but there is much work left to do. Members of the WEAll network and the policy makers involved in the WEGo partnership know that they are far from being in a position to tout themselves as having *delivered* on this front. Sociologist and philosopher Zygmunt Bauman reportedly once observed that "*a good society is one that knows it is not yet good enough*". If he knew about these alliances, he might have added "*an even better society is one that wants to work with others to get better*" (Trebeck 2020b).

REFERENCES

Beyond COVID (2020). *How can economies prioritise our wellbeing?* Beyond COVID: The Discussion Series. Retrieved from https://www.youtube.com/watch?v=Sh16yL4ujFo&feature=emb_logo.

Boyes, R. (2009). *Meltdown Iceland: Lessons on the world financial crisis from a small bankrupt island.* GetAbstract. Retrieved from https://www.economist.com/media/pdf/meltdown-iceland-boyes-e.pdf.

Bramley, G., Hirsch, D., Littlewood, M., & Watkins, D. (2016). *Counting the cost of UK poverty.* Joseph Rowntree Foundation. Retrieved from https://www.jrf.org.uk/report/counting-cost-uk-poverty.

Ceballos, G., Ehrlich, P. R., & Raven, P. H. (2020). *Vertebrates on the brink as indicators of biological annihilation and the sixth mass extinction.* PNAS. Retrieved from https://www.pnas.org/content/117/24/13596.

Citizens' Assembly of Scotland. (2020). *The basics.* Citizens' Assembly of Scotland. Retrieved from https://www.citizensassembly.scot/how-it-works/the-basics.

Coady, D., Parry, I., Sears, L., & Shang, B. (2015). *IMF working paper: How large are energy subsidies?* International Monetary Fund (IMF). Retrieved from https://www.imf.org/external/pubs/ft/wp/2015/wp15105.pdf.

Costanza, R., Atkins, P., Bolton, M., Cork, S., Grigg, N., Kasser, T., & Kubiszewski, I. (2017). Overcoming societal addictions: What can we learn from individual therapies? *Ecological Economics, 131*, 543–550.

Edelman. (2020). *Research: Edelman trust barometer.* Retrieved from https://www.edelman.com/trustbarometer.

Government of Iceland. (2019). *Indicators for measuring wellbeing.* Prime Minister's Office. Retrieved from https://www.government.is/lisalib/getfile.aspx?itemid=fc981010-da09-11e9-944d-005056bc4d74.

Hirschman, D., & Berman, E. (2014). Do economists make policies? On the political effects of economics. *Socio-Economic Review, 12*(4), 779–811. https://doi.org/10.1093/ser/mwu017.

Jackson, T. (2017). *Prosperity without growth: Foundations for the economy of tomorrow* (2nd ed.). London; New York: Routledge, Taylor & Francis Group.

Jakobsdóttir, K. (2019). Building an inclusive economy. *International Monetary Fund Finance & Development, 56*(1). Retrieved from https://www.imf.org/external/pubs/ft/fandd/2019/03/gender-equality-in-Iceland-inclusive-economy-jakobsdottir.htm.

Living Wage Scotland. (2020). *What is the real living wage?* Retrieved from https://scottishlivingwage.org/what_is_the_living_wage.

Marinósdóttir, M., & Erlingsdóttir, R. (2017). *This is why Iceland ranks first for gender equality.* World Economic Forum. Retrieved from https://www.weforum.org/agenda/2017/11/why-iceland-ranks-first-gender-equality/.

McKay, A. M. (2018). Fundraising for favors? Linking lobbyist-hosted fundraisers to legislative benefits. *Political Research Quarterly, 71*(4), 869–880. Retrieved from https://journals.sagepub.com/doi/10.1177/1065912918771745.

Mortensen, L., & Petersen, K. (2017). Extending the boundaries of policy coherence for sustainable development: Engaging business and civil society. *The Solutions Journal, 8*(3). Retrieved from https://www.thesolutionsjournal.com/article/extending-boundaries-policy-coherence-sustainable-development-engaging-business-civil-society/.

New Zealand Government. (2020). *Budget 2020: Budget policy statement.* Retrieved from https://www.budget.govt.nz/budget/2020/bps/wellbeing-priorities.htm.

OECD. (2018). *6th OECD world forum on statistics, knowledge and policy.* Retrieved from https://www.oecd-6wf.go.kr/eng/main.do.

OECD. (2020). *How's life? Create your better life index.* Retrieved from http://www.oecdbetterlifeindex.org/#/11111111111.

Philipsen, D. (2015). *The little big number: How GDP came to rule the world and what to do about it*. Princeton: Princeton University Press.

Scottish Government. (2020a). *Climate change*. Gov.Scot. Retrieved from https://www.gov.scot/policies/climate-change/.

Scottish Government. (2020b). *Gross domestic product (GDP) monthly estimate: June 2020*. Retrieved from https://www.gov.scot/publications/monthly-gdp-june-2020/.

Scottish Government. (2020c). *Just transition commission*. Gov.Scot. Retrieved from https://www.gov.scot/groups/just-transition-commission/.

Tan, G. (2018). *How human-centred policy helped Iceland overcome the Great Financial Crisis*. Asia and the Pacific Policy Society. Retrieved from https://www.policyforum.net/10-year-recovery-lessons-iceland/.

Trebeck, K. (2020a). European health forum: Recovering from the COVID-19 pandemic. *Health Europa*. Retrieved from https://www.healtheuropa.eu/european-health-forum-recovering-from-the-covid-19-pandemic/103114/.

Trebeck, K. (2020b). Here we go. *Mint Magazine*. Retrieved from https://www.themintmagazine.com/here-we-go.

Trebeck, K., & Williams, J. (2019). *The economics of arrival: Ideas for a grown-up economy*. Bristol: Policy Press.

United Nations. (2020). *Goal 12: Ensure sustainable consumption and production patterns*. Sustainable Development Goals. Retrieved from https://www.un.org/sustainabledevelopment/sustainable-consumption-production/.

Welsh Government. (2015). *Consultation: How do you measure a nation's progress?* Gov.Wales. Retrieved from https://gov.wales/sites/default/files/consultations/2018-02/151022-fg-act-consultation-document-en.pdf.

Zero Waste Scotland. (2020). *Building a circular economy for Scotland*. Zero Waste Scotland. Retrieved from https://www.zerowastescotland.org.uk/research-evidence/report-building-circular-economy-for-scotland-2012-16.

CHAPTER 10

In Well-being We Trust: The Nova Scotia Quality of Life Initiative

Michael Flood and Éloi Laurent

INTRODUCTION: LOCALIZING THE WELL-BEING TRANSITION

All over the world, at all levels of government (United Nations, European Union, countries like Germany or Italy, regions like Wallonia, metropolises like Copenhagen or Los Angeles, medium-sized cities like Santa Monica or Bristol) a dynamic movement to overcome growth as a social project and put human well-being at the heart of common horizons, goals, and policies has emerged. This 'well-being transition,' accelerated by the adoption of the 'Sustainable Development Goals' by the United Nations in

M. Flood (✉)
Lee Kuan Yew School of Public Policy, National University of Singapore, Singapore, Singapore

OFCE/Sciences Po, Paris, France
e-mail: michael.flood@sciencespo.fr

É. Laurent
OFCE/Sciences Po, Ponts ParisTech, Paris, France

Stanford University, Stanford, CA, USA
e-mail: eloi.laurent@sciencespo.fr

© The Author(s), under exclusive license to Springer Nature Switzerland AG 2021
É. Laurent (ed.), *The Well-being Transition*,
https://doi.org/10.1007/978-3-030-67860-9_10

September 2015, aims not only at rebuilding our understanding of economic, social, and ecological realities in the twenty-first century but also and above all at thoroughly renewing our institutions and policies and the way in which citizens can actively participate in their design.

Exploring human well-being means articulating a multidimensional vision of human welfare casually referred to as "quality of life" (Laurent 2018) where the quality of life in question depends on individual dimensions (health, education, happiness, etc.) as well as collective ones (institutions, infrastructures, trust, etc.), going beyond income and material possessions or the increase in gross domestic product (i.e., economic growth). But to be fully meaningful, this plural human well-being needs to be dynamic: it should be maintained over time, which implies taking into account its environmental underpinning (biodiversity, ecosystems, climate) here and now (e.g., air quality) but also tomorrow and the day after (e.g., the impact of climate change on health).

Within this framework, territorial (or local) well-being can be simply defined as the well-being of people resulting from the locality (the place) where they reside, work, and spend their free time. Human well-being is, in fact, place-based.

There are at least three reasons that make localities (regions, metropolises, cities, villages, communities) important vectors of the well-being transition. The first is linked to their emergence and growing power under the double revolution of globalization and urbanization which has accelerated in the last 30 years, leading to a third phenomenon: agglomeration. Localities are no longer administrative subdivisions of the national space; they have become autonomous drivers of human development.

Brezzi et al. (2016) indeed point to the fact that 40% of total public expenditures in OECD countries occurred at the subnational level in 2014 and 70% of this territorial public spending is spent on education, health, mobility, social protection, and public services in general.[1] This important level of discretionary authority places a heightened pressure on local authorities to make effective and impactful decisions—it also affords them the privilege of greater policy autonomy with which a well-being agenda can be comprehensively implemented.

---

[1] Expressed as a percentage of GDP, Canada had the second highest level of subnational government expenditures (31.6%) after Denmark (34.8%) and well above the OECD total average (16.2%).

Second, the need to measure and improve human well-being as close as possible to the realities experienced by people gives an even stronger relevance to the local level. The quality of life varies from one region to another, from one city to another, from one neighborhood to another, within seemingly identical space. In fact, more and more robust academic work shows how the specific place where people live determines their chances in life (Chetty et al. 2018). Geography is certainly a result of history, but it reciprocally becomes—and increasingly so—one of its key determinants.

The "Measure of America" project, for instance,[2] adapting the methodology of the UN Human development index at three US territorial levels (states, metropolitan areas, and counties), provides some striking illustrations of this reality. When differences in human development between US states are considered, while the average score of the United States as a nation is around 5 (in index value), the highest ranked state, Connecticut, reaches 6.17, more than one and a half times the level reached by Mississippi, located at the bottom of the ranking. This gap in human development may seem small but it is actually roughly equivalent to the one that separates the United States and Sao Tome and Principe, respectively ranked 3rd and 156th in terms of human development index by the United Nations. National averages are indeed misleading, as Veneri and Edzes (2017) acknowledge.

While national initiatives, generally housed in central government ministries, have been implemented in countries such as New Zealand, Ecuador, France, Italy, Scotland, Sweden, Australia, and the United Kingdom, local initiatives led by charities/NGOs and/or municipal or regional governments have been given less attention (Exton and Shinwell 2018; Brezzi et al. 2016).

The OECD has commissioned a number of *How's Life in Your Region?* studies which present data on a long list of domains of well-being across all OECD countries (OECD 2014). In addition, they have administered a regional well-being tool that generates comparisons on 11 domains of well-being at subnational levels for a total of 395 regions.[3] This is part of a wider swell of ongoing initiatives that look to better understand the local well-being of citizens in order to tailor and improve policymaking.

---

[2] Measure of America: http://www.measureofamerica.org/.
[3] OECD Regional Well-being: https://www.oecdregionalwellbeing.org/.

The *Thriving Places Index* (United Kingdom) is one such program that looks at the well-being of localities across the country but goes a step further and assesses whether the conditions for well-being are sustainable.[4] Instead of ranking localities against one another, scores are plotted along a high-medium-low range and broadly categorized into three domains: Equality, Local Conditions, and Sustainability, each consisting of a small number of indicators.[5]

While they cannot all be included here, a number of initiatives at the national and subnational level have spawned: the 2013 edition of Measures of Australia's Progress was published by the Australian Bureau of Statistics;[6] the Walloon Institute for Evaluation, Prospective and Statistics (IWEPS) published a similar report in 2013–2014.[7] The emerging world is not to be overlooked; since 1998, the Atlas of human development in Brazil has calculated the Human Development Index (HDI) of all states administrative Brazilians, based on data provided by Curitiba. And countries ranging from Costa Rica to Bhutan to Mexico have utilized well-being as a pillar of policymaking in varying capacities, and at various levels of governance (OECD 2015).

In that spirit, the Council of the European Union (2019) adopted conclusions promoting 'Economies of well-being' across the Union, and their horizontal implementation through cross-sectoral activities that address well-being challenges and the UN 2030 agenda.

All these initiatives matter, but when it comes to policymaking, a key argument must be made: measuring human well-being at the local level only makes sense if the preferences of people are taken into account to be reflected in public policies. In other words, democracy is not only an important dimension of well-being, but also the method which must govern its governance.

Trust, as it sustains social cooperation, thus appears crucial in the process of measuring, defining, and improving local well-being. Cooperation is the ability to act together to solve our problems and fulfill

---

[4] Centre for Thriving Places (Previously Happy City): https://www.thrivingplacesindex.org/results/england.

[5] The Centre for Thriving Places team operates in a dual capacity insofar as they collect and consult, leveraging well-being measurements to help inform and build local capacity alongside in-community partners and government.

[6] Measures of Australia's Progress: https://www.abs.gov.au/ausstats/abs@.nsf/mf/1370.0.

[7] https://www.iweps.be/wp-content/uploads/2019/02/RR23-1.pdf.

our desires: man is a cooperative animal. Trust is the key to cooperation because it transforms uncertainty into risk and accelerates reciprocity between individuals and groups. What makes humans so different from other animals is their ability to pass on collective intelligence through institutions of cooperation[8] (cities, State, schools) and develop through generations the ability to interact and learn from others outside of the family circle (Laurent 2019).

This chapter aims at contributing to the local well-being transition literature by underscoring the role of trust. It offers a three-fold presentation of the Nova Scotia Quality of Life Initiative, by emphasizing its unique focus on building a local, spatialized understanding of well-being; creating an understanding of inequalities in well-being across regions in order to improve well-being in every region, before finally demonstrating how putting trust at the center of the design and operationalization of initiatives that measure well-being may lead to a greater propensity for implementation of their metrics in decision-making. We start by presenting the Nova Scotia Quality of Life Initiative.

THE NOVA SCOTIA QUALITY OF LIFE INITIATIVE

The Nova Scotia Quality of Life Initiative (NSQoL hereafter) is a local, NGO-led movement borne out of a collective exercise whereby Nova Scotians assembled to consider what kind of action could be imagined that would inspire new social, economic, cultural, and political frontiers for the Canadian province. Along the way, Engage Nova Scotia ('Engage' hereafter), the organization at its helm, and those who participated in public engagements, surveys, and online interactions, offered a clear message: that what matters, above economic and pecuniary qualities, is the quality of relationships, of life, of the environment, and of institutions.

---

[8] Where humans and other animals part ways is in the unique ability of humans not only to collaborate (for survival and reproduction) but also to cooperate in building, sharing, and passing on to future generations common knowledge. There is a fundamental difference between the human species and the others in the capacity we have not only to reproduce cooperative behaviors observed among our elders, but to build sustainable and flexible institutions that allow cooperation of every human with every other, beyond the bonds of blood. The lionesses teach their offspring very early, through play, to hunt in packs. But it's still same way that lion cubs learn and that, become lions, they will hunt. And they will never hunt with strangers. Humans can change the rules of the social game at each generation.

In other words, a measure of human well-being.[9] In this sense, their movement is characterized as a process based on citizen input and multi-stakeholder engagement with the ultimate goals of bringing out long-term, systemic change. The initiative's bottom-up approach in advancing the well-being agenda is unlike other regional initiatives documented in OECD countries (Exton and Shinwell 2018).

The same participatory approach has informed the design and delivery of the most extensive well-being survey collected in Canada to date.[10] Using the Canadian Index of Well-being ('CIW') Framework of domains[11] and indicators (informed from a separate, extensive process of Canada-wide public engagement), Engage, at the outset, looked to collect a sample of 8000 responses to the 230-question survey. This—based on the CIW's standard 10% response rate—would require requesting roughly 80,000 households to fill out the voluntary survey, or roughly 20% of the households in Nova Scotia (which has a population close to 1 million). In the end, nearly 13,000 households responded (response rate of ~ 16%), making it the largest dataset using CIW metrics ever gathered (see Appendix, Map 10.1). The target, which was significantly increased as the initiative benefitted from new funding and stakeholder buy-in, was tailored to generate a statistically significant response rate in each of ten 'Functional Economic Regions' as defined by Statistics Canada and the Province of Nova Scotia. Province-wide consultations confirmed that these regions, with some exceptions, represented indeed the areas where most residents 'live, work, and play.'

In its approach to well-being, NSQoL shares a common concern with the OECD framework: to reflect the plural, multidimensional reality of human well-being (Table 10.1).

The remaining differences between the two approaches should not be seen as a hindrance to the local well-being transition, on the contrary: indicators need to be contextualized through the involvement of local actors and informed by local research—indeed, this defines the NSQoL and the expectation is that subject focus areas will emerge as the initiative evolves.

[9] Engage Nova Scotia: https://engagenovascotia.ca/.

[10] Engage staff reference the IAP2 model for public participation as a useful model for stakeholder   engagement: https://iap2canada.ca/Resources/Documents/0702-Foundations-Spectrum-MW-rev2%20(1).pdf.

[11] See the CIW framework of domains and indicators at https://uwaterloo.ca/canadian-index-wellbeing/what-we-do/domains-and-indicators.

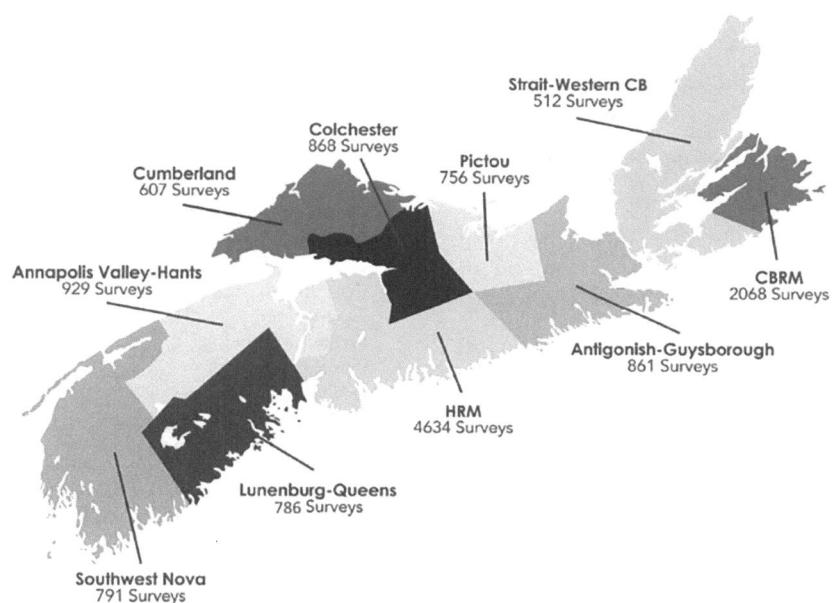

Map 10.1 Response rate of Nova Scotia Community Well-being survey by region. (Source: Engage Nova Scotia: https://engagenovascotia.ca/)

It is indeed reasonable to suggest that these local adaptations have contributed to the successful response rate and meaningful level engagement with Nova Scotians. This experience highlights how the choice of measurement tool—in terms of both how it is used in the field and communicated back to the public—is imperative to the trust-building process, and to the overall success of well-being initiatives.

UNDERSTANDING LOCAL WELL-BEING IN NOVA SCOTIA, CANADA

Nova Scotia lies on Canada's easternmost seaboard, comprising a population with Scottish and Irish heritage but also African Nova Scotian, Indigenous, and Immigrant minorities. Indeed, the province's population growth has been fueled by the latter groups in recent years (CIC News 2019).

Table 10.1 Mapping the CIW domains against the OECD conceptual framework for current well-being (Exton and Fleischer 2020)

OECD conceptual framework for current well-being	CIW domain
Income and wealth	Demographic profile; living standards
Work and job quality	Living standards
Housing	Demographic profile
Health	Healthy populations; leisure and culture
Knowledge and skills	Education
Environmental quality	Environment
Subjective well-being	Overall well-being[a]
Safety	Community vitality
Work-life balance	Living standards
Social connections	Community vitality; time use
Civic engagement	Democratic engagement

[a]This section was added to the Canadian Index of Well-being Community Survey to include the life satisfaction and eudemonic measurements of overall well-being, in addition to asking respondents to evaluate overall well-being on each of the domains, generally

In advance of the Community Well-being survey, the CIW produced an index report that looked at broad-level well-being across Nova Scotia when compared to Canada. The findings highlighted both promising trends in well-being, and areas where policymakers might devote more attention (ENS and CIW 2018).

More precisely, the report highlights how Nova Scotia outperforms national averages on Living Standards (overall poverty and income inequality are lower than the national average), the Environment, Leisure and Culture, Community Vitality, and Time Use during the Index years (1994–2014).[12] While the Democratic Engagement and Healthy Populations domains improved over the period, they did so at a lower rate than the national average. For instance, the percentage of Nova Scotians rating their overall health as 'very good' or 'excellent' dropped by roughly 10% between 1998 and 2014' and at the same time only 1 in 4 Nova Scotian reported having confidence in Parliament (federal government) by

[12]For a full version of the Nova Scotia Quality of Life Index: https://engagenovascotia. ca/2018-quality-of-life-index.

2014 (lower than the national average). These are mere previews of much more acute findings that the later 2019 household survey, hereafter introduced, presents.

Building a Uniquely Nova Scotian Well-being Project

One key advantage of Engage's role as overseer of this initiative is their understanding of the human geography of the province, which helped them establish a framework for collecting well-being measurements based on ten unique regions. This partitioning was done with statistical and spatial analysis provided by the Provincial government in partnership with Statistics Canada, and eventually amended by Engage after local engagements with key stakeholders in each region. The regions are outlined in Table 10.2 and portrayed in the Appendix, Map 10.1.

While the regional populations are far from uniform, the preference was to consider salient regional identities as places where people 'live, work, and play.' These regional delineations are in fact supported by robust social and economic boundaries with which citizens can identify.

As efforts to divide the province into 'measurable regions' were biased toward community cohesion rather than equal socioeconomic weightings, it is important to also consider demographic profiles. Results of the survey were weighted to take these differences into account. Broadly speaking, the province is divided into urban and rural tracts, HRM and CBRM comprising the former (Table 10.3), the remainder being rural because research on well-being in Canadian communities has shown a significant relationship between rural livelihoods and greater levels of happiness (overall satisfaction with life) as compared to their urban counterparts (Helliwell et al. 2018).

Table 10.2 The ten regions of the NSQoL Initiative

HRM Halifax Regional Municipality	**Cumb**. Cumberland
CBRM Cape Breton Regional Municipality	**Lun.-Q** Lunenburg-Queens
AV-H Annapolis Valley-Hants	**Pictou** Pictou
Ant-Guy Antigonish-Guysborough	**SWN** Southwest Nova
Colc Colchester	**SA-WCB** Strait Area-Western Cape Breton

Table 10.3 Population
of Nova Scotia's func-
tional economic regions

Region	Weighted population
Nova Scotia	727,631
HRM	323,545[a]
CBRM	72,861[a]
AV-H	97,479
Ant-Guy	21,272
Colc	39,794
Cumb.	23,546
Lun.-Q	45,784
Pictou	32,688
SWN	44,309
SA-WCB	26,353

[a]Defined as *urban regions*

Understanding Local Well-being Inequality

Inequalities in well-being—here defined by subjective well-being—have been understood as potentially more indicative of how a population is doing than widely used indicators such as objective levels of health or income (Helliwell et al. 2020).

From this perspective, localizing well-being across all eight domains of the CIW is of great importance. Moreover, as the tool is implemented with the help of civil society partners (in this case, the Engage-led NSQoL network and ten local leadership teams representing each region), this localization is endowed with community meaning.

How Far Are NS Regions Apart on Each Dimension

There is a general consistency in scores among regions across all indicators. Most score highly on Environment, Leisure and Culture, and Communsity Vitality, while Democratic Engagement and Education lag behind (Table 10.4).

Appendix, Table 10.7 provides statistical (multivariate regression) analysis of the overall results, stressing the importance of key drivers of local well-being.

In the social well-being model, overall sense of community (strength of bonds and sense of community belonging) is a strong predictor of well-being, while social isolation scores (e.g., loneliness) are negatively correlated with well-being. Civic well-being looks at perceived political

Table 10.4 Composite scores across the CIW eight domains of well-being for all ten regions on a 7-point scale (Smale et al. 2019)

Well-being domain	Nova Scotia mean (Std)	HRM	CBRM	AV-H	Ant-Guy	Colc.	Cumb.	Lun.-Q	Pictou	SWN	SA-WCB
Environment	5.33 (1.32)	5.31 (1.31)	5.16 (1.45)	5.51 (1.15)	5.57 (1.15)	5.40 (1.30)	5.12 (1.50)	5.50 (1.24)	4.82 (1.46)	5.33 (1.34)	5.58 (1.24)
Community vitality	4.83 (1.40)	4.74 (1.38)	4.89 (1.48)	4.87 (1.34)	5.03 (1.31)	4.89 (1.41)	4.84 (1.44)	4.95 (1.46)	4.74 (1.48)	4.90 (1.45)	5.10 (1.32)
Healthy populations	4.75 (1.46)	4.71 (1.44)	4.81 (1.54)	4.79 (1.43)	4.87 (1.35)	4.83 (1.47)	4.63 (1.56)	4.83 (1.48)	4.64 (1.49)	4.66 (1.54)	4.96 (1.39)
Leisure and culture	4.73 (1.27)	4.77 (1.25)	4.68 (1.35)	4.74 (1.21)	4.85 (1.23)	4.93 (1.23)	4.52 (1.38)	4.76 (1.24)	4.52 (1.35)	4.59 (1.33)	4.56 (1.29)
Livings standards	4.66 (1.63)	4.69 (1.60)	4.52 (1.73)	4.70 (1.60)	4.82 (1.52)	4.74 (1.55)	4.54 (1.71)	4.66 (1.66)	4.46 (1.75)	4.53 (1.63)	4.76 (1.55)
Time use	4.59 (1.51)	4.51 (1.49)	4.67 (1.57)	4.61 (1.51)	4.79 (1.36)	4.71 (1.55)	4.66 (1.55)	4.70 (1.45)	4.46 (1.51)	4.61 (1.54)	4.80 (1.45)
Education	4.47 (1.60)	4.55 (1.55)	4.42 (1.66)	4.60 (1.56)	4.67 (1.62)	4.55 (1.64)	4.23 (1.67)	4.29 (1.69)	4.36 (1.63)	4.21 (1.63)	3.98 (1.66)
Democratic engagement	3.88 (1.49)	3.92 (1.42)	3.39 (1.58)	4.07 (1.44)	4.20 (1.47)	4.07 (1.47)	3.90 (1.60)	3.94 (1.45)	3.67 (1.57)	3.80 (1.60)	3.78 (1.57)
Overall well-being	4.66 (1.13)	4.65 (1.12)	4.57 (1.20)	4.74 (1.07)	4.85 (1.05)	4.77 (1.16)	4.56 (1.21)	4.71 (1.11)	4.46 (1.17)	4.58 (1.16)	4.69 (1.04)

efficacy (sense of influence on government) and democratic engagement; while the former is a relatively small predictor of overall well-being, there is still a positive and significant relationship; the measure of democratic engagement shows a strong degree of predictability with overall well-being.

The 'Making Time' model considers the extent to which people are satisfied with the time they have to set aside for themselves and others (TU), their access to leisure and culture activities (LC), and their degree of work-life balance. TU and LC show significant and positive scores in predicting well-being, while work-life balance shows a strong, negative relationship with well-being (intuitive as a higher score indicates less work-life balance).

Finally, in the economic well-being model, where overall job fit and work-life balance are considered, the latter is significantly more important than the former in predicting overall well-being. In essence, whether one has time for a life outside of work is seemingly more important than the extent to which their work and interests match. Each of the composite indicators of well-being included in this study shows an important relationship with overall well-being; each far more important than income, age, or sex, all of which are controls. However, income and length of residency in community (COMYEARS) show some—albeit minor—degree of significance in each model.

Two additional models (1) environmental well-being and (2) community vitality and democratic engagement are given more attention below (see Tables 10.5 and 10.6).

Some overall regional scores stand out, and help communities identify where they are falling behind their neighboring jurisdictions and where they may be setting the pace (Table 10.4):

Falling Behind
- Environmental well-being in Pictou sits well below the provincial average (4.82, 5.33)
- Educational well-being in SA-WCB lies significantly below the provincial average (3.98, 4.47)

Setting the Pace
- Democratic Engagement is significantly higher in Ant-Guy than the provincial average (4.20, 3.88)
- Community Vitality is significantly above the provincial average in SA-WCB (4.83, 5.10)

Table 10.5 Environmental well-being

Model 1: Environmental well-being

	Coefficient	Std. error
Age	0.016***	0.043
Sex	-0.002	0.001
Income	0.063***	0.002
COMYEARS	0.002***	0.000
ENV	0.581***	0.006

Adjusted *R*-squared: 0.588
Significance codes: 0 '***' 0.001 '**' 0.01 '*'

Table 10.6 Community and democratic vitality

Model 2: Community versus democratic vitality

	Coefficient	Std. error
Age	0.008***	0.000
Sex	-0.001	0.002
Income	0.036***	0.002
COMYEARS	-0.000**	0.000
CV	0.503***	0.004
DE	0.282***	0.003

Adjusted *R*-squared: 0.8153
Significance codes: 0 '***' 0.001 '**' 0.01 '*'

Comparing Environmental Well-being and Community Vitality and Democratic Well-being with Overall Well-being

The role that the environment plays in shaping local well-being and well-being inequality has been the recent focus of scholarly attention (Laurent 2018; Helliwell et al. 2020). The latest edition of the World Happiness focuses on "Environments for Happiness." Krekel and MacKerron (2020, pp. 95–107) show that environmental attitudes and well-being are closely related, as is the quality of the natural environment, with one's overall life evaluation. Moreover, they observe important effects across OECD countries whereby climate and air pollutant emissions lead to lower life evaluations.

It is not surprising, then, that the well-being of Nova Scotians—with their abundance of natural amenities but also concern for environmental degradation—is significantly informed by environmental quality. Indeed, of all the composite indicators, *Satisfaction with the Environment domain* (ENV) appears to be the best predictor of overall well-being (composite of all domains) and explains much of the variance in overall well-being scores (Table 10.5).

Nova Scotians care about their environment and it is reflected in the way they evaluate their lives—that is, to say, a 1-point increase in one's environmental well-being increases overall well-being by 0.581 points (out of 7).

Involvement in community and in democracy also shows strength in predicting well-being. A 1-point increase in satisfaction with the Community Vitality domain and the Democratic Engagement domain increase overall well-being by 0.503 and 0.282 points, respectively (out of 7). The former domain reflects "what is happening in…neighbourhoods, how safe [people] feel, and whether [they] are engaged as citizens or…becoming socially isolated", while the latter reflects "whether a democracy is strong and healthy or in decline" by measuring citizen engagement with instruments of democracy at the local, regional, and national level (CIW 2012). The strength of these models is reflected in their overall predictive power, describing over 80% of the variance in overall well-being scores. What these statistics tell us about Nova Scotian communities is that engagement is a rich resource that can be tapped into to improve well-being in localities. It is a mirror reflection of the Engage model, which builds upon these community bonds to move forward a well-being agenda at the speed of trust.

ADVANCING WELL-BEING AT THE SPEED OF TRUST: A NEW APPROACH

The importance of *trust and social capital* in evaluating well-being—and indeed, wealth—received significant attention over the past decade (see Laurent 2019; Woolcock et al. 2016; Helliwell et al. 2016; OECD 2017b; Akaeda 2020).

For example, a recent study by Akaeda (2020) looking at 29 European countries finds that high levels of contextual social trust have the effect of reducing well-being inequality by virtue of increasing *satisfaction with life* of those in relatively lower income and education categories. Daskalopoulu (2019) shows that there is an important interrelation between institutional and social trust, proving that micro-level trust (in individuals) has an effect on macro-level trust (in large institutions, such as national governments). Many have illustrated the importance of trust in predicting overall well-being (Helliwell et al. 2016; Yagi 2017; Helliwell and Putnam 2004) and even in predicting wealth (Hamilton 2016).

The connection between trust and social capital is most prominently introduced by Coleman (1988) in his seminal paper arguing that one's social capital is comprised of (1) trust and obligations, (2) information channels, and (3) norms and sanctions. Leung et al. (2011) describe how researchers have 'built out' this triangular understanding of trust; the first category having been broadened to cover trust levels between two individuals or between an individual and an institution. Information channels reflect the information gains through bonds and interactions with family and friends and through civic engagement (participation in sport, professional, civic, or volunteer organizations), while norms and sanctions reflect commonly accepted values and behaviors that foster activities beneficial to society (ibid., p. 446).

Internationally, the OECD (2017a) has advanced both micro and macro conceptualizations of trust within the broader context of public policy and policymaking, identifying the drivers of trust as "(i) competence or operational efficiency, capacity and good judgement to actually deliver on a given mandate; and (ii) values, or the underlying intentions and principles that guide actions and behaviours" (p. 21). The OECD study demonstrates that trust levels are highly contingent on a government's capacity to deliver services that meet public needs, but that trust cannot be fostered if only in such a top-down, unilateral way. Strengthening "integrity for trust" means aligning values in the public sector with the public interest writ large, and this requires building up "local integrity systems" where trust is built in the first place (pp. 29–30). This is Engage's bread and butter. The more included citizens are in the processes that filter into policymaking, the more they will see themselves in the outcomes, and the more effective those outcomes will be in improving quality of life (ibid.).

The Nova Scotia approach to measuring well-being (including indicators of trust and social capital) operationalizes these concepts. In the N.S. model, the Coleman and OECD conceptualizations are relevant; trust is instrumentalized by building and bridging links within and across communities, based on pre-existing values and obligations within those communities. Moreover, in order to generate the capacity to measure and utilize well-researched indicators that have largely been constructed by academics and statistical organizations, Engage needed to find partners who could effectively communicate this nascent area of inquiry to an audience who would then need to empower their stakeholders to 'carry the

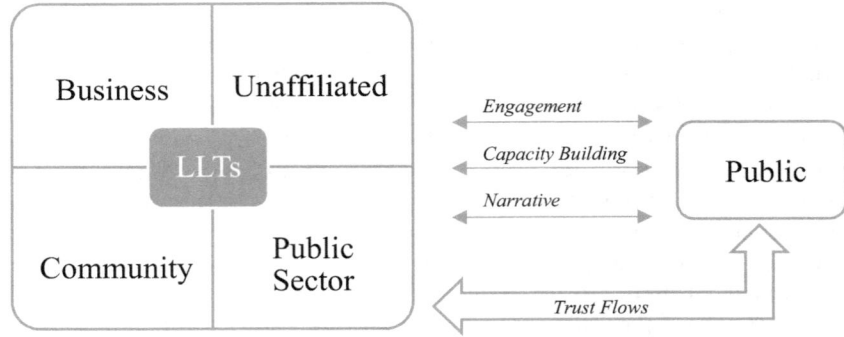

Fig. 10.1   NSQoL local leadership team structure and *trust flows*

torch.' Despite well-being studies being well-established in the literature, the lexicon used to illustrate its importance can be confounding to actors in civil society and local and regional government. Therefore, Engage needed to bridge links between individuals and between ideas, with the help of trusted and competent institutions at the local and regional level.

In order to achieve this, local leadership teams (LLTs) were established in the ten regions where survey data would be collected (see Appendix, Map 10.1). A total of 150 individuals make up the teams, with an average of 15 individuals per region. They represent a more/less equal weighting of representatives from the business sector, the community sector, the public sector, and unaffiliated members of the public (depicted in Fig. 10.1). The members, each representative of their own cross-section of stakeholders, readily engage their constituents (colleagues, students, customers, users, etc.) through pre-established and trusted channels of communication.

It is clear that community attachment is demanding and selective: in looking at overall trust scores from the survey results (see Appendix, Table 10.9), Engage's position as a convener of the initiative benefits from public perception on the credibility of specific institutions. This is in line with a global trend whereby non-governmental organizations are increasingly being seen as trusted leaders of change. According to Edelman (2020), NGOs were the most trusted type of institution (compared with Business, Government, and Media) to do what is right. At the same time, NGOs score poorly when assessed on their partnerships with other institutions to address today's challenges. The Engage model directly addresses this concern with their three-pillared approach to bring about systemic change: Engagement, Capacity Building, and Narrative work (ENS 2020).

Engagement

This pillar demands that the work (1) be inclusive in processes of engagement and decision-making with a recognition of the diversity of their community of stakeholders; (2) facilitates exchanges of information among stakeholders; and (3) empowers those involved to become aware, inspired, and articulate with regard to the initiative.

Capacity Building

Enhancing the capacity of the community to own the well-being agenda in their own right is perhaps the most central tenant of the initiative, which involves (1) adequate resourcing; (2) providing volunteer opportunities; (3) strengthening technical leadership; (4) empowering thought leadership and learning; (5) increasing opportunities for learning and access to tools and resources; and (6) engaging partnerships and stakeholders to bring about change.

Narrative

Contributing to an evolving provincial narrative is about building empathy with stakeholders, creating opportunities for sharing and reflection within and across communities, and ultimately contributing to changing perceptions about what progress means for the province. The *Engagement* and *Capacity Building* pillars directly feed into the overall narrative work of the organization.

Engage is committed to a robust evaluation framework that ensures these three pillars are met using both qualitative and quantitative performance indicators. What is unique about this approach is that—as the organization's name may already suggest—few components of their work are purely internal. The assertion is that their success is directly tied to the ability of the community to carry out some of the operations. While this poses challenges insofar as it requires potentially more time and the management of expectations that accompanies cross-sector collaborations, it is in the spirit of *moving at the speed of trust* and paramount to their success thus far.

A fourth and last pillar of great potential for local well-being initiatives is *inter-regional cooperation*. The CIW tool illustrates areas where deeper collaboration may be conducive to increasing well-being in one region that is falling behind, or in learning why another region is performing well. The NSQoL has set the table for this collaborative approach with the mandate of local leadership teams. More pointedly, the element of shared ownership which defines their efforts to advance a well-being agenda makes their case stand out globally. Putting well-being measurements in the hands of those whose day job is to improve local quality of life is as intuitive a practice as any and ought to be a cornerstone of regional well-being initiatives. Indeed, it is this feature that inspires trust by arming those with repute in the community to share and use measurements in a way that connects with citizens.

CONCLUSION

National statistical agencies play an invaluable role in documenting important indicators of well-being and should continue to broaden the scope of their measurement exercises over time. That said, it is unrealistic to expect that measurement exercises will necessarily translate into trust from and among the public. This chapter has attempted to demonstrate that moving at the speed of trust can help legitimize well-being initiatives by including the communities whose quality of life is being measured, even if that means a more elongated roll-out of key interventions. This requires designing, implementing, and interpreting data with the individuals and organizations it is intended to empower, as well as those whose lives' well-being agendas seek to improve.

The Nova Scotia model has relied on a tested framework for well-being and built buy-in from a network of cross-sector partners to implement *trusted change*. While project evaluations of such initiatives may not necessarily lead to quantifiable gains in quality of life in the near term, it is important to consider the strides they do make in terms of local capacity and trust-building between and within communities and across sectors, in addition to the propensity for this approach to spur new initiatives that are focused on improving local well-being in the long term.

Acknowledgments The contributions of the Canadian Index of Wellbeing and Dr. Bryan Smale are invaluable to this chapter. Indeed, they are integral to the success of the Nova Scotia initiative and, more broadly, to the well-being agenda in Canada and beyond. It is with utmost appreciation and gratitude that we use, with approval, CIW research (completed with Engage Nova Scotia) in this chapter.

Comments and contributions from Engage Nova Scotia have been instrumental to this case study, which relies heavily on the insights from their staff, including Danny Graham, Hailey Vidler, and Taylor Hill.

Appendix

Table 10.7 Predictors of overall well-being controlled for age, sex, income, and years lived in community

(1) Environmental well-being			(2) Social well-being		
	Coefficient	Std. error		Coefficient	Std. error
Age	0.016***	0.043	Age	0.023***	0.001
Sex	-0.002	0.001	Sex	-0.005	0.003
Income	0.063***	0.002	Income	0.055***	0.004
COMYEARS	0.002***	0.000	COMYEARS	0.001	0.000
ENV	0.581***	0.006	OVERALL_SOC	0.443***	0.012
Adjusted R-squared: 0.588			SOC_ISO	-0.186***	0.009
			Adjusted R-squared: 0.418		

(3) Civic well-being			(4) Making time		
	Coefficient	Std. error		Coefficient	Std. error
Age	0.016***	0.001	Age	0	0.001
Sex	-0.003	0.002	Sex	0.009	0.005
Income	0.056***	0.003	Income	0.043***	0.005
COMYEARS	0.004***	0.000	COMYEARS	0.006***	0.001
DE	0.448***	0.005	LC	0.324***	0.014
POLEFFICACY	0.062***	0.009	TU	0.363***	0.013
Adjusted R-squared: 0.5356			WL_BALANCE	-0.153***	0.017
			Adjusted R-squared: 0.5406		

(5) Economic well-being			(6) Community versus democratic vitality		
	Coefficient	Std. error		Coefficient	Std. error
Age	0.013***	0.107	Age	0.008***	0.000
Sex	-0.010*	0.005	Sex	-0.001	0.002
Income	0.056***	0.005	Income	0.036***	0.002
COMYEARS	0.002***	0.001	COMYEARS	-0.000**	0.000
OVERALL_JF	0.211***	0.013	CV	0.503***	0.004
WL_BALANCE	-0.547***	0.015	DE	0.282***	0.003
Adjusted R-squared: 0.4142			Adjusted R-squared: 0.8153		

Significance codes: 0 '***' 0.001 '**' 0.01 '*'

Table 10.8 Data dictionary for variables included in regression models

Variable name	Description
COMYEARS	Length of residency in community
ENV	Satisfaction with Environment domain
OVERALL_SOC	Overall measure of sense of community
SOC_ISO	Feelings of social isolation (measure embedded in OVERALL_SOC scale)
DE	Satisfaction with Democratic Engagement domain
POLEFFICACY	Overall perceived political efficacy (i.e., people's sense of their influence on government)
LC	Satisfaction with Leisure and Culture domain
TU	Satisfaction with Time Use domain
OVERALL_JF	Overall job fit
WL_BALANCE	Work-life balance
CV	Satisfaction with Community Vitality domain
DE	Satisfaction with Democratic Engagement domain

Table 10.9 Rankings of feelings of trust in institutions by region and province-wide

Institution	Province-wide ranking	HRM	CBRM	AV-H	Ant-Guy	Colc.	Cumb.	Lun.-Q	Pictou	SWN	SA-WCB
NGOs	1	1	1	2	2	3	2	2	2	2	2
Business	2	2	2	1	3	1	1	1	1	1	1
Local/municipal/band government	3	3	3	3	1	2	3	3	3	3	3
Media	4	4	4	4	4	4	4	4	4	4	4
Federal government	5	5	5	5	5	5	6	6	5	6	5
Provincial government	6	6	6	6	6	6	5	5	6	5	6

REFERENCES

Akaeda, N (2020) Contextual Social Trust and Well-being Inequality: From the Perspectives of Education and Income. *Journal of Happiness Studies 21*: 2957–2979. https://doi.org/10.1007/s10902-019-00209-4

Brezzi, M., de Mello, L., & Laurent, E. (2016). Au-delà du PIB, en-deçà du PIB. *Revue de l'OFCE, 145*, 13–32.

Canadian Index of Wellbeing. (2012). *How are Canadians really doing? The 2012 CIW report.* Waterloo, ON: Canadian Index of Wellbeing and University of Waterloo.

CIC News. (2019, December 27). Record immigration drives Nova Scotia's population to all-time high. Retrieved October 10, 2020, from https://www.cic-news.com/2019/12/record-immigration-drives-nova-scotias-population-to-all-time-high-1213404.html.

Coleman, J. M. (1988). Social capital in the creation of human capital. *American Journal of Sociology, 94*, 95–120.

Council of the European Union. (2019, July 15). The economy of wellbeing – Council conclusions. Brussels. Retrieved from https://data.consilium.europa.eu/doc/document/ST-11164-2019-INIT/en/pdf.

Daskalopoulu, I (2019) Individual-level Evidence on the Causal Relationship Between Social Trust and Institutional Trust. *Social Indicators Research 144*: 275–298. https://doi.org/10.1007/s11205-018-2035-8

Edelman. (2020). Edelman Trust Barometer 2020. Retrieved November 23, 2020, from https://www.edelman.com/trustbarometer.

Engage Nova Scotia. (2020). Quality of life initiative evaluation framework. Retrieved from direct correspondence with organization. Permitted for use.

Engage Nova Scotia, & Canadian Index of Wellbeing. (2018). Nova Scotia quality of life index report. Retrieved from https://engagenovascotia.ca/2018-quality-of-life-index.

Exton, C., & Fleischer, L. (2020). *The future of the OECD well-being dashboard.* OECD Statistics Working Papers, OECD Publishing, Paris.

Exton, C., & Shinwell, M. (2018). *Policy-use of well-being metrics: Describing countries' experiences.* Organization of Economic Cooperation and Development. Working Paper No. 94: 20–21.

Hamilton, K. (2016). *Social capital, trust and well-being in the evaluation of wealth.* National Bureau of Economic Research.

Helliwell, J. F., & Putnam, R. D. (2004). The social context of well-being. *Philosophical Transactions (Biological Sciences), 359*(1449), 1435–1446.

Helliwell, J. F., Huang, H., & Wang, S. (2016). *New evidence on trust and well-being.* National Bureau of Economic Research.

Helliwell, J., Shiplett, H., & Barrington-Leigh, C. P. (2018). How happy are your neighbours? Variation in life satisfaction among 1200 Canadian neighbourhoods and communities. *PLoS ONE, 14*(1), 1–24. https://doi.org/10.1371/journal.pone.0210091.

Helliwell, J. F., Layard, R., Sachs, J., & De Neve, J.-E. (Eds.). (2020). *World happiness report 2020.* New York: Sustainable Development Solutions Network.

Krekel, C., & MacKerron, G. (2020). How environmental quality affects our happiness. In *World happiness report* (pp. 95–111). New York: Sustainable Development Solutions Network.

Laurent, É. (2018). *Measuring tomorrow: Accounting for well-being, resilience, and sustainability in the twenty-first century.* Princeton; Oxford: Princeton University Press. https://doi.org/10.2307/j.ctvc7727v.

Laurent, É. (2019). *Économie de la confiance.* Paris: La Découverte.

Leung, A., Kier, C., Fung, T., Fung, L., & Sproule, R. (2011). Searching for happiness: The importance of social capital. *Journal of Happiness Studies, 12*(3), 443–462.

OECD (2014), *How's Life in Your Region?: Measuring Regional and Local Well-being for Policy Making.* Paris: OECD Publishing. https://doi.org/10.1787/9789264217416-en.

OECD. (2015). *Measuring well-being in Mexican states.* Paris: OECD Publishing. https://doi.org/10.1787/9789264246072-en.

OECD. (2017a). *Trust and public policy: How better governance can help rebuild public trust. OECD Public Governance Reviews.* Paris: OECD Publishing. https://doi.org/10.1787/9789264268920-en.

OECD. (2017b). *How's life? 2017: Measuring well-being.* Paris: OECD Publishing. https://doi.org/10.1787/how_life-2017-en.

Chetty, R., Friedman, J., Hendren, N., Jones, M. R., & Porter, S. R. (2018). *The opportunity atlas: Mapping the childhood roots of social mobility.* NBER Working Paper No. 25147.

Smale, B., Gao, M., & Jiang, K. (2019). *A profile of wellbeing in Nova Scotia: A summary of results from the Nova Scotia quality of life survey.* Waterloo, ON: Canadian Index of Wellbeing and the University of Waterloo.

Veneri, E. & Edzes, Arjen J.E. (2017). Well-being in cities and regions: Measurement, analysis and policy practices. *Region (Louvain-la-Neuve) [Online], 4*(2), E1–E5. Retrieved from https://openjournals.wu.ac.at/ojs/index.php/region/issue/view/12.

Woolcock, M., Helliwell, J. F., & Hamilton, K. (2016). *Social capital, trust and well-being in the evaluation of wealth.* National Bureau of Economic Research.

Yagi, T. (2017). Moral, trust and happiness: Why does trust improves happiness? *Journal of Organizational Psychology, 17*(1), 83–94.

PART IV

Well-being Policies, from Global to Local

CHAPTER 11

Can Global Capitalism Produce Global Well-being?

Xavier Ragot

INTRODUCTION

We are witnessing the spectacular end of a second period of globalization and the return of states in the definition of international order. The project of a gradual erasure of borders and international coordination through rules produced by benevolent international institutions has lived. Borders are back. In Europe, Brexit is the first real failure of the initial European project. Growing tensions between China and the United States herald a polarization of the world (Allison, 2017). Likewise, the exit of the United States from the Paris Agreement is then the sign of a renationalization of the environmental debate. Moreover, the Coronavirus disease (Covid) crisis first led to a renationalization of the economy on a national basis, before a slow and progressive international cooperation.

The decline of multilateralism, the return of states and borders can be seen as the failure of an economic project of international coordination through competition, which would aim at the disappearance of borders.

X. Ragot (✉)
OFCE/Sciences Po, Paris, France
e-mail: xavier.ragot@sciencespo.fr

This economic globalization would give way to the return of politics, borders and States as the only means of allowing the survival of the social body. If the election of Joe Biden is the start of a new and more cooperative global capitalism, then it is far too early to say whether this new trend will offset the deleterious effects of Donald Trump's presidency.

Within this dynamic of global capitalism, the possibility of an environmental transition or a transition toward an economy of well-being (Laurent 2017; Stiglitz et al. 2018; Nozal et al. 2019) respectful of the environment is as much an economic as a political issue. The aim of this text is not to define precisely the notion of an economy of well-being, which is done in other chapters of this book. Suffice it to say that it is an economy where an important role is given to the health sector, to education, to the reduction of inequalities, to the increase of opportunities and finally to an environment-friendly growth. Other names have been put forward to define this economy, in particular by Robert Boyer (2020) who defines it as a model of *anthropogenic* development, which places human beings at the heart of its accumulation dynamic. The peculiarity of this development model is that it is based largely on non-market sectors or highly regulated sectors, such as health and education, where externalities are significant. In other words, these are sectors where competition alone can reduce well-being and put entire populations at environmental risk. The well-being economy is, therefore, based on a new articulation between the state, regulation and the market. The purpose of this chapter is to question the capacity of global capitalism to effectively allow for a transition to a well-being economy.

The main idea of the chapter is to distinguish what is national in the transition to the economy of well-being, from what is based on international coordination, the prime example of which is the ecological transition. One can be optimistic about the transformations requiring the mobilization of welfare states or national social states. As shown in the first part of this chapter, these social states are now developed in all countries of the world, due to the integration of the social question into capitalism in the twentieth century. As a result, the transition to a well-being economy is "only" a reorientation of existing public policies. The environmental issue and the management of international risks pose far more complex challenges for which our social states are not suited.

A first solution to the problems of international coordination linked to the transition to an economy of well-being is the reactivation of multilateralism, of which the Paris Agreement showed the way. The election of Joe

Biden indicates that this option is not to be abandoned. A second solution does exist, however, which is cooperation between economic areas large enough to internalize the global effects of their decisions. The United States, China and the European Union could implement policies that are more respectful of the environment, either in a cooperative manner, within the framework of a bi- or trilateral relationship, or in a less cooperative manner within the framework of fixing of pricing policies. From this per-spective, the issue of carbon taxes at borders is as much an "internal" tool as an international signal for trade policy that is more favorable to the environment. Likewise, environmental clauses in all trade treaties serve the same purpose. This chapter is made up of three parts. The first quickly returns to the integration of the social question into capitalism in the twentieth century, emphasizing the regulatory aspect which led to the reduction of working time. The first conclusion is that capitalism in the twentieth century did not maximize growth but allowed an increase in well-being by the spectacular reduction of working hours, the fruit of the course of social movements. The second part focuses on social states. It shows the growing international trend of the latter in all countries throughout the XXth century. From these two parts, a positive tone can emerge, one can impose a transition to the well-being economy as one could achieve a transition to a less brutal capitalism on the social level. The third concluding part of the chapter shows, however, that the global nature of the environmental transition creates new challenges compared to the social question.

Can Global Capitalism Be Transformed into an Economy of Well-being? A Look Back at the Evolution of Working Time

We have to adapt our lifestyles and our economy to the energy transition to preserve the environment. Is capitalism compatible with the energy transition and the protection of biodiversity? How can economics be use-ful in thinking about this necessary change?

To think about the very possibility of an adaptation of capitalism to the environmental question, we must first turn to the history and geography, the diachrony and synchrony of capitalism, in other words: History, first of all, to observe the evolution of capitalism in the twentieth century in the face of the main question then, which was the social question; Geography then to compare the diversity of capitalisms. What was the great transformation of twentieth-century capitalism? Has capitalism maximized growth through increased predation on the lives of workers? No, not really. Capitalism in all developed countries has not maximized growth. Indeed, he used part of the productivity gains to reduce working time, contributing to the invention of mass consumption and the leisure society, which Veblen (1899) first identified. However, Veblen identified the leisure class as subset among the wealthiest, while leisure has become a general social fact in the twentieth century. The annual working hours per worker were 3000 hours in 1840, now reaching around 1500 hours for all workers, a reduction by two. Second, capitalism did not maximize the accumulation of capital; it led to the emergence of mass consumption, which is a different concept. In fact, maximizing capital accumulation requires investment. This represents less than 20% of the value produced each year against 80% for total consumption in France. For the record, the investment rate is over 40% in China, mainly due to public support. To take the measure of this development, the economic system valuing heroic working time, in the person of Stakhanov and the accumulation of capital with the ambitious goals of the Plan, was not capitalism. The battle between the two economic systems, capitalism and communism, was fought in part by valuing leisure within capitalism and not work.

Of course, this transformation of capitalism does not come from the economic system itself but from the body of legislation, social conflicts, the emergence of trade unionism at the beginning of the twentieth century (Hobsbawm 1994, *among many others*). The integration of the social question into capitalism is not a strict economic necessity but a political and social outcome. Observation of the twentieth century cannot lead to the conclusion that capitalism is inherently progressive, but to the conclusion that it is politically plastic. Then, the comparison between countries shows a great diversity of capitalisms, which have been studied by institutionalists and the School of Regulation (Boyer and Saillard 2002) or theory of the diversity of capitalism (Amable 2003). In short, that we can qualify both Sweden and China as capitalism shows the diversity of social compromises compatible with an economy described as capitalist. Faced with such diversity, one can even wonder if the word still retains an intellectual effectiveness. Twentieth-century capitalism did not lead to the highest growth. He partly used the productivity gains to create a leisure society, increasing the well-being of all workers. The question is rather to identify what will be the social forces that will lead to the transformation of our economic system in order to place the environmental question at its heart. As with the social question, all aspects of the economy are concerned—labor law, taxation, economic policy, corporate accounting, finance and so on. It is a similar systemic change.

Compared to the ecological question, the social question had the obvious advantage that the conflict was localized in companies. Forms of protest, such as strikes, and changes in the organization of work concerned the same actors, the workers. This is correct, but the institutionalization of European social states has required a generalization and nationalization of local institutions, produced in large part by the Bourse du Travail movement in France (Pelloutier 1902).

Another question concerns the usefulness of economics itself for understanding the efforts required for environmental transition. Here precision is essential, echoing the historical approach mentioned above. No economist should think that the goal of the economy should be to maximize growth or a measure of it like GDP. On the contrary, economic science, both marginalist and institutionalist economics, was built against this productivist vision. It was built on the idea that well-being is the ultimate goal, not growth. The latter is of course always difficult to measure, but all material objects and services are only means. Thus, if society really sets itself the goal of reducing its environmental footprint, economics must allow, modestly but usefully, to identify the levers. As with any discipline dealing with environmental issues, economics generates sometimes contradictory intentions and work, which must be used wisely. However, economics will be a powerful tool for thinking through the necessary transitions. Let's be more concrete: Should we introduce a carbon tax, a carbon tax at borders, or ban certain goods or air travel? How to think about the evolution of the carbon price or the emission rights market currently in Europe? To give an example, a particularly useful contribution of economics to this reflection is the study of the effects of a carbon tax on French households between the poorest and the richest (Ademe et al. 2019). The approach also considers territories and people to understand, and therefore compensate for, the effects of a change toward consumption compatible with the energy transition. The expert has a large number of indicators, GDP, of course, but also CO_2 emissions, different forms of inequality, measures of well-being. It is also the responsibility of the economist to transform these elements into evaluation procedures, useful for political debate and public decision-making. It is this effort that Éloi Laurent (2020) is making when considering indicators to guide public action to measure the efforts made or, unfortunately, the lack of efforts, on this difficult path of environmental transition. It is also the responsibility of the economist to provide monetary quantifications of the efforts required.

The Social State and Ecological Transition

The role of the state in the economy is difficult to grasp in all its generality. The state regulates markets, owns companies or chooses taxation. The measure I will choose is the simplest: public spending. It corresponds to the part of the national wealth, which is taken each year by the state to be either redistributed (for the most part) or used by the state to invest in public goods and provide services to the population, such as education, health, justice, the police or the army. The measurement of public expenditure may differ between countries, which makes it difficult to interpret international comparisons of expenditure levels.

However, we can still note global and global trends. When observing the trends in public spending over the world, what is surprising at first is the overall upward trend in public spending[1]. These are financed by a growing increase in compulsory levies, and by an increase in public debts. All countries, from Sweden to the United States, are experiencing an increase in public spending over the whole twentieth century, until now. In other words, an increasing share of the resources produced by countries is allocated by political choices and not by strict market mechanisms. These political choices concern both the nature of spending and the structure of the tax system necessary to finance the state.

The French rate of compulsory levies is now over 44% of GDP (which is here the right measure of the overall fiscal base for the state). This rate is now the highest in the world, as it recently passed that of Denmark. On the contrary, a vast protest movement asserts that we live in a neoliberal economy, which we will have to understand.

The interesting point is the overall trend. How to explain a similar trend in countries with such different political traditions? Such trends

[1] See Mauro, P., Romeu, R., Binder, A. and Zaman, A. (2015). A modern history of fiscal prudence and profligacy. Journal of Monetary Economics, 76, 55-70. The data are available in Esteban Ortiz-Ospina and Max Roser (2018)—"Public Spending". Published online at OurWorldInData.org. The French data can be obtained from INSEE after 1960 and before come from Christine André and Robert Delorme, "Le Budget de l'Est", in Cahiers français, no 261.

reveal features common to capitalisms, which can be summed up in one sentence: a growing trend toward socialization on a national basis. I use the word "socialization" in a narrow but precise sense. It is the share of national income, which is levied by the state for redistributive or productive purpose. It is thus a measure of national income, which is not allocated by the market.

Where does this trend of socialization come from? In taking over American Nobel Prize winner Paul Krugman, the government must "be seen, and this is not original, as a giant insurance company with an army". This civil service reveals a fundamental financial imperfection of market economies, which leads to economic insecurity to which our welfare states respond.

France is a perfect example of the state's insurance function. France is one of the most socialized countries in the world. The main risks, illness, occupational diseases, retirement (which includes widowhood and loss of autonomy), employment, housing and poverty go through some form of public insurance. In other countries, some risks are left to the private sector market, in the form of private insurance, or pension funds for example. What is best? The state or the market for each of these risks? The answer is primarily political and depends on the acceptance of risks and inequalities by populations. Strictly speaking about economic efficiency, the debate rages on. For my part, reading the literature leads me to think that there is no general answer to this question. It depends on the strength of states and the efficiency of the administration. It also depends on the organization of the private sector. Highly aggregated comparisons on national data are not informative.

Let us take a more concrete example. Social security spending is largely health and pension spending. In France, these two items represent nearly half of public spending and 23% of GDP. In the United States, these amounts correspond to 14.6% of the GDP. However, when we add public and private spending for these two functions, we reach 28.4% of GDP in the United States and 25.5% in France. Americans, therefore, spend more on their retirement and health, without it being said that their system is more efficient.

Recently, a report by US economic advisers to the White House tried to assess the opportunity cost of "socialism". By socialism, the authors mean the Nordic countries with a strong distribution. This report is most entertaining as the demonstration effort ended in failure. Their main measure for comparing the relative efficiencies of social systems is the cost in terms of the working week to buy a pickup car, which is lower in the United States. This measure reveals more the national preference for this type of car than any economic efficiency. In terms of life expectancy, wealth per capita and a measure of equal opportunity, the evidence is not convincing. I am not saying that strong socialization is necessarily better, only that there is no indication that lower socialization is obviously better.

Then, with such amounts passing through the state budget, we must be vigilant for the proper use of public money. If the effectiveness of public action is called into question, this ultimately results in a lower propensity to pay taxes, which is most dangerous.

Finally, socialized does not mean more egalitarian in itself. I wrote above that a significant part of the national wealth is allocated by the state. This does not mean that the state makes these transfers to reduce inequalities. Some transfers are known to reduce inequalities, such as the taxation of capital rather than labor. Other transfers can have neutral effects on inequalities or even increase them. The data show that income after transfers and taxes is less unequal than before these transfers. However, the degree of reduction in income inequality differs across countries. Redistribution in the United States reduces income inequalities by 22%, while this amounts to 40% in France and nearly 50% in Finland. The weak relationship between the total amount of public expenditure and the effect on inequalities is also confirmed in the course of the twentieth century. Numerous works (Pikettty 2014) show in the long time a strong inequality in the United States before the Second World War, then a reduction during the period described as the glorious thirties, from 1950 to 1980 approximately, then a continuous rise in inequalities since 1980. These long-term changes do not automatically follow the amounts of public expenditure. It is of course necessary to look at the details of the expenses and the nature of the means used. As our economies are highly socialized, redistributions depend on political perceptions of the concept of fairness, which largely determine inequalities and the efficiency of the distribution system.

The conclusion of these first two parts is that market economies can adapt to strong political constraints such as those imposed by the treatment of the social question. So, it seems that the issue is more political than economic. It is necessary to make emerge a social force carrying the project of reinstitutionalization of capitalism around the ecological question. This reinstatement has two components. The first is the evolution of the current institutions of our social states. It is relatively easy to implement, because the instruments of national democracies can transform them. For example, the French and German recovery plans to combat the economic effects of Covid-19 are based on public investments for the energy transition, such as the thermal renovation of buildings. Likewise, the French state is now carrying out an assessment of the impact of the budget on the environment. If the amounts in terms of public money are still low, we see that the environmental issue can find its way into national institutions. The second component is much more difficult. It concerns the creation of an international institution for the energy transition.

INTERNATIONAL COORDINATION FOR WELL-BEING

The main difficulty in a global economy of well-being concerns the issues that have externalities across the border of our social states. International sharing of economic risks is fairly well achieved through national issuance of public and private debt (Baxter 2012). However, the necessary condition is a resilient financial and international system. The situation is quite different with environmental issues for which international coordination is absolutely necessary, in order to share the differentiated cost of efforts, to share the effects of growing climate risks on the poorest countries. In this matter, two complementary strategies are possible.

The first is investment in multilateral forums, which allow international agreements like the Paris Agreements. These agreements are weakly binding for countries, because the core legal obligations are mainly procedural for the preparation and enhancement of individual climate plans. The countries can be accountable only for their national plan (Bodle et al. 2016).

In addition to these international efforts, non-coordinated tools must be put in place to restrict both CO_2 emissions and any threats to biodiversity with international spillover effects. The border carbon tax mechanism is the most operational example of such a mechanism.

The idea is to introduce a tax at the borders of the European Union to increase the price of imports of goods produced with high carbon emissions compared to European averages. It is part of the European Commission Green Deal, which is scheduled for adoption in the second quarter of 2021 to date. There are different rationales for this Border Adjustment Mechanism (BAM). The first and obvious one is the existence of leakages. These ones are due to the ability of European consumer to import less-expansive carbon-intensive goods, which would increase the carbon footprint of Europe and generate an unfair competition for European firms. The magnitude of these leakages is still under debate as they depend on measurement techniques (Zachmann and McWilliams 2020). A second rationale relies on political economy considerations in front of other trading partners, and within Europe. CO_2 emissions are concentrated on three major international players, the United States, China and the European Union, obviously in varying amounts. Unilateral climate action by large economic zones, consistent with international agreements, is more likely to accelerate the global climate effort, by strategic reactions of global trading partners. A BAM is a commitment device at the international level. Another argument is that the condition for the acceptability by Europeans of an increase in carbon price is that others don't benefit from this increase in price, not paying the cost. Even if the economic amounts are small, the very idea that some foreign firms may benefit from a higher carbon price (say in China) and thus pollute more in China is politically devastating. The BAM would also be an internal commitment device for the firms to prepare for higher cost of carbon.

The technical and organizational difficulties of such a mechanism are not negligible. The main idea is to have an assessment of the carbon content of imported goods to increase the selling cost in Europe to compensate for the carbon price in Europe and in the exporting countries. The assessment of the carbon content is challenging. In addition, one has to check the consistency of the BAM with national carbon taxes and with the EU Emission Trading System. However, all of these difficulties are surmountable. But as the commission noted, under the European Trading Scheme (ETS), a system of harmonized EU-wide benchmarks has been developed for industrial processes.

As a consequence, to the extent that a sector is covered by the EU ETS, a border measure could be based on similar methodological considerations as for ETS. This method relies on benchmark values, unless the exporter certifies a lower carbon content and/or a higher carbon cost at origin. The idea is thus to start with Carbon intensive sectors covered by the ETS, like steel, cement or aluminum.

Any increase in carbon price is likely to be regressive, and a BAM is no exception (Ademe et al. 2019). At this stage, it is difficult to assess the budgetary return of the BAM for each member state. The compensation of this undesirable adverse redistributive effect should be compensated by member states considering the overall effect of the fiscal system. However, this economic cost is likely to be small and depends on the final chosen mechanism. Indeed, only some sectors would initially be concerned, and European industrial innovations would mitigate the negative social impact of an increase in the price of imports.

The border adjustment mechanism (to increase the price of carbon-intensive imports) is only one concrete example of a not-internationally coordinated answer to a global problem for well-being, which is climate change. International coordination is better than unilateral change in one economic zone. However, the difficulty to reach international agreement should not be an excuse for inaction.

CONCLUSION

In conclusion, the question of the transition from global capitalism to a well-being economy is first a question of political economy before being a question of economic policy. We need to explain the necessary constraints, which have to be imposed on social states by the democratic process, in which the middle classes and the mobilized youth are essential. Concerning climate change, the perception of a fair distribution of efforts is essential, and a carbon adjustment mechanism including a social dimension is an essential tool. The interest of Such a mechanism would help to promote a different form of globalization based on a well-being objective.

REFERENCES

Ademe, Paul M., Ruben, H., Emeric, N. (2019). La fiscalité carbone aux frontières: ses impacts redistributifs sur le revenu des ménages français, report.

Allison, G., (2017), Destined For War: Can America and China escape Thucydides's Trap, Houghton Mifflin Harcourt, Boston.

Amable, Bruno. (2003). The diversity of capitalism. Oxford University Press, 2003 - Business & Economics.

Baxter, M. (2012). International risk-sharing in the short run and in the long run. *The Canadian Journal of Economics, 45*(2), 376–393.

Bodle, R., Lena, D., & Matthias, D. (2016). The Paris agreement: Analysis, assessment and outlook. *Carbon & Climate Law Review, 10*(1), 5–22.

Boyer, R. (2020). Les capitalismes à l'épreuve de la pandémie, La Découverte.

Boyer, R., & Saillard, Y. (Eds.). (2002). *Régulation theory. The state of the art.* London & New-York: Routledge.

Hobsbawm, E. (1994). The age of extremes: The short twentieth century, 1914–1991, Michael Joseph editor.

Laurent, E. (2017). *Measuring tomorrow: Accounting for well-being, resilience, and sustainability in the twenty-first century.* Princeton: Princeton University Press.

Laurent, E. (2020). The New Environmental Economics. Cambridge: Polity Press.

Nozal, A., Martin, N., & Murtin, F. (2019). The economy of well-being creating opportunities for people's well-being and economic growth, SDD WORKING PAPER No. 102

Pelloutier, F. (1902). Histoire des bourses du travail, Paris

Pikettty, T. (2014). *Capital in the 21st century.* Harvard: Harvard Edition.

Stiglitz, J., Fitoussi, J.-P., & Durand, M. (Eds.). (2018). *For good measure: Advancing research on well-being metrics beyond GDP.* Paris: OECD Publishing.

Veblen, T. (1899). The theory of the Leisure class: An economic study of institutions. Penguin twentieth-century classics. Introduction by Robert Lekachman. New York: Penguin Books, edition de 1994.

Zachmann, G., & McWilliams, B. (2020). A European carbon border tax: much pain, little gain, Policy Contribution 05/2020, Bruegel.

CHAPTER 12

Integrating Environmental Justice into EU Policymaking

Marie Toussaint

INTRODUCTION

We live in times of crisis. Even before the COVID-19 pandemic, all environmental signals were turning red in Europe and globally:[1] climate change is accelerating, biodiversity is disappearing at a breathtaking pace, resources are being overconsumed and wasted, people are dying prematurely from pollution exposure and four out of nine planetary boundaries have been exceeded (nitrogen and phosphorus cycles; biosphere integrity; climate change and land system change) (Rockström et al. 2009; Steffen et al. 2015). On the social front, inequalities are rising,[2] and although

---

[1] See EEA (2019) UNEP Global Environment Outlook 6 (2019).
[2] See UN Department of Economic and Social Affairs (DESA), World Social Report 2020: Inequality in a rapidly changing world.

M. Toussaint (✉)
European Parliament / International Alliance of Parliamentarians for the Recognition of Ecocide, Paris, France

© The Author(s), under exclusive license to Springer Nature Switzerland AG 2021
É. Laurent (ed.), *The Well-being Transition*,
https://doi.org/10.1007/978-3-030-67860-9_12

217

poverty had been declining in recent years, in a matter of a few months 150 million people could fall into poverty around the world.[3]

Times of crisis are opportunities to take a step back and think about what is important and even essential. While renewed interest in the measurement and advancement of well-being has arisen during the last decades in all corners of the world, including in the European Union (EU), focusing on well-being should be our compass for rebuilding Europe in these demanding times.

For decades, the EU has been developing concepts, tools and policies to embrace the well-being transition. While the EU has embraced the 'Beyond Growth' idea since its High-Level Conference in 2007,[4] 2015 was a global turning-point, with the adoption of the Sustainable Development Goals (SDGs) by the UN and the beginning of their integration within EU policy. Despite the European Commission's commitment to the SDGs in 2016, linking social and environmental concerns, progress was weak and the policies pursued arguably lacked consistency. Against this background, we must consider the promise of the Commission, led by Ursula von der Leyen, to deliver a 'Green Deal which leaves no one behind', both as a positive step and as a renewed binding commitment (European Commission, 2019).

In fact, in October 2019 the Council of the EU, chaired by Finland, published its conclusions on 'The Economy of Well-Being', setting out a path towards a renewed European public policy inspired by OECD guidelines. Yet the Commission did not include in its work programmes for 2020 and 2021 any new legislation on well-being.

If the EU sincerely intends to deliver on a well-being economy and a just transition, it must embrace environmental rights and address environmental justice. To do so, this chapter argues, the EU should question its current approach to collective success (section 1), and decide to renew its global framework so as to respect planetary boundaries as well as global and local environmental justice (section 2).

---

[3] See World Bank Group, Poverty and Shared Prosperity 2020: Reversals of Fortune.

[4] See European Communities (2009), Beyond GDP: Measuring progress, true wealth and the well-being of nations, Conference proceedings.

FROM 'BEYOND GDP' TO THE ENVIRONMENTAL ACTION PROGRAMMES: STRENGTHS AND WEAKNESSES OF THE EU'S APPROACH TO THE WELL-BEING TRANSITION

An Uncertain and Long Overdue Revolution

In 1997, the EU enshrined in Article 2 of the Treaty of Amsterdam its determination to promote sustainable development. As early as in 2001, the Commission published a communication entitled 'A Sustainable Europe for a Better World: A European Strategy for Sustainable Development' (European Commission, 2001).

In 2007, the European Commission, the European Parliament, the Club of Rome, the OECD and the WWF hosted a high-level conference entitled 'Beyond GDP'. In his opening speech at the conference, the then Commission President, José Manuel Barroso, called for a 'breakthrough' in promoting alternative visions of wealth and development. In 2009, the Commission adopted a communication containing a roadmap entitled 'GDP and Beyond: Measuring Progress in a Changing World', aimed at complementing GDP with high-level indicators on environmental protection, quality of life and social cohesion. This communication referred to 'clean environment' among other indicators that need to be developed, as well as establishing a comprehensive environmental index and promoting quality of life and well-being.

In 2010, in the aftermath of the financial crisis and the great recession, the Europe 2020 strategy aimed at 'smart, sustainable and inclusive growth'. However, the pieces of legislation concerned missed the opportunity to address social and environmental injustices, as well as to truly challenge the concept of 'growth'.

After the 2014 European elections, as the issue of sustainable development was gaining momentum, the Commission, then presided by Jean-Claude Juncker, was to commit to the SDGs. Indeed, in 2015 the world leaders had adopted the '2030 Agenda for Sustainable Development', 17 SDGs and 169 related targets in order to integrate the three dimensions of sustainable development. The set of goals range from the eradication of poverty and inequality to the protection of the environment and climate and the sustainable use of resources. The Commission published, in November 2016, a communication entitled 'Next Steps for a Sustainable European Future—European Action for Sustainability', while European Parliament addressed the policy gaps and trends and the inconsistencies and deficiencies of the current policies and urged the Commission and Council to step up their work, in its resolution on 'EU action for sustainability' (European Parliament, 2017).

A study carried out by the Oko-Institut for the Commission's DG Environment in the context of the evaluation of the Seventh Environment Action Programme published in January 2019 offered a polite but severe assessment of the progress made since 2016, highlighting that several sustainability objectives were either overlapping or conflicting. The Oko-Institut made a number of structural recommendations: in aiming for the absolute decoupling of growth from its environmental impacts, the EU institutions should end harmful subsidies, ensure stronger environmental safeguards and inclusiveness within trade agreements, reform agricultural policy, focus on the replacement of harmful infrastructures with environmentally friendly and 'resource-light' ones and work at greening the digital market.

Just before the end of his term as Commission President, Jean-Claude Juncker released a Reflection Paper entitled 'Towards a Sustainable Europe in 2030', which put forward three scenarios to advance sustainable development in the EU (European Commission, 2019). The most ambitious scenario proposed a strategic framework to guide all actions and establish a mechanism of reporting and monitoring. This was endorsed by the European Parliament in its resolution of 14 March 2019.

In 2019, the European Green Party achieved a historic score in the European elections, amid rising environmental concerns and growing mobilisations in civil society. The new Commission had to acknowledge this new political context. In her speech to the European Parliament on the day of her election as the new Commission President, Ursula von der Leyen promised a 'Green Deal for Europe' which would leave no one behind (Ursula von der Leyen, 16 July 2019).

In October 2019, the European Council, led by the progressive Finnish government, published its conclusions on an 'economy of well-being' (European Council, 2019), strengthening the commitment made by the Commission. However, major uncertainties remain as to what precisely 'well-being' means. The OECD defines a well-being economy as one with 'capacity to create a virtuous circle in which citizens' well-being drives economic prosperity, stability and resilience, and good macroeconomic outcomes allow to sustain well-being investments over time' (OECD, 'The Economy of Well-Being', 2019). However, this definition is not widely shared or agreed upon. For instance, in 2019, Hough-Stewart,

Trebeck, Sommer and Wallis defined a well-being economy as character-ised by an equitable distribution of wealth, health and well-being, while protecting the planet's resources for future generations and other species[5]. More importantly, there was also no consultation of the EU population regarding their definition of 'well-being'.

As a result of this confusion, the Commission decided to stick with the (already defined) SDGs. In its communication 'The European Green Deal' of 11 December 2019, it proposed 'to integrate the United Nations' SDGs, to put sustainability and the well-being of citizens at the centre of economic policy, and the SDGs at the heart of the EU's policymaking and action'. In its resolution of 15 January 2020, the European Parliament called for greater clarity and precision, stating that 'the Green Deal must lead to social progress, by improving the well-being of all' and calling for a 'just transition towards a carbon-neutral economy based on the highest social justice criteria so that no one and nowhere is left behind'.

The Need for Urgent Action

In its recent report on the 'state of nature in the European Union' (European Commission, 14 October 2020), based on the technical 'State of Nature' report from the European Environment Agency (EEA), the Commission admitted that the decline of protected habitats and species still continues. In its proposal for a 'General Union Environment Action Programme to 2030', released on the same day, the Commission further admitted that 'progress related to nature protection, health and policy integration was not sufficient'.

In fact, in almost every sector, the EU is failing to reach its goals, and there is a deficiency as regards relevant indicators and monitoring.

In November 2018, the Environment indicator report published by the EEA gave more insight into the progress made on each priority objective: natural capital, resource-efficient and low-carbon economy, and people's health and well-being (EEA, 2018). In December 2019, the EEA pub-lished its 5-year state of the environment and outlook report which offers a comprehensive assessment of how the state of environment has changed over the past 10–15 years as well as future prospects Europe's environ-ment and the transitions to sustainability. Another study from the EEA

---

[5] See Hough-Stewart, Lisa and Trebeck, Katherine et al., (2019) What is a well-being economy?

reveals decreasing but persistent air pollution, exposure to a large share of population to noise, as well as impacts of climate change, many issues with a clear link to inequalities.[6]

Conclusions from these studies are clear: among the indicators, many are red; many are orange and too few are green. And the future prospects are even less promising given the scale of the challenges Europe faces and the influence of global developments largely outside Europe's control: there are 'no policies in place to promote the necessary reductions to the rate of land loss', the use of Europe's seas with regard to fish stock is 'not sustainable', 'the EU is not on track to meet the objective of halting bio-diversity loss', etc. The reports further add that the EU is almost on track to reach its energy goals but needs 'renewed efforts' while 'there are no quantitative targets for improvement in resource productivity' and indica-tors are seen as 'limited'. It is underlined that some indicators are used as proxies, for instance in the case of resource efficiency, since the EU has no real strategy to reduce overall material consumption in the economy.

Several scientists have also pointed out that the current goals of the EU are anyway too low, the 40% objective for 2030 giving us only a 50% chance to limit global warming to 3.2 °C,[7] while the EU and its Member States continue to delocalise production and thus import CO_2 emissions for which no rules have yet been set. In 2018, the EU27's carbon foot-print was 7 tonnes per person, with 1 tonne being imported from abroad (Eurostat 2020). That tonne is not subject in any way to public policy. A change in the European strategy is obviously needed.

THE NEED FOR A NEW EUROPEAN WELL-BEING CONTRACT

Achieving Climate and Environmental Justice Through the Concept of Planetary Boundaries

There can be neither effective protection of the planet nor environmental equity in the world if the EU does not return to a decent level of con-sumption and uptake of natural resources. Over the last two decades, the ecological footprint of countries has received growing attention. This indicator, developed by the Global Footprint Network, has the merits of

---

[6] See EEA (2020), 'Healthy environment, healthy lives'.
[7] See Robiou du Pont and Meinshausen (2018) Warming assessment of the bottom-up Paris Agreement emissions pledges. *Nature Communications* 9, 4810.

relying on existing solid data. It indicates the overall resource demand of European societies, taking into account the capacity of ecosystems to produce useful biological materials and to act as sinks of carbon emissions. The outcome is as bad as unsurprising for the EU: the total ecological footprint of the EU Member States (the UK still included) is too high, exceeding more than twice the biocapacity available in the EU's territory. According to the EEA, this not only prevents the Union from asserting a true position of leadership on the environmental battlefield, but also endangers the ability of other countries, peoples and generations to come to hope for a better future.

The ecological footprint could have been a useful indicator for the EU governance and convergence frameworks. However, it regrettably ignores crucial factors which impact strongly on the environment, such as social well-being, the use of non-renewable resources, for example, oil, gas or metal deposits, unsustainable activities, for example, the release of heavy metals, radioactive materials and persistent synthetic compounds, ecological degradation and the resilience of ecosystems (EEA). However promising, the ecological footprint is therefore not an adequate indicator on which to base our well-being and environmental policy.

In 2009, the Stockholm Resilience Centre released a first study entitled 'Planetary Boundaries: Exploring a Safe Operating Space for Humanity' (Rockström et al. 2009), which was followed by a second one in 2015, on 'Planetary Boundaries: Guiding Human Development on a Changing Planet' (Steffen et al. 2015). These two reports established a scientific framework of interrelated and interdependent boundaries, which is suitable to address the challenges of the Anthropocene.

Since its introduction, the concept of planetary boundaries and a safe operating space for humanity has attracted and stimulated considerable discussions among policy leaders, even at the UN level.[8] It is a driving force for change towards a more sustainable global policy governance.

The fifth objective of the EU's Seventh Environment Action Programme (2013–2020) directly addressed the issue of planetary boundaries. Indeed, improving the 'knowledge and evidence base for Union environment policy' requires, in particular, 'coordinating, sharing and promoting research efforts at Union and Member State level with regard to addressing key

[8] See UN GSP, UN High-Level Panel on Global Sustainability, Report for the 2012 Rio+20 Earth Summit (2012) Resilient People, Resilient Planet: A Future Worth Choosing, United Nations, New York.

environmental knowledge gaps, including the risks of crossing environmental tipping-points and planetary boundaries"[9].

In 2018, the Stockholm Resilience Centre published, for the EEA, a
new report on 'Operationalising the concept of a safe operating space at
the EU level—first steps and explorations' (Häyhä et al. 2018). The report
was not optimistic: it revealed that the EU is not living within the limits of
our planet and that its per capita contribution to reaching planetary
boundaries' maximum thresholds is significantly higher than the global
average. From a dynamic perspective, the report also shows how the
improvements made within the European territory are offset by the externalisation of the EU's environmental footprint, ultimately depriving these
EU internal measures from having any net positive impact on planetary
boundaries.

The report called for further research with a view to the integration of
planetary boundaries into EU policymaking. This was answered by the
launch of a three-year research programme by the EEA. Another report,
'Is Europe Living Within the Limits of Our Planet?' (EEA, 17 April 2020),
once again concludes stressing the transgression by the EU of its safe
operating space, and emphasises that there is a great need for further
research in order to design scientific operating tools to measure these
boundaries and create the legal framework necessary to transform those
tools into policy instruments.

This last report shows quite clearly why the concept of planetary
boundaries matters for global justice: first, the concept can be used to
reduce the environmental pressure exerted by the EU on the rest of the
world and especially on developing countries; second, it opens up a necessary and highly political discussion on the global allocation of effort shares
in relation to these planetary boundaries.

Höhne et al. (2014) propose considering four allocation criteria: historical responsibility, capabilities, equality per person and cost-effectiveness.
Sabag-Muñoz and Gladek (2017) have developed four categories of
approaches at country and company level: egalitarian approaches, economic throughput, economic capacity and efficiency, and historical justice

---

[9] Article 73 of the Annex to Decision No 1386/2013/EU of the European Parliament
and of the Council of 20 November 2013 on a General Union Environment Action
Programme to 2020 'Living well, within the limits of our planet'.

and inertia (including the polluter pays principle). Den Elzen and Lucas (2005) mention 'sovereignty' as a staged category. The EEA has made its own selection of criteria: equality (equal share per capita), needs (different resource needs depending on age, location or other criteria), right to development (convergence of welfare), sovereignty (based on internal policy rules) and capability (different levels of economic wealth) and did not apply the historical responsibility principle.

Following the equality principle (per capita ratio of the European share of the world population), the EU's share of the global safe operating space (to determine a European safe operating space) amounts to 8.1%. The latter drops to 4.1% if one adopts the right to development principle. On the contrary, if instead one adopts the sovereignty principle (assuming that Europe's relative economic strength necessitates its proportionally greater use of the global commons), the EU's share rises to 12.5% (EEA 2020).

An Opportunity for a New Approach to Global Environmental Justice

This discussion on allocation criteria clearly shows that the framework elaborated by the Stockholm Resilience Centre should be linked to considerations of global environmental justice and to existing international legal principles such as the notion of 'common but differentiated responsibilities' introduced in principle 7 of the UN's Rio Declaration of 1992. Further, the principle of intra- and inter-generational equity—also to be found in the 1992 Rio Declaration, principle 3—emphasises that development cannot be based on short-term ends but must also encompass and ensure protection of the environment for present and future generations.

Since their adoption, these principles have not fulfilled their promise. These concepts translated intuitions for global justice and gave the impression of opening up multiple opportunities for differential treatment (technology transfer, development and climate aid, financial compensations, etc.).

Carbon footprint and imported CO_2 emissions can be used as an illustration. In its report 'Controlling France's Carbon Footprint' published on 6 October 2020, the French High Council for the Climate underlined that imported emissions have been rising steadily since 1995 and are 70% higher than domestic CO_2 emissions and called for a strategy for action to reduce imported emissions. Another report drafted by the social enterprise IDH—Sustainable Trade Initiative—focusing on deforestation, revealed that for 12 European countries, imported deforestation is estimated to amount to more than 50% of national agricultural emissions. The EU's responses to the externalisation of its environmental impacts are diverse: a legal framework for halting deforestation is expected for adoption in 2021, but the way the EU apprehends its imported emissions will be based in the coming years entirely on a market-based solution, namely a carbon adjustment mechanism.

The theory of ecologically unequal exchange supports a critical approach to neoliberalism and its consequences by postulating that there are asymmetric net transfers of resources from peripheral to core areas of the global economic system, in diverse fields such as materials, energy, land and labour[10]. Just before the pandemic, the use of natural resources was still growing (Krausmann et al. 2018), as was also the volume of international trade because of increasing demand for non-domestic materials, energy, land and labour (Wiedmann and Lenzen 2018). As a result, the asymmetry of international trade has had a huge impact on global equity, but also on environmental sustainability. Experts have denounced: an environmental burden-shifting to poorer nations (Wiedmann and Lenzen 2018); the displacement of extractive frontiers (Schaffartzik and Pichler, 2017), linked to socio-environmental conflicts affecting agriculture and the mining and manufacturing sectors (Temper et al., 2015); and issues relating to waste (Hein and Faust 2014).

In a recent and solid article (Dorninger et al. 2021), various experts provide evidence to support the theory of ecologically unequal exchange. They state: 'On aggregate, ecologically unequal exchange allows high-income countries to simultaneously appropriate resources and to generate a monetary surplus through international trade. This has far-reaching implications for global sustainability and for the economic growth prospects of nations'.

According to Martínez-Alier (2002), ecological debt is an economic concept that arises from distribution conflicts of two kinds: firstly, ecologically unequal exchange understood as 'the fact of exporting products from poor regions and countries, at prices which do not take into account the

---

[10] See among others Hornborg and Martínez-Alier (2016).

local externalities'; and secondly, the tendency of wealthy countries to dis-proportionately use environmental space without paying for it'. Ecological debt significantly exceeds the financial debt of Southern countries (Emelianoff 2008); yet it cannot be costed, owing to its intrinsic, cultural and non-monetary value (Emelianoff 2008; Temper and Martínez-Alier, 2013) but also because of its impacts on health (toxic chemicals) and well-being (privation of use of areas) (Blanchon et al. 2009) concepts including ecocide (Zierler 2011), an international environmental crimes tribunal (complementary to demands for civil liability), corporate accountability (Utting 2008; Broad and Cavanagh 1999) and the rights of nature. Rather than market-based solutions and approaches, rather than focusing on growth, there is a growing call for a shift towards a new legal framework to ensure global ecological justice.

We are currently experiencing a historic pandemic, which was born in an ecological crisis. A zoonotic virus spread throughout the world and created a health crisis which then became a huge economic crisis, increasing inequalities and hampering well-being. The low ambition, fragmentation and poor implementation of European environmental policy is one of the reasons for the failures of the EU in its attempts to attain a well-being society. And, as is underlined by Kelly F. Austin, externalisation of environmental costs to less developed countries through unequal trade relationships and cross-national patterns in resource use explains how consumers in the Global North contribute to the emergence of zoonotic disease.[11]

If the academic discussion is still very much alive, the definition given by Martínez-Alier should encourage the EU to develop a policy which takes responsibility for both past and cumulative crossing of planetary boundaries. Articulating the concepts of planetary boundaries and global environmental justice could give rise to a renewed framework for EU development aid and policy, based on the actual historical responsibility of the EU in the Anthropocene.

For the time being, research and inclusion of the planetary boundaries within the EU governance framework are part neither of the Green Deal policy proposals, nor of the EEA work programme for 2021–2023. The Green Group of the European Parliament presented an amendment to the 2021 budget of the EU to grant the EEA the necessary budget to pursue

---

[11] See Kelly F. Austin (2021), Degradation and disease: Ecologically unequal exchanges cultivate emerging pandemics.

its work, which now has to be endorsed by the Council. The rising concepts of planetary boundaries, global environmental justice and ecocide/ environmental accountability still have to emerge as legitimate legal instruments within the European institutions.

Promoting Environmental Rights and Justice Within the EU

Despite the study carried out for the Commission in 2008, 'Addressing the Social Dimensions of Environmental Policy: A Study on the Linkages Between Environmental and Social Sustainability in Europe', the EU has not really apprehended the issue of environmental justice and rights within its social policy. As we will see, some recent studies by the EEA give some hope for change, but political support is still needed after more than a decade of absence of action.

The 2008 study was promising in addressing three dimensions of environmental justice: the distribution of environmental quality, the drivers of environmental quality (which socio-economic groups pollute, and how do they pay proportionately for the resulting impacts?) and, finally, the equity of environmental policy (the financial burden of environmental policies).

This European environmental justice approach has recently been developed by Éloi Laurent (Laurent 2011),[12] who suggests a fourfold structure of environmental justice. Laurent distinguishes categories as the following: firstly, inequality of exposure and access: whether negatively (exposure to environmental risk and hazard) or positively (access to environmental amenities); secondly, inequality of policy effect: that is, the unequal distribution, not of environmental 'goods' or 'bads', but of the effects of environmental regulatory or tax policies; thirdly, inequality of impact: the unequal environmental impact of different individuals and groups as a result of their income and/or lifestyle; and lastly, policymaking inequality: unequal access to environmental policymaking, that is, the unequal degree of involvement and empowerment of individuals and groups in relation to decisions regarding their immediate environment.

Different case studies have highlighted the relevance of questioning environmental justice in the EU on the lines Laurent suggests. Lucie Laurian showed that poor and immigrant minorities are disproportionately exposed to environmental risks and hazardous facilities (Laurian

---

[12] See Laurent (2011). Issues in environmental justice within the European Union, *Ecological Economics*, Elsevier, vol. 70(11), 1846-1853.

2008; Laurian 2014). The same trends are visible in Italy[13] or in Germany, where, as Tamara Steger shows, Turkish immigrants, for example, work in unsafe conditions and live near highly polluting factories (Steger 2007). With others, Steger has also revealed the same trends in Central and Eastern Europe, while the Roma people (and especially the Romani from Central and Eastern Europe) seem to be the most impacted population (Harper et al. 2009).

Environmental injustices are thus found within Member States, but also between them, as shown by D. Petric (2019). Regarding indicators as diverse as ecological footprint, hazardous waste, air quality or energy poverty, Petric has underlined the disproportion between the historically and still today polluter countries of the EU centre compared to the eastern and central European Member States. He argues that market-based solutions such as 'cap-and-trade' disregard, also in the EU, the social conditions of those suffering directly from emissions, and calls for new legislation that will acknowledge 'the EU centre's disproportionate—historical and contemporary—contribution to environmental degradation, its superior capacities and resources (financial and technical) to address environmental problems, and the EU periphery's economic and ecological vulnerability'. Such legislation could also require changes to the Treaties. Petric does not examine another indicator, namely the disproportionate levels of CO_2 imports per Member State (the centre importing far more carbon than Eastern and Central Europe), but it only reinforces his views (Global Carbon Project[14]).

In a report published in February 2019, the EEA makes the call concerning compiling data and defining policy in the field of environmental justice. The agency drew attention to the uneven distribution of the impact of air pollution, noise and extreme temperatures on the health of Europeans, which reflects the sociodemographic differences within our society; together with the strong regional differences in social vulnerability and exposure to environmental health hazards across Europe. It also pointed out inequalities in exposure to environmental health hazards and their impacts on European society, which are only partially addressed by current policy and practice. The report underlined the fact that the impacts of and exposure to environmental health hazards are likely to continue in

---

[13] See Martuzzi et al. (2010), Inequalities, Inequities, Environmental Justice in Waste Management and Health.

[14] Global Carbon Project. Last data available date from 2014. Accessed 15 October 2020.

the future and thus require increased recognition in policy across governance levels; and at last the need for a better alignment of social and environment policies and improved local action to tackle environmental justice issues.

In 2020, two members of staff at the EEA elaborated a fivefold framework for further studies on environmental justice in the EU, drawing on discussions of the Scientific Committee of the EEA in 2018, distinguishing from Laurent's proposal through precisions on environmental inequalities across generations,[15] by stressing the unequal distribution of environmental risks across generations, underlining particularly the risks of chemical pollution and climate change for future generations.

Yet, despite this work, a study commissioned by the Committee on Employment and Social Affairs of the European Parliament on 'Social Sustainability' (European Parliament, 2020) once again missed the opportunity to pave the way towards a general environmental justice approach. As we are still lacking the tools to measure the environmental inequality and to monitor the effectiveness of the measures addressing the inequalities, EEA is currently developing approaches to presenting and analysing socio-environmental inequalities in order to address this gap, which need to be taken into account as soon as possible.

As underlined by academic work and research, this environmental justice strategy could rely on the recognition of environmental rights and people's rights in order to guarantee that real and concrete action is undertaken, both on programmes aimed at correcting the current environmental injustices, and on new horizontal norms to ensure that each single environmental policy takes into account the need to fight injustices.

From Environmental Rights to the Rights of Nature

This academic work was echoed by numerous 'climate justice' mobilisations, among them: the Urgenda case in the Netherlands, in which the Dutch Supreme Court underlined the link between the rights to life and to privacy as enshrined in the European Convention on Human Rights and climate change; the People's Climate Case led by ten families from the EU and beyond denouncing the climate inaction of the European Union and the violation of their fundamental rights; or even the 'yellow vests'

---

[15] Ganzleben and Kazmierczak (2020), Leaving no one behind—understanding environmental inequality in Europe, in Environmental Health.

movement in France, which demanded fairness in environmental fiscal policy.

At the global level, the integration of social and environmental issues is making progress: the UN dedicated the 2020 edition of the International Day for the Eradication of Poverty to achieving 'social and environmental justice for all'. The UN Special Rapporteur on Extreme Poverty and Human Rights released his first report, entitled 'The "Just Transition" in the Economic Recovery: Eradicating Poverty Within Planetary Boundaries', on 9 October 2020 (De Schutter, 2020).

At European level, within its evaluation of the Seventh Environment Action Programme (EAP), the Commission had concluded that 'the integrated approach to policy development and implementation should be strengthened with a view to maximising the synergies between economic, environmental and social objectives, while paying careful attention to potential trade-offs and to the needs of vulnerable groups'. On 14 October 2020, Commission Vice-President Franz Timmermans presented a new Communication on Access to Justice for Environmental matters (European Commission, 2020) as well as a new legislative proposal. This new development was welcomed, although it does not overcome all the obstacles to access to justice in the framework of Article 263 Treaty on the Functioning of the European Union (TFEU).

On 15 January 2020, the right to a stable climate was adopted in the 'Green Deal Resolution' of the European Parliament. On 22 October 2020, the latter decided to call for the universal recognition of the right to a healthy environment and for the protection of environmental defenders, measures which would open up the path towards a revitalised approach to social and environmental justice at both local and global level.

The Council of Europe, whose work sometimes influences the EU's policies and public debates, defined environmental protection as a priority on 27 February 2020, during a High-Level Conference on Environmental Protection and Human Rights. Lastly, on 14 October 2020 the European Commission published a chemicals strategy for sustainability as part of the EU's zero pollution ambition. This constitutes another opportunity to mobilise the European Environment Agency (EEA) and other scientific agencies to examine the issues of planetary boundaries and environmental justice.

CONCLUSION

On 14 October 2019, ATD Fourth World Movement and the University of Oxford released a research document three years in the making, entitled 'The Hidden Dimensions of Poverty' (ATD Fourth World Movement/ Oxford, 2019). The research was conducted in six different countries with the participation of people facing poverty. Not only did the researchers find that everywhere the environment and its safety is one of the dimensions raised by the most vulnerable as a condition for well-being and the fight against poverty: they also found that 'suffering in body, mind and heart, disempowerment, and struggle and resistance' are at the centre of the conceptualisation of poverty. If the European Union truly wants a 'Green Deal which leaves no-one behind', the participation of the poorest among us is a prerequisite.

The EU also has to understand that well-being is conditioned by our ability to live in harmony with the biosphere which is our habitat. While environmental justice theories and practices raise the need for the condemnation of environmental loss, damage and crime, various groups and researchers have also called for a philosophical, juridical and political revolution: the recognition of the rights of nature.

In 2019, the Greens addressed the different weaknesses of the EU's approach to well-being in a proposal for a new treaty. This Environmental Treaty would turn its back on the focalisation of growth and would confront ecological debt and unequal exchange, raising at the highest level of the hierarchy of norms the question of fair respect for planetary boundaries. It would compel the EU as a whole to develop distributive and corrective ecological justice, recognise both the rights of nature and the environmental rights of the people, and establish a firm and definitive environmental accountability while focusing its environmental action on the most vulnerable.

This chapter has shown how much the EU needs such a treaty for genuine well-being, drawn up in cooperation with the poorest among us. By following this path, the EU could at last find a new way to ensure coherence among its different policies.

REFERENCES

Austin, K. F. (2021). Degradation and disease: Ecologically unequal exchanges cultivate emerging pandemics. *World Development, 137*, 1. https://doi.org/10.1016/j.worlddev.2020.105163.

Blanchon, D., Moreau, S., & Veyret, Y. (2009). Understanding and building environmental justice. *Annales de géographie, 665-666*(1), 35–60. https://doi.org/10.3917/ag.665.0035.

Broad, R., & Cavanagh, J. (1999). The corporate accountability movement: Lessons and opportunities the corporate accountability movement: Lessons and opportunities. *Fletcher Forum of World Affairs, 23*, 1.

Varga, C., Kiss, I., & Ember, I. (2002). The lack of environmental justice in Central and Eastern Europe. *Environmental Health Perspectives, 110*(11), A662–A663.

Den Elzen, M. G. J., & Lucas, P. L. (2005). The FAIR model: A tool to analyse environmental and costs implications of regimes of future commitments. *Environmental Modeling and Assessment, 10*(2), 115–134. https://doi.org/10.1007/s10666-005-4647-z.

Dorninger, C., Hornborg, A., Abson, D. J., von Wehrden, H., Schaffartzik, A., Giljum, S., Engler, J.-O., Feller, R. L., Hubacek, K., & Wieland, H. (2021). Global patterns of ecologically unequal exchange: Implications for sustainability in the 21st century. *Ecological Economics, 179*, 106824. https://doi.org/10.1016/j.ecolecon.2020.106824.

Emelianoff, C. (2008). The issue of environmental inequalities: A new conceptual landscape. *Ecologie and politique, 35*(1), 19–31. https://doi.org/10.3917/ecopo.035.0019.

Environment European Agency. (2019a). The European environment—State and outlook 2020, https://www.eea.europa.eu/soer; and UN Environment Programme Global Environment Outlook 6 (2019), https://www.unenvironment.org/resources/global-environment-outlook-6

Environment European Agency. (2019b). Unequal exposure and unequal impacts: social vulnerability to air pollution, noise and extreme temperatures in Europe.

European Environment Agency, Indicator Assessment: Ecological Footprint of European Countries, SEBI 023, 20. (2020, April). https://www.eea.europa.eu/data-and-maps/indicators/ecological-footprint-of-european-countries-2/assessment

Environment European Agency. (2020a). State of Nature in the EU, https://www.eea.europa.eu/publications/state-of-nature-in-the-eu-2020

Environment European Agency. (2020b). Healthy environment, healthy lives. Retrieved November 21, 2020, from https://www.eea.europa.eu/publications/healthy-environment-healthy-lives.

Environment European Agency. (2020c), Is Europe living within the limits of our planet?

European Communities. (2009). Beyond GDP: Measuring progress, true wealth and the well-being of nations, Conference proceedings. https://doi.org/10.2779/54600

European Commission. (2007). Summary notes from the Beyond GDP conference, https://ec.europa.eu/environment/beyond_gdp/download/bgdp-summary-notes.pdf.

European Commission, study carried out for the Directorate-General for Employment, Social Affairs and Equal Opportunities. (2008). Addressing the social dimensions of environmental policy: A study on the linkages between environmental and social sustainability in Europe.

Eurostat. (2020). Statistics Explained, Greenhouse gas emission statistics—carbon footprint. Retrieved October 15, 2020, from https://ec.europa.eu/eurostat/statistics-explained/pdfscache/10389.pdf.

Ganzleben, Catherine, & Aleksandra, Kazmierczak. (2020). Leaving no one behind—understanding environmental inequality in Europe, in Environmental Health. https://doi.org/10.1186/s12940-020-00600-2

Harper, K., Steger, T., & Filčák, R. (2009). Environmental justice and Roma communities in Central and Eastern Europe. *Environmental Policy and Governance, 19*, 251–268. https://doi.org/10.1002/eet.511.

Haut Conseil pour le climat. (2020). Maîtriser l'empreinte carbone de la France. https://www.hautconseilclimat.fr/wp-content/uploads/2020/10/hcc_rapport_empreinte-carbone.pdf.

Häyhä, T., Cornell, S.E., Hoff, H., Lucas, P., van Vuuren, D. (2018). Operationalizing the concept of a safe operating space at the EU level—first steps and explorations. Stockholm Resilience Centre Technical Report, prepared in collaboration with Stockholm Environment Institute (SEI) and PBL Netherlands Environmental Assessment Agency. Stockholm Resilience Centre, Stockholm University, Sweden.

Hein, J., & Faust, H. (2014). Conservation, REDD+ and the struggle for land in Jambi, Indonesia. *Pacific Geographies, 41*, 20–25.

Höhne, N., den Elzen, M., & Escalante, D. (2014). Regional GHG reduction targets based on effort sharing: a comparison of studies. *Climate Policy, 14*, 122–147. https://doi.org/10.1080/14693062.2014.849452.

Hornborg, A., & Martínez-Alier, J. (2016). Hough-Stewart, Lisa and Trebeck, Katherine et al., (2019) What is a well-being economy?, https://wellbeingeconomy.org/wp-content/uploads/2019/12/A-WE-Is-WEAll-Ideas-Little-Summaries-of-Big-Issues-4-Dec-2019.pdf.

IDH. (2020). The urgency of action to tackle tropical deforestation. February 2020. Prepared for IDH by FACTS Consulting, COWI A/S and AlphaBeta

Singapore. IDH: Utrecht, the Netherlands. https://www.idhsustainabletrade.com/tacklingdeforestation.

Krausmann, F., Lauk, C., Haas, W., & Wiedenhofer, D. (2018). From resource extraction to outflows of wastes and emissions: the socioeconomic metabolism of the global economy, 1900–2015 Global Environmental Change 52 131–40, and OECD/IEA (2018) World Energy Outlook 2018. Retrieved from www.iea.org/weo2018/.

Laurent, É. (2011). Issues in environmental justice within the European Union. *Ecological Economics, Elsevier, 70*(11), 1846–1853.

Laurian, Lucie. (2008). Environmental injustice in France, *Journal of environmental planning and management.*

Laurian and Funderburg. (2014). Environmental justice in France? A spatio-temporal analysis of incinerator location, *Journal of Environmental Planning and Management.*

Martuzzi, M., Mitis, F., & Forastiere, F. (2010). Inequalities, Inequities, Environmental Justice in Waste Management and Health. *European Journal of Public Health, 20*(1), 21–22.

Martínez-Alier, J. (2002). *The environmentalism of the poor. A study of ecological conflicts and valuation.* Cheltenham: Edward Elgar Publishing Ltd..

Petric, Davor. (2019). Environmental Justice in the European Union: A Critical Reassessment 15 CYELP 215 200.

OECD. (2019). The Economy of Well-Being. Retrieved October 15, 2020, from http://www.oecd.org/social/economy-of-well-being-brussels-july-2019.htm.

Pichler, M., Schaffartzik, A., Haberl, H., et al. (2017). Drivers of society-nature relations in the Anthropocene and their implications for sustainability transformations. Current opinion. *Environmental Sustainability, 26-27,* 32–36.

Rockström, J., Steffen, W., Noone, K., et al. (2009). A safe operating space for humanity. *Nature, 461,* 472–475. https://doi.org/10.1038/461472a.

Robiou du Pont, Y., Jeffery, M., Gütschow, J., et al. (2017). Equitable mitigation to achieve the Paris Agreement goals. *Nature Climate Change, 7,* 38–43. https://doi.org/10.1038/nclimate3186.

Robiou du Pont, Y., & Meinshausen, M. (2018). Warming assessment of the bottom-up Paris Agreement emissions pledges. *Nature Communications, 9,* 4810. https://doi.org/10.1038/s41467-018-07223-9.

Steger, Tamara. (ed.) (2007). Making the case for environmental justice in Central and Eastern Europe. Brussels: Central European University, Center for Environmental Policy and Law (CEPL), (Budapest, Hungary) and the Health and Environment Alliance (HEAL): 10.

Steger, T., & Filčák, R. (2008). Articulating the basis for promoting environmental justice in Central and Eastern Europe. *Environmental Justice, 1,* 49–53. https://doi.org/10.1089/env.2008.0501.

Steffen, W., Richardson, K., Rockström, J., et al. (2015). Planetary boundaries: Guiding human development on a changing planet. *Science, 1*, 437.

Steininger, K., Lininger, C., Meyer, L., et al. (2016). Multiple carbon accounting to support just and effective climate policies. *Nature Climate Change, 6*, 35–41. https://doi.org/10.1038/nclimate2867.

Temper, L., del Bene, D., & Martínez-Alier, J. (2015). Mapping the frontiers and front lines of global environmental justice: The EJAtlas. *Journal of Political Ecology, 22*, 255–278.

Utting, P. (2008). The struggle for corporate accountability. *Development and Change, 39*, 959–975. https://doi.org/10.1111/j.1467-7660.2008.00523.

UN Department of Economic and Social Affairs (DESA), World Social Report. (2020). Inequality in a rapidly changing world, https://www.un.org/development/desa/dspd/wp-content/uploads/sites/22/2020/02/World-Social-Report2020-FullReport.pdf

Wiedmann and Lenzen. (2018). Environmental and social footprints of international trade, Macmillan Publishers Limited, part of Springer Nature.

Wolff, F., & Öko-Institut. (2019). Coherence between the 7th EAP, the Juncker priorities and the Sustainable Development Goals, https://ec.europa.eu/environment/action-programme/pdf/Issue_Paper_7th_EAP_Juncker_Priorities_SDGs_190125_final.pdf

World Bank Group. (2020). Poverty and Shared Prosperity 2020: Reversals of Fortune, https://www.worldbank.org/en/publication/poverty-and-shared-prosperity

World Wildlife Fund, Sabag-Muñoz, O., & Gladek, E. (2017). One planet approaches—Methodology mapping and pathways forward. Swiss Federal Office for the Environment. *Metabolic* website (Netherlands), https://www.metabolic.nl/

Zierler, D. (2011). *The invention of ecocide.* Georgia: University of Georgia Press.

CHAPTER 13

European Indicators and Governance for the Twenty-First Century

Xavier Timbeau

INTRODUCTION

One of the strong messages of the Stiglitz-Sen-Fitoussi report, Stiglitz et al. (2009), was that "*what we measure shapes what we collectively strive to pursue—and what we pursue determines what we measure*". In other words, designing the measures of societies and the uses associated with those measures is of the utmost importance. More generally, the kind of information we acquire, the way the resulting indicators are disseminated and how they are used by every actor in society determine which policies are chosen and how they are implemented.

Unfortunately, the way we construct indicators is not only a question of will: we measure what we can, with scarce measurement resources that have to be allocated wisely. We use a flow of information produced for other purposes because it is available and is occupying some space in the information landscape. And we harbour some preconceptions about what is needed that originate from other eras where different concerns prevailed.

X. Timbeau (✉)
OFCE, Sciences Po, Paris, France
e-mail: xavier.timbeau@sciencespo.fr

© The Author(s), under exclusive license to Springer Nature Switzerland AG 2021
É. Laurent (ed.), *The Well-being Transition*,
https://doi.org/10.1007/978-3-030-67860-9_13

237

Quantification is about producing knowledge. As Lord Kevin supposedly said, in a statement inscribed on the pediment of the Social Sciences building of the University of Chicago "*when you cannot express it in numbers, your knowledge is of a meagre and unsatisfactory kind*". It is said that Franck Knight, wandering around, replied: "*Yes, and when you can express it in numbers your knowledge is of a meagre and unsatisfactory kind*". Those two witticisms summarize perfectly the internal inescapable conflict in the construction of rules or policies and the use of numbers to drive them. These result from ancient beliefs, reflect a current balance of power and yet will crystallize what can be done for the future.

This chapter starts by showing that European governance does not escape this circularity and its consequences. European governance is indeed an interesting case study, as it is a rather young construction and has relatively straightforward economic governance objectives (as it deals mainly with public finance stability at an aggregate level) and a framework that is the fruit of intense negotiations between the Member States. Yet, I will argue that, in the recent period, these negotiations have been increasingly motivated by mutual distrust and an approach to economic governance and the definition of indicators that is becoming less and less productive and relevant.

In the second section, I will offer a way out of this European crisis of distrust by exploring possible evolutions of European governance and their implications for building information systems. Going beyond a narrow economic perspective is in fact essential, because the European Union (EU) must take care of its overall sustainability instead of focusing on chasing free riders among its Member States. But sustainability is a concept that is hard to define, precisely because it encompasses many dimensions. In my view, the EU's sustainability has to be understood in the early twenty-first century as a mixture of the stability of the Union as a political construction (resisting forces that tend to provoke its collapse) together with environmental sustainability, that is to say, the ability left to future generations of Europeans to lead a decent life. To face both challenges, European governance must include new objectives, such as social issues and the transition to a zero-net emissions society, along with new instruments better suited to efficient collective action.

SURVEILLANCE GOVERNANCE AND DISTRUST POLICY

Two main goals have been pursued by European governance since the establishment of the Maastricht Treaty and the common currency in 1992: the first is surveillance, and the second is structural reform. These two goals join in one at an abstract level: As European Union Member States share common goods such as the single market and the single currency yet lack a common government able to coerce Member States in case of a conflict over political choices, distrust between Member States reigns, demanding some way to prevent the damage of moral hazard. Surveillance is a simple monitoring process based on quantitative thresholds and goals to judge national policies procedurally. The framework underlying structural reforms is fuzzier; however, it is based on a rather narrow conception of the economic sustainability of each Member State.

There is far more fear than facts about the abuse of European common goods by Member States. This is nevertheless the driver for surveillance and structural reform. Most EU common goods are beyond the reach or advantage of any free rider. As direct monetary creation is in the hands of the European Central Bank, it is not clear how a Member State would be able to generate inflation and affect its neighbours. Default on public debt would surely trigger harmful spill-overs from the defaulting Member to other Member States, but a default event would also have direct, first-order consequences on the defaulting country itself. In most cases, there is at least a weak convergence between preserving EU common goods and the country's own interests. Moral hazard is thus probably bounded by peer pressure and the repeated game of European negotiations.

Surveillance Governance

Surveillance is unpleasant, especially when it leads to excessive and costly demands to correct what is judged as incorrect behaviour. Everything can be contested, from the poor rationale of the rules to the short-term bias induced by the correction policies demanded. However, at least for the European Union, surveillance has been a rather simple business in the past years; it has been based on a small number of indicators, follows a clear procedure and pursues a simple objective.

Surveillance is focused mainly on euro area Member States, but the motives of the single market, the circulation of capital and future entry into the single currency have combined to justify the application of surveillance to all EU Member States.

As Member States share, or in the case of non-euro area Members will share in the future the same currency, the goal of surveillance is to deal with the possibility that some adopt a "free rider" strategy. Based on such a strategy, some country may abuse the protection offered by the monetary union to conduct an expansive fiscal policy without concern for the sustainability of their public finances over the long term. Benefiting from low interest rates, thanks to an active central bank guaranteeing low inflation and a low default probability on public debt, such a policy could impose a cost on other countries without their consent or control.

Such a possibility is remote, and this chapter is not the place to discuss the validity of this line of thinking. However, a common narrative about the 2009–2012 debt crisis in Greece is based on this fear.

Thus, surveillance concerns the financial stability of each Member State's public finances, and more specifically about a core indicator: public debt over GDP (Gross Domestic Product). This explains the centrality of macroeconomic indicators, as displayed by the AMECO (Annual MacroECOnomic) database and the European Commission analysis. Everything is about the debt dynamic and its drivers, from public sector deficit to GDP. As stated frankly in a technical document from the Commission in 2016 (European Commission 2016): "*A rules-based system is the best guarantee for commitments to be enforced and for all Member States to be treated equally. The two nominal anchors of the Stability and Growth Pact—the 3% of GDP reference value for the deficit ratio and the 60% of GDP reference value for the debt ratio—and the medium-term budgetary objectives are the centerpiece of multilateral surveillance*". This has determined the simplicity of the surveillance branch of European Governance for many years.

Attempts have been made to introduce a broader view of a country's economic sustainability, with the introduction of the *Macroeconomic Imbalance Procedure* in 2011.[1] The innovation was intended to take into account a broader view than the initial criteria to assess a country's situation, including: external imbalances, current account surpluses being treated symmetrically with deficits, private debt as well as public debt, and social indicators as well as aggregate and macroeconomic ones. The

---

[1] The legislation defining the Macroeconomic Imbalance Procedure is the Six Pack, EU Regulation No 472/2013 and EU Regulation No 473/2013.

innovation was limited in scope and ambition, as the dashboard was mostly macroeconomic, and the social part was limited to unemployment, with no consideration for, for instance, inequality, poverty or access to education. Environmental issues and the question of political representation were totally absent, even though the dashboard was extended in 2011, after the fourth assessment report from the IPCC (Intergovernmental Panel on Climate Change) in 2007. Despite its limited ambition, the extension of the dashboard has not been a success. Never-ending discussions about the German surplus and its legitimacy have stalled the rebalancing of economic governance. The multiplication of criteria has led to confusion and, in the end, core criteria, that is mainly the public debt to GDP ratio, have had to be reinforced and, more importantly, debate about objectives, sound sustainability, and various possibilities to improve the macroeconomic imbalances procedure have been lost in the sands.

Distrust Policy

Besides surveillance, the other arm of the EU governance scheme is policy guidance. That arm takes material shape through the Country Specific Recommendations (CSR) that are established and discussed throughout the process of the European Semester. Policy guidance is richer than surveillance in terms of economic indicators. Policy recommendations include a more causal representation of economic functioning, even if competitiveness is a matter for which there is much concern. This brings to mind the *dangerous obsession* pointed out by Paul Krugman (1994), for whom competitiveness is one of the less relevant factors for prosperity. Even more striking is the fact that competitiveness in the EU takes place mainly between Member States of an Economic Union where most Members share the same currency. Repeated calls for fiscal devaluation, an usual message in a CSR, are a process that exacerbates fiscal competition and does not produce any productivity gains, especially if one considers that common goods and their financing are necessary to the functioning of complex societies (Fitoussi et al. 1999 and Timbeau et al. 2013–2019).

Policy guidance is another term for structural reform. Reforms respond in a sense to the surveillance arm by applying over the long-term policies aiming to reform economies towards a more "sustainable" state. Of course, the concept of sustainability used and the selection of which policies have an impact are not innocent notions. They are embedded in the same economic paradigm and the same economic goals as the concepts used to build the indicators used in their pursuit. Because of that, it is difficult to escape from the intertwining of the doctrines, goals and quantifications used to assess progress towards those goals (Porter 1995).

One other innovation in the European Semester has been to shift from an obligation of results—reaching nominal targets—to an obligation of diligence—showing effort and accounting for external events. This was indeed a recommendation of many economists and was materialized by the extensive use of a structural concept. The aim is to identify what lies beyond the will of Member States (the so-called cyclical part of the evolution of any indicator, like the public deficit) and what is the intended policy of a Member State (for instance, the variation in the structural or "cyclically adjusted" deficit). Diligence in reducing the deficit is then appreciated through looking at structural evolution and not at effective evolution. In theory, this makes it possible to be countercyclical and tolerate evolutions in the deficit that would have been considered faulty.

However, this innovation has led to a complexification of the process. It is as difficult to make real-time estimates of structural evolutions as it is to make *exact* forecasts of the future. Consequently, attempts to apply explicit and stable procedures are leading to absurd decisions. Procyclicality is one example of such absurd decisions, surging back precisely from where it was supposed to be buried. The evaluation of potential activity (or potential growth) is correlated to past observations of activity (say a five-year lag), and thus a long phase of slow activity translates into a lower evaluation of potential, which leads to the evaluation that stability of the public finances calls for greater consolidation. Persistent consolidation may replace short-term pro-cyclicality and, by relying on a supposedly scientific evaluation of potential growth, political decisions about fiscal policy are captured by administrations or bodies of experts.

Lessons Learned from the 2008 and 2012 Crises: From Surveillance to Responsibility

The surveillance and guidance arms both share the distrust trait on which they are built. The European Union has been forged on the idea that the political project was sound and beyond debate. Thus, Member States were, at best, suspected of being willing to take advantage of this by becoming free riders. A slightly over-optimistic view of the evolution of European governance could lead one to hope that distrust is a failure of the past. Two points can be made in that respect, illustrated by the twin crisis of 2008 and 2012.

The first is that there is no strong divergence between countries' interests and what is under surveillance. This has led to severe disputes, for instance over the conduct of fiscal policy, as some countries viewed respect of strict fiscal criterion to be overshooting the very needs of the Union. The European framework can work to treat any deviance from fiscal orthodoxy as the route to a default. But when a country needs to respond to a crisis, the brakes implied by surveillance are counterproductive and undermine the possibility for a Member State's national debate to deal with the long-term stability of the public finances or any subject related to prosperity or sustainability in the broad sense of an economy.

The second point is that countries' stability is at the core of the guidance and surveillance mechanism. But the real question is not the stability of a given country inside a perfectly and forever stable Union. The real question is the stability of the Union and its ability to deliver a framework in which each Member State derives some benefit. Complying with some unpleasant rules to ensure the functioning of the Union is not repulsive in itself. But, in exchange, so to speak, the Union must provide a framework that is positive for each member. This is the condition for the Union's stability. This balance between avoiding free riders and building a stable and useful Union has been difficult to establish, if it has indeed happened. The 2012 debt crisis demonstrated to each Member State that failing to balance the pros and cons of the Union for each Member State could lead to the disintegration of the Union. This may be the reason why in 2020, amidst an extraordinary health crisis, all the old fiscal rules have been set aside. Free riding should no longer be the primary fear and obsession of policy makers in Europe, and as political construction slowly matures, surveillance should consume less political time, to the advantage of matters like the Union's stability and sustainability.

Sustainability and the prevention of free riding are key to ensuring mutual trust among all stakeholders in Europe. Fear of paying for others is a European obsession that is shared at every level of the emerging European society. The crises in 2008 and 2012 have made clear that a sound currency, a stable financial system, constant access to financial markets and a solid lender of last resort are paramount for the Union—and they are attractive achievements for the Member States. This gives a first group of common goods to be managed.

Given the national political layer on which the Union is built, the list of common goods must be kept as minimal as possible, but it should include all externalities that operate at the European level. Indicators, as means of monitoring these externalities, should reflect this broader scope. This includes subjects such as:

1. Currency and inflation, current accounts, public-private financial stability, the financial system.
2. A social dimension. As there is competition between Member States and because social systems are financed at the national level, social issues are part of that competition. The Philadelphia declaration, ILO (1944), reminds us that "there is no peace without social justice" and probably no Union possible without peace. That means that social justice is not only delivered by a "generous" social system but also by a society in which remaining inequalities are considered fair by a vast majority (Forsé and Parodi 2010).
3. More generally, everything that is related to the competition between Member States should be managed at the European level and considered as common goods. These include topics such as global taxation and base erosion and profit-shifting OECDs (Organisation for Economic Co-operation and Developments) BEPS (Base Erosion and Profit-Shifting), fiscal shopping inside the Union, norms, research, large-scale infrastructure (Trans-European Networks for Energy or Transport) and so on. The emergence of new common goods will be discussed below.

A second important lesson from the 2008 and 2012 crises is that to take one step beyond the narrow surveillance of countries, information is a better driver of reform than endlessly repeated recommendations. The OECD's PISA (Programme for Internation Student Assesment) is a pertinent template for a completely different approach. Instead of the top-down elaboration of policy by a technocratic body speaking only to administrations and governments and hoping from this intermediate layer to explain to the people that there is no alternative to these policies, the aim is to fuel a debate with information and benchmarks that provokes a change in policy (OECD 2020). The aim is not to dictate policy, but to trigger a critical look at the national level at the state of things and what could be done. Of course, building a dashboard and choosing indicators is applying an ideology to a problem, which is not all that far from designing policy from the top. Many criticisms have been made of the PISA programme and the choices made in drawing up the reports and selecting and constructing the indicators (Grek 2009). Those choices are never innocent and result from deeply anchored beliefs in what is a good policy. Hence, compiling indicators and promoting ideology-driven analysis is not completely different from pure top-down policy making (Sjøberg 2015).

However appealing and informed these criticisms may be, two points stand out. The first is that information is a two-sided weapon of manipulation. It can be used in a biased way but, slowly, it opens the way to an in-depth discussion of the policy. The main difference between an ideology-based policy and an information-based manipulation is that one can discuss an analysis based on quantitative information. It is more difficult to contest a policy when the grounds for that policy are not explicit. Defenders of a policy will not attempt to justify themselves on circumstantial evidence. To the contrary, claiming to prove the necessity of a policy based on quantitative grounds is a call to discussion. It is an open approach to building the underlying knowledge instead of a closed discussion of the execution of a policy. More information, more quantitative data, the evaluation of past experience or even the design of the experimental setup to assert the validity of a theory may produce results that are not expected by the initial promoters of the reform. In that respect PISA has proven to be a flexible and two-sided tool, shifting for instance from the general benchmarking of education systems to the more subtle quantification of inequalities produced by education systems. The attention is more on education as a producer of workers than as a system providing tools to citizens to participate in a living democracy. But, nevertheless, year after year, as demonstrated by the various reports, PISA is helping to develop a richer, whilst still partial, view of the faults of education systems.

Moreover, the process of PISA is not simply a controlled manipulation of public beliefs about the functioning of the education system. It is at the margin a transparent debate that is open to everyone and to every opinion, even if the quantitative dogma is limiting the analysis to what is quantifiable. In that way, it is a breach, albeit a small one, in a process that makes national democracies clash with technocracies.

The PISA process, applied to other fields, may be used as a substitute for the recurrent call to structural reform for which the main levers lie at the national level. From various subjects ranging from cost competitiveness, employment protection legislation, education, local public investment, local governance, immigration policies and so on, the PISA approach could relax the pressure on Member States and could appear as a sound investment for the future, by delivering more reforms than any diligent technocrat could dream about. One could also reasonably expect that those reforms might well have more solid scientific and quantitative foundations and that they could also reflect a greater diversity of appreciation of what is a "good" policy.

Towards a Sustainable Union

Sustainability without considering ecosystems at large and without serious consideration of the long term is devoid of any sense. Obviously, the imperative of climate mitigation and adaption calls for new targets. But this involves more than a simple extension of the scope of things to consider. We are going to argue that the concern of sustainability has been removed from economic reasoning. Thus, sustainability is more and more a notion *external* to economic consideration, opposed to what it was when the key issue was defining trade-offs, such as efficiency versus equity. Moreover, monitoring sustainability policies will call for much more detailed information, which converges here with concern for social issues. Building a sound micro-based information system is key for the possibility of the environmental transformation of modern societies. Hence, the practice of aggregate quantification must be deeply amended.

The SDGs as a New Development Paradigm?

Published in 2015 (UN 2015), the Sustainable Development Goals (SDGs) look like they are fulfilling everything that could be desired about indicators and targets. With 17 goals ranging from the eradication of poverty and hunger (SDGs 1 and 2) to gender equality (SDG 5) and education (SDG 4), including health and well-being (SDG 3), SDGs deal with nearly everything from social justice, political fairness (SDGs 10, 16 and 17) and labour (SDG 8) to environmental sustainability (SDGs 7, 11, 12 and 13) and biodiversity (SDGs 6, 14 and 15). Elaborated with the broad participation of governments, NGOs and civil society, they provide an ambitious classification and a range of indicators suited to the full income range of countries. They impose on countries an agenda for the publication of data with an exigence of transparency, auditing and quality that is essential to trust in the quantification process.

The statistical value of the SDGs is beyond any doubt, and the stress they impose on the national statistical bodies is a confirmation that the exclusively economic approach of the System of National Accounts is a relic of the past. One positive outcome of the SDGs will undoubtedly be to document much more extensively and regularly issues on which light has only been intermittently shed. Fuelling the public debate with quantitative elements will influence the representations we make about the functioning of society and public policies as well. Extending the criticisms made of the PISA programme, one can regret that certain dimensions of the education system are still neglected, especially when their quantification is more difficult, such as the important instruction of future citizens able to think for themselves and immunized against gross manipulation, which is a little more important than the more easily quantified goal of being a productive worker. A more careful examination of the set of selected indicators may raise some concerns about the potential uses and consequences of a strict application of the SDG framework.

The national application of SDGs 3, 4, 8 and 10 to France led the National Institute to pick regional heterogeneity as an indicator of the distance to the goal of equal access to health (INSEE 2020). However, spatial heterogeneity at a rather small scale could mean many things and will always appear as non-zero. But the differences observed in, for instance, the population mortality rates by French region do not necessarily bear any significance. These differences may be small and even negligible when compared to differences between other groups, which are not clearly identified by the regional breakdown. Spurious effects may even appear, bringing the conclusion that mortality is higher in one place, but for inescapable reasons—average age would be a good candidate—masking other differences, linked to real discrimination. Assessing a diagnosis of equal access to health services is a rather complicated issue that cannot be understood by means of a simple quantification of spatial heterogeneity. As a matter of fact, this diagnosis would probably require building up a panel of individuals and being careful to sample without excluding some categories of the population—homeless people are difficult to survey, for instance, but children could be a blind spot when the base unit of the survey is the household. So this is not a question of indicators, but rather the architecture of an information system, which is open to research and administrative exploitation to provide pioneering analysis but also periodic assessments of a policy, causalities and policy evaluation. The cost of such information-gathering devices is so high that *ad-hoc* strategies cannot immediately be ruled out. The allocation of statistical and information production resources is also a critical element, and unfortunately, is totally absent from the SDG recommendations.

Drawing from this example, one can grasp the danger of freezing the association between a goal—one of the 17 or its breakdown—and an indicator associated with it, despite the pride that every national statistical institute displays when publishing a number for an SDG. While it may help to materialize what the goal will imply as policies or to provide a first attempt to measure the distance between the reality of a society and the goal, there are many reasons and examples of the complete inadequacy of an out-of-the-box indicator to guide policy. Actually, what we need is an in-depth understanding of the causal schemes that explain why we are in some distance from a given goal and what kind of policies, based on those causal links, may induce change. Without that analysis, indicators are pure window-dressing. Sticking to a poor indicator may land us in the same kind of dead-ends that we have observed for fiscal policy and the Stability and Growth Pact rules. The damage may even be greater, because the causal schemes underlying the selection of the poor indicator may be even more wrong than they were for fiscal policy.

But a collection of goals does not indicate what should be the allocation of resources for change. Progress towards the achievement of some goals can probably be made in parallel or even, in some cases, in a way that is mutually reinforcing. However, some goals may be contradictory, and the ability to change the society on both grounds may be limited by the design of the goals. This implies, for different reasons, being able to establish a hierarchy and to deal with trade-offs between goals. One can then decide an agenda that can reach a consensus in the society to promote real change rather than living with never-solved frustrations. Producing an agenda for reform based on the SDGs would be a positive outcome of building goals and measuring them with indicators. But, based on the PISA experience and the relative failure of European governance to produce cooperation beyond surveillance, this road is a long one. Evaluating and elaborating causal schemes, based on in-depth information, is the job of the social sciences. The toolbox includes large datasets, panels, rigorous sampling techniques and statistical tools suited to causal inference with big data—modern machine learning. But data and computing power alone will not be sufficient. A social science cannot be summarized by causal inference and quantification, and humility is the first step in the scientific method. All those elements, made clear in the 20+ years' experience with

PISA, are strangely absent from the SDG approach, which, by default, implicitly promotes a mechanical view of the main political issues of the century.

The Carrying Capacity of the Planet

Having dismissed the SDGs as a valid method for solving political issues, some basic facts need to be stated. The environmental constraint is defining urgent matters in the preservation of common goods. Basically, those common goods have been defined by the synthetic work on the carrying capacity of the planet (Steffen et al. 2015 extending Rockström et al. 2009). They evaluate limits on human activity so as to preserve the fundamental grounds for human activity on earth. These limits are global, climate being the prototype or local, like soil erosion, or both, for instance, biodiversity. The limits cannot be traded for anything else. A non-liveable climate cannot be compensated by educating more people. Irreversibility, radical uncertainty and tipping points justify the complementary nature of limits to human activity. As pointed out by some authors, Costanza (1989) and Daly (2005) for instance, this does not limit human activity but forms a closed space in which human activity should remain and develop. Following other scholars (Ratworth 2018), one may add an inner limit to human activity, defined by the guarantee that everyone has access to a decent way of living. Those two sets of limits represent an important paradigm shift, because there are no trade-offs possible with either the outer limits or the inner one. In a long-standing tradition, economics was thought of as the encompassing framework for everything. This ranges from the early project of general equilibrium economics to the work of Nordhaus and Tobin (1973) or even more recently the Stiglitz-Sen-Fitoussi Commission (Stiglitz et al. 2009). Extending the concept of GDP to include damages, natural wealth accounts and the pricing of externalities will not acknowledge the major changes that have operated since the emergence of the environmental question. To paraphrase Keynes (Arts Council 1946), the day has come when the economic problem will take the back seat where it belongs. Instead of life, human relations or religion or the problem of creation, it is the carrying capacity of the planet that is now in the driver's seat. The ecological sciences and knowledge are helping to understand what those limits are.

The role of the economic science is not nil: it could be to deliver humanity inside the carrying capacity of its planet, a task towards which all human ingenuity must be mobilized. Whether it is through a centralized and planned economy or by using regulated markets to coordinate multiple free entrepreneurs is not the subject of this chapter. Staying inside the outer circle of the ecological limits and building a society able to deal with the inner circle of social justice is not merely a scientific or social engineering problem: It is the mother of all policy debates to come.

Conclusion: Efficiency in a "Glocal" World

What economy and indicators can bring to this reversed paradigm is no longer the usual cost-benefit analysis using monetary value as a single scale for everything: it is what is called a cost-efficiency analysis, where given a set of constraints, one defines the best path—usually the least costly one—to maximize material well-being. Hence, all the work intended to better define what is well-being is not lost, but it is a huge transformation; it is a secondary objective.

The carrying capacity limits are to be understood as global constraints. Even their regional breakdown remains global when compared to the decision space individuals face. This gives two supplementary motives for indicators. The first is surveillance of the borders implied by the outer and inner circles. The second is related to the tools and policies that can be used to force individual behaviour to stay inside those tools.

The kind of surveillance involved there is not very far in principle from the surveillance process that was put in motion by the Stability and Growth Pact. There is, however, a slight nuance to add to a future surveillance scheme. It will not only involve surveillance of Member States to stay within the limits of, let's say, the CO_2 emissions allocations that are granted to countries in order to respect a general commitment to transit towards a zero-net economy. But the surveillance has to be done at all levels of decision making, so as to be able to monitor decentralized actions, whether those are the actions of a subnational authority, such as a city, or even an individual if decentralization of the action process goes that far. Respecting the global limits to human activity is not a global policy. It is a spectrum of policies, where actors range from supra-national entities to the smallest granularity. Smooth coordination of all those levels is by its very nature a quite new challenge. This is the collision between global limitations and multilevel decision layers.

Such surveillance will rely not only on aggregate indicators but also on indicators suited to monitor actors at all decision-making levels and provide feedback. As the requirement of respect for global limits may breed a multilevel free rider problem, transparent and open surveillance is critical to its good functioning. This level of information transmission between actors, to inform them that their actions are efficient in staying inside the outer circle and that all other actors are also behaving accordingly, is unknown today and may be needed in the future.

To make more concrete the need for a sophisticated monitoring scheme, one can consider the transition towards a zero-net emissions society. This transition implies, for instance, being able to monitor emissions at the finest level possible with good accuracy. The point is to know early the level of emissions even at the level of individuals, and thus to be able to assert that the policies undertaken are producing the expected results. Reducing the carbon footprint of residential buildings can be done by improving the energy efficiency of buildings. But to be sure that strategy is sufficient, one needs to know, building by building, flat by flat, what the energy consumption is before and after any investment policies. The aim is not to simply estimate the carbon footprint of an average individual but to measure nearly real-timewise where the carbon leaks are. This is necessary to track any rebound effect or unexpected behaviour that may hamper the final objective. The constraint is so strong that half-measures will be insufficient and constant monitoring of nearly everything will be necessary. The aim of this surveillance is not to create an Orwellian nightmare where everyone's every move is monitored and controlled by coercion. What is needed is to reach a high level of decentralization and to allow for assessment of policies that are under the responsibility of local decision-making levels.

Parallel to the need for surveillance, there is the need for knowledge about the effective policies. The point here is not only to monitor and inform actors but also to identify the levers that can be used for curbing individual behaviour within the planet's limits. This question is not different from those customarily dealt with in the social sciences, and especially in public economics. But the urgency of reversing current trends and the enormous efforts required to achieve zero-net emissions is such that acting to develop the information necessary to produce this knowledge is critical.

Monitoring behaviour closely, for instance accurately measuring residual CO_2 sources, will raise many privacy issues. Here again, the contribution of the social sciences to building a transparent society where individuals are informed more than designated as sinners will be decisive.

REFERENCES

Arts Council. (1946). *First annual report of the Arts Council.* Retrieved November 20, 2020, from https://www.artscouncil.org.uk/arts-council-great-britain-1st-annual-report-1945.

Costanza, R. (1989). What is ecological economics? *Ecological Economics, 1*(1), 1–7. https://doi.org/10.1016/0921-8009(89)90020-7.

Daly, H. (2005). Economics in a full world. *Scientific American,* September issue. Retrieved November 20, 2020, from https://www.scientificamerican.com/article/economics-in-a-full-world/.

European Commission. (2016). *Specifications on the implementation of the stability and growth pact and guidelines on the format and content of stability and convergence programmes.* Retrieved November 20, 2020, from https://ec.europa.eu/economy_finance/economic_governance/sgp/pdf/coc/code_of_conduct_en.pdf.

Fitoussi, J. P., et al. (1999). *Rapport sur l'Etat de l'Union Européenne.* Presses de Sciences Po, Fayard Paris.

Forsé, M., & Parodi, M. (2010). Une théorie empirique de la justice sociale, Hermann, coll. « Société et pensées », 347 p., EAN: 9782705669614. Paris.

Grek, S. (2009). *Governing by numbers: The PISA 'effect' in Europe.* Education and Society, Edinburgh University, Edinburgh.

INSEE. (2020). *Indicateurs pour le suivi national des objectifs de développement durable.* Retrieved November 20, 2020, from https://www.insee.fr/fr/statistiques/2654944?sommaire=2654964.

International Labour Organization. (1944). *ILO declaration of Philadelphia.* Retrieved November 20, 2020, from https://www.ilo.org/legacy/english/inwork/cb-policy-guide/declarationofPhiladelphia1944.pdf.

Krugman, P. (1994). Competitiveness: A dangerous obsession. *Foreign Affairs, 73*(2), 28. https://doi.org/10.2307/20045917.

Nordhaus, W., & Tobin, J. (1973). Is growth obsolete? In *The measurement of economic and social performance,* NBER.

OECD. (2020). *Education at a glance 2020: OECD indicators.* Paris: OECD Publishing. Retrieved November 20, 2020, from https://doi.org/10.1787/69096873-en.

Porter, T. M. (1995). *Trust in numbers, the pursuit of objectivity in science and public life.* Princeton University Press.

Ratworth, K. (2018). *Doughnut economics: Seven ways to think like a 21st-century economist.* Random House Business Books.

Rockström, J., et al. (2009). Planetary boundaries: Exploring the safe operating space for humanity. *Ecology and Society, 14,* 32. http://www.ecologyandsociety.org/vol14/iss2/art32/.

Sjøberg, S. (2015). PISA and global educational governance – A critique of the project, its uses and implication. *Eurasia Journal of Mathematics, Science & Technology Education, 11*(1), 111–127.

Steffen, W., et al. (2015). Planetary boundaries: Guiding human development on a changing planet. *Science, 347*, 1259855. https://doi.org/10.1126/science.1259855.

Stiglitz, J. E., Sen, A., & Fitoussi, J.-P. (2009). *Report by the Commission on the measurement of economic performance and social progress.* Paris. Retrieved November 20, 2020, from https://www.vie-publique.fr/sites/default/files/rapport/pdf/094000427.pdf.

Timbeau, X., et al. (2013–2019). *independent Annual Growth Survey.* Retrieved November 20, 2020, from https://www.iags-project.org/.

United Nations. (2015). *Transforming our world: The 2030 agenda for sustainable development.* Resolution adopted by the General Assembly on 25 September 2015. A/RES/70/1, New York.

CHAPTER 14

Is Resilience Measurable?

Magali Reghezza-Zitt

INTRODUCTION

Resilience is a relatively fuzzy, plastic and elusive term. It can be broadly defined as the ability to cope with, respond and adapt to and recover from a disturbance, which may be a slow stress or a sudden shock. Resilience is sometimes understood as a process, sometimes as a state resulting from this process. Within environmental concerns, resilience has gradually emerged in the field of disaster risk reduction (DRR), moving from a scientific descriptive concept to a normative imperative in international political agendas (Weichselgartner and Kelman 2015). Resilience is also widely used in the climate change field, in connection with adaptation (Fisichelli et al. 2016).

Resilience is closely related to well-being. Shocks and stresses directly affect well-being, both during the crisis and in the aftermath. Disasters worsen people's quality of life and access to the resources essential to their functionings (Quinn et al. 2020). Resilience is nothing but misused if well-being is not preserved or even enhanced. Resilience and sustainable development are therefore intertwined. Community resilience is

M. Reghezza-Zitt (✉)
École normale supérieure, Paris, France

French High Council for Climate, Paris, France
e-mail: reghezza@mercator.ens.fr

© The Author(s), under exclusive license to Springer Nature Switzerland AG 2021
É. Laurent (ed.), *The Well-being Transition*,
https://doi.org/10.1007/978-3-030-67860-9_14

considered as an indicator of social sustainability, and societal well-being can be strengthened by designing sustainable and resilient organizations, infrastructures and so on (Fiksel 2006). Conversely, components of human well-being are generally seen as key determinants of the capacity to cope with and recover from shocks and stresses—that is, resilience.

In academic use, the concept cuts across several disciplines, each of them having their own definitions and methods to characterize, understand and measure resilience (Chandler and Coaffee 2017).

While resilience studies now cover a very broad spectrum with numerous scientific publications, the shift from the academic to the operational spheres remains problematic: resilience has spread in the discourse of political, institutional and economic stakeholders, both at local (particularly urban), national and international levels but almost of the time without any clear conceptualization (Reghezza-Zitt and Rufat 2016).

Practitioners and scholars alike stress the need to measure resilience to monitor success of programming and justify investments. Guides, indicators, indices are increasing in number, in both academic and operational fields. Among the most recent: Rockefeller Foundation's City Resilience Index (2015), the Net Vulnerability Resilience Index (NVRI), the United Nations Demographic Exploration for Climate Adaptation (DECA) measuring resilience to climate change (2016), the FEW-Nexus City Index (2017), this in addition to earlier attempts such as FAO's Resilience Index (2012) or Food Security Information Network (FSIN) (2014). But even active promoters of resilience acknowledge that their assessments are still very far from universal measurements or consensual metrics and that their tools remain rudimentary.

In this chapter, I emphasize the necessity for a critical insight into the ongoing development of indicators reflecting the current operational turn in resilience studies. I defend three main arguments. First, the inability to produce universal indices or to agree on relevant indicators challenges the very possibility of measuring resilience. Second, the proliferation of indicators, methods and tools reflects the theoretical impasses of resilience, but also its eminently political nature. How resilience is defined reflects subjective judgments, values, beliefs, ideologies, which vary across individuals, places and times. I therefore finally recommend that resilience be considered not as an objective, but as a method for de-compartmentalizing public policies, transforming security governance and initiating the structural transformations necessary for a fair transition, with well-being improvement as horizon.

RESILIENCE AND WELL-BEING

Defining Resilience

Resilience is essentially a descriptive concept, used in many sciences and academic fields, that each has attempted to define, measure and sometimes strongly criticize resilience, forming a dense theoretical and methodological corpus (Chandler and Coaffee 2017).

Resilience studies share common features. They consider their research objects as systems. Whatever the system (individual, social group, community, technical system, productive system, socio-ecological system, socio-spatial system, etc.) or the disruption considered, they generally tackle resilience *ex post*, identifying *a posteriori* the different phases of the recovery process to retrospectively shed light on the drivers that explain resilience pathways. Addressing the complexity of those processes in a holistic perspective, they emphasize their non-linearity, the relationships between the system's resilience and that of its components, and the interactions between the different resilience drivers (Reghezza-Zitt and Rufat 2016).

Resilience has particularly flourished in environmental studies. As stated by Bourbeau (2017), "a large strand of literature employs resilience to analyze how co-evolving societies and natural/ecological systems can cope with, and develop from, disturbances". Stemming from the ecological sciences, studies focus on socio-ecological systems response to environmental change, especially global climate change and its impacts, and so-called natural hazards.

In the fields of ecological or social systems, resilience has been interpreted in two different ways (Cutter et al. 2008; Cutter 2016a). Numerous works define resilience in terms of capacity for resistance: a resilient system will prove robust to disturbance and return to the initial state after the disruption. Resilience is then determined by the ability of "bouncing back", which underlies the Latin etymology of the word and refers finally to stability and equilibrium maintaining. Intrinsic resilience can be seen as an attribute which pre-exists triggering events.

Other interpretations, on the contrary, emphasize learning and innovative processes to highlight actual transformation. Resilience then means emergence, creation and structural changes. This so-called adaptive resilience is based on self-organization and flexibility as with the imperative to "build back better" used in international frameworks of action (Cutter 2016b). In this perspective, resilience is dynamic, not static.

Resilience and Well-being

World damage distribution maps show a clear link between GDP and disaster impacts. Economic inequalities are generally seen as root causes of vulnerability. The 2010 earthquake in Haiti, which hit one of the poorest nations in the world, shows that income inequalities were a critical driver of damage. The poorest often inhabits high-risk areas. Informal, illegal and precarious housing are very sensitive to shocks. Poverty may also hamper resilience: the poorest are not insured and have difficult access to relief, emergency aid or health care. Material and economic capitals are therefore resilience drivers.

However, wealth and GDP are not good predictors of sensibility to shocks and post-crisis resilience. People with low economic capital can be extremely resilient. When Hurricane Irma hit the island of Saint Martin in 2017, slums were very exposed to marine submersion and wind, but their inhabitants were able to shelter in safe places using their social capital. These neighborhoods were quickly cleaned up, and people implemented immediately effective adjustments to overcome the drinking water, power and communication networks collapse. However, disasters reduce incomes and physical capital and push many households into poverty. In the long aftermath, resilience of the poorest households often consists of severe deteriorations in their living conditions and well-being.

Beyond GDP and household income, inequalities in their multi-dimensional and intersectional nature are critical drivers of susceptibility to harm and coping capacities. Both vulnerability and resilience are based on a dynamic combination of interacting factors such as age, gender, education, access to power and decision-making, quality of living environment, social capital and so on. Most of them are constitutive dimensions of well-being, explaining why certain groups can be severely affected in rich countries. For instance, in France, the Coronavirus disease 2019 (COVID-19) crisis impact was significantly higher in underprivileged neighborhoods; co-morbidities (diabetes and obesity) are more frequent due to an inferior quality diet, access to health care is more uneasy, degraded housing conditions encourage promiscuity and contagion. What is more, low-skilled jobs, for which teleworking is impossible, and precarious incomes have forced residents to commute, often by public transport, during lock-downs. In addition, these people have been hit harder by the economic and social crisis, which hampers their resilience. Children are particularly affected: not only have their material living conditions deteriorated, but domestic violence, school dropouts and mental health problems have also increased.

Finally, disasters reduce individual well-being, disproportionately for those with reduced economic and material capital. But low incomes do not condemn people to be helpless victims, precisely because other resilience drivers, who resonate with well-being indicators.

Competing Narratives

Similar conclusions were drawn regarding climate change, which is seen as a major risk booster for the poorest. Climate change worsens the universal, irreducible material conditions that are essential for achieving human well-being (Guivarch and Taconet 2020).

Resilience can then be regarded as a new narrative which echoes the criticism of "modernity" and is anchored in the debates about "planetary boundaries", entry into the Anthropocene, development ethics and environmental justice. Growth is based on unlimited pressure on finite environmental resources, modifying planetary dynamics and creating global environmental disruptions. These major disturbances interact with economic and social crises, producing shocks and stresses which destroy the well-being that material wealth was aimed to create and sustain. "Modern" societies have based their security on growth, which was supposed to favor the science and technology progress needed to eradicate threats and hazards. Not only does growth produce risks, but wealth is disconnected from invulnerability. Hurricane Katrina, the 2003 heat wave in Europe, the Tohoku tsunami and the Fukushima disaster, big fires in Australia and California, the COVID-19 crisis, all demonstrated the huge sensibility of rich regions and countries.

Resilience can, in fact, be interpreted as an alternative to growth. Designing resilient societies or places requires to strengthen not just economic and material capacities, but well-being, based on new relationships to natural resources and biosphere. Resilience is therefore underpinned by medium- and long-term sustainable development. This interpretation also highlights the potential regressive effects of vulnerability reduction, mitigation or adaptation policies on the well-being.

This narrative is however contested. Linking resilience and well-being highlights the role of structures and overarching context that undermine well-being and reduce coping capacities. In this perspective, resilience building aims to create agency, local communities' empowerment, promoting participatory and bottom-up approaches (Gaillard 2010). On the contrary, resilience can be regarded as an intrinsic attribute of individuals or communities, based on adaptive and auto-organization capacities. Numerous scholars have criticized this interpretation as neo-liberal and inherently conservative (Reid 2012; Joseph 2013; Pugh 2014). They argue that the "resilience turn" in public policies and international frameworks is actually a step backward which imposes on individuals the moral responsibility for their vulnerable condition, without tackling its root causes and initiating structural transformations. Resilience then becomes an alternative to well-being increase, ecological transition and sustainable development.

IMPLEMENTING RESILIENCE

Enthusiasm for Resilience

Resilience was adopted into Disaster Risk Reduction (DRR) field with Hyogo Framework for Action 2005–2015, which was the global blueprint for DRR produced by the World Conference on Disaster Reduction (WCDR). It was also gradually introduced in the Intergovernmental Panel on Climate Change (IPCC) reports, in connection with adaptation. In both cases, resilience has been linked to vulnerability, but the relationship between the two is still debated and remains controversial (Cutter 2016a). However, most scholars converge on the fact that improving resilience requires tackling pre-existing vulnerabilities, a premise that underpins several resilience-building programs, which often consist of vulnerability reduction measures.

For the past two decades, resilience has also been introduced into public policies at different territorial levels. For instance, cities adopted the concept, sometimes under private actors' impetus as with the 100 resilient cities network, initiated and financed by the Rockefeller foundation. Paris designed its "resilience strategy" in 2017, implemented through 30 operational actions. Other French cities such as Lyon have also put resilience on their governance agenda. In parallel, a growing number of non-governmental organizations use resilience as one of their new programmatic pillars, resilience either becoming the core of new strategies or introduced as complement to existing policies and programs, sometimes in a purely cosmetic way.

The enthusiasm for resilience, widespread in political and institutional discourse, can be explained both by the concept's plasticity and by its positive connotation. Resilience constitutes a non-fatalistic response to uncertainties and unavoidable crisis. Positive connotation gives the opportunity to acknowledge one's vulnerability, but also to overcome it. Plasticity makes resilience consensual and helps to recycle old practices under a new label. In France, resilience is the new name for natural hazards prevention, polluted soil treatment, industrial reconversion, urban renovation, sustainable urban planning or critical network vulnerability reduction.

Arguable Assumptions

Resilience operationalization is based on several beliefs, which were never really been discussed and must be challenged.

First, resilient systems are thought to possess intrinsic characteristics that determine their capacity to cope and recover. Acknowledging this premise leads to move from the *ex post* assessment of a given system resilience to the *ex-ante* design of resilient systems. If the properties that increase coping capacities for a given system can be identified, then it will be possible to create or replicate them within other systems, either because they are similar or because they face similar disturbances. This assumption implies that resilience can be built, reinforced or enhanced *before* the shock or the stress. System's responses to disturbance can then be anticipated, planned and integrated into strategies (Reghezza-Zitt and Rufat 2019). But resilience paths are neither linear nor unique. Resilience patterns are multiple and the label "resilient" applies to very different post-disaster situations. Some systems will recover quickly, while others will experience long phase of decline or even temporary collapse. In 1902, Mount Pelée's eruption destroyed the city of Saint-Pierre, in Martinique. Saint-Pierre disappeared for several years, even losing its status as a municipality. The city was gradually rebuilt and repopulated, but never regained its economic and demographic dynamism, even if Saint-Pierre is presented by local authorities as an archetype of resilience.

Second, the resilience capacity is often regarded as a generic property of systems. But a resilient system *per se*, that is a system that is able to respond to any disturbance, in any time and any places, does not exist. Pompeii recovered from a major earthquake but disappeared ten years later when Vesuvius erupted. The system's resilience does not necessarily imply the resilience of its components, which follow their own recovery patterns. In New Orleans, devastated by Hurricane Katrina in 2005, some neighborhoods have been rebuilt very quickly, while others are still in ruins 15 years later. Therefore, even before knowing what the resilience drivers are in order to define corresponding indicators, there is a need to agree on what resilience is, depending on the type of system in question (resilience of what?), the disturbance faced (resilience to what?) and the temporal and spatial scale considered.

Third, while decision-makers and practitioners discourse start from the premise that resilience is about positive transformation, resilience is not necessarily desirable. Post-disaster reconstruction often provides economic rebound with positive impacts on employment or reinforcement of protective infrastructure. But recovery means also exclusionary processes, due to expropriation, land speculation, rent increases or rise in the price of basic commodities. New Orleans has been held up as a model of resilience: after Hurricane Katrina, incomes and GDP per capita increased, homicide rate collapsed, unemployment decreased. But access to health care, education and housing for the poorest was severely deteriorated. The COVID-19 pandemic revealed that the city's resilience has never tackled the structural causes of its vulnerability. France has not experienced disasters on a similar scale. However, Guadeloupe after the Soufrière eruption in 1976 or places devastated by floods in South of France suffered demographic and economic decay. Beyond the radiant tale of a resilience that would allow systems to transform in a better, fairer and more sustainable way, numerous post-disasters feedbacks show that resilience often consists in the deterioration of initial conditions, mal-adaptation and vulnerabilities increases.

MEASURING RESILIENCE WITH INDICATORS AND SYNTHETIC INDEX

The very fact of talking about a desirable state relies on a value judgment. Calling a system resilient system involves a degree of subjective appreciation. However, many tools attempt to assess resilience objectively, by measuring it. Resilience measurement is characterized by a proliferation of methods, tools and frameworks. Cutter (2016b) considers that resilience assessment approaches can be divided in three categories: indicators, scorecards and toolkits. Indicators are quantifiable variables representing a selected characteristic of resilience. They are combined to produce indices, which condense the multi-dimensional nature of resilience in a single numerical value. Scorecards are based on surveys where each question is related to the presence or absence of characteristics, elements, actions, associated with resilience. Qualitative assessment is then converted into scores, which can be expressed in numerical values, letters scores or descriptors. Toolkits are expected to provide simplified and easily usable measurement instruments.

Level of Resilience and Indicators

Resilience assessments can be divided schematically into two categories: those that look at outcomes, which occur after the disturbance (real or simulated) and those that deal with outputs, which can be observed before the disturbance (Winderl 2014). Depending on the approach, by outcomes or by outputs, the indicators differ.

Estimates based on outcomes attempted to measure the system's resilience following a major disruption. They aim to assess the degree of recovery achievement, mainly through physical reconstruction and restoration of economic functions. They compare the state prior to the disturbance with the current state of the system. Widely used in post-disasters feedbacks, these studies finally address adaptive resilience. Resilience measurement is then based on various indicators such as mortality, rate of displaced return, employment, household income, GDP, the rebuilding rate of buildings and critical infrastructure and so on. Some estimates also include well-being indicators as physical and mental health, access to public services or assets, crime rates, individual perceptions of quality of life and so on.

Most resilience assessments seek, however, to estimate resilience *ex-ante* through outputs. These works aim to produce baseline and evaluation tools for planning, programs' monitoring, or support and incentives' efficiency assessment. They address intrinsic resilience, assuming on the arguable premise that intrinsic and adaptive resilience are positively correlated (Tierney and Bruneau 2007). *Ex-ante* estimates often favor a circular logic. Most of them are based on inductive approaches: they define *a priori* the variables that lead to system resilience. In doing so, the conclusions are likely to be largely driven by initial selection of variable (Cumming et al. 2005).

Resilience Metrics: Quantitative Versus Qualitative Approaches

Resilience measurement raises debates on the value of quantitative assessment compared to qualitative approach. Quantitative approaches are perceived by practitioners and decision-makers as more "objective", easily accessible and therefore more policy relevant. They generally select indicators, assign them numerical values, weight them and finally combine them to obtain a resilience score. The main limitations lie in choosing the dimensions of resilience to be considered, the variables to represent each dimension, the ranking of indicators and the weighting of variables. Rufat (2018) points to the current inflation in the set of indicators, but their quantity is not a guarantee of quality.

Qualitative approaches, based on words and narratives, are generally presented as more specific-context and, for this reason, better suited to tackle complexity and multi-layered reality. Qualitative approaches use marks, scores or descriptors for a list of items, which has led Bahadur et al. (2015) to state that they prioritize "processes" over "assets". These approaches provide information about motivational or cultural value systems and beliefs, which influence behavior and decision-making processes and for that reason are often perceived as better able to integrate social networks, relationships, interactions or capital. Finally, many scholars stress the need to include subjective approaches to grasp resilience, even if qualitative and subjective information must be distinguished. For instance, measures of well-being are also subjective and can be captured through self-assessment or ranking.

It remains that quantitative and qualitative methods are often combined: qualitative information can be used to produce quantitative instruments; qualitative information can also be relevant to explain the results of a quantitative analysis.

Top-down or Bottom-up Method?

Access to data and methodology determines the general scope of the estimates. Scholars distinguish three approaches: top-down or nomothetic methods, generally quantitative, leading to synthetic indices; bottom-up or idiographic methods, more qualitative, which involve local actors; mixed methods, which seek to combine both approaches.

Top-down approaches aim to produce resilience synthetic indices through standardized and quantitative methodology. In this approach, resilience indicators are derived from theoretical frameworks and are not related to case studies. The data come from national or international databases, which constrain the scale of analysis. Numerous scholars underline that there is no consensus on any index provided by this method. For Schipper and Langston (2015), difficult access to data explains the impossibility of arriving at a "universal" resilience index.

Conversely, bottom-up approaches are essentially qualitative (Pfefferbaum et al. 2013). They often use scorecards, based on resilience surveys and favor stakeholders' self-evaluation. Though they overcome the problem of access to data and provide abundant information, they make comparisons and changes of scale difficult, because they are highly dependent on the field.

Finally, mixed methods combine the two previous ones. They use so-called participatory approaches to select dimensions of resilience that must be considered or the variables chosen to represent each dimension of resilience. Participation is based on interviews with experts and local actors. These interviews are also used to classify the indicators or to weight the variables. This approach allows to produce synthetic indices for which the choices seem less arbitrary than for top-down approaches.

Should We Give Up Measuring Resilience?

Although frameworks, indices and measurements flourish, most of the methods have not been empirically validated—even institutions that promote resilience and produce "best practice" guides recognize that "no general framework for measuring disaster resilience has yet been empirically verified" (UNDP, 2014: 19). Bahadur et al. (2015) add that almost half of all frameworks they reviewed are not based on clear empirical evidence to support the approach chosen.

Despite the multitude of analytical frameworks, application guides and action plans, there is no consensual methodology for estimating resilience and monitoring capacity building. This challenges the very possibility of actually measuring resilience in a meaningful and robust way.

Can Resilience Be Measured?

To use Béné's (2013b) words, "we are still not sure exactly what resilience is", even though it is clearly becoming a major new paradigm for development, planning or security. However, Béné noted that other realities (poverty, vulnerability, etc.) with conflicting definitions have nevertheless been measured, even if the resulting metrics have been strongly criticized.

Resilience measurement is hampered by the inherent contradiction in using an analytical approach to capture a systemic reality. Resilience refers fundamentally to complexity: it is multi-dimensional, multi-component, multi-scalar. Frameworks developed to measure resilience need to be sufficiently generic to allow them to be scaled up and compared, whereas resilience by its very nature is a matter of time, space, communities, livelihoods, assets and so on (Béné 2013a).

Existing estimates capture less resilience than its drivers (poverty, development, inequality) or proxies (vulnerability, exposure). Since many resilience indices recycle methodologies used to assess hazard impacts, social vulnerability, risk perception, level of development and so on, it is, as Rufat (2018) remarked, almost impossible to guarantee that it is resilience that is being measured and not something else.

Interpreting Failure to Measure Resilience

Failure to produce universal and, above all, empirically validated indicators results first from the weakness of the theoretical basis of the methodologies employed. Meerow et al. (2016) notice, for example, that resilience measurement has resulted in a multiplicity of indicators, or even meta-indicators, without any real theoretical justification for the choices made. The increase in the number of indicators shows the difficulty of choosing which dimensions of resilience should be included in the measure and which should not. In this regard, the proliferation of indicators reveals the ambiguities of resilience, a point made by Rufat (2018) who notes: "the profusion of indices and methodologies only serves to conceal the theoretical impasses of resilience".

Above all, one must admit that the selection of indicators is not politically neutral, any more than their interpretation. Defining the desirable state of resilience involves options and decisions that are anything but obvious or consensual. The selection of indicators can, for instance, neglect deliberately the vulnerability root causes, the role of socio-economic structures or of individual decisions. It also results in overlooking the exclusion and vulnerability processes of the most fragile households or territories.

The use of figures and the claim to objectivity serve to justify decisions, programs' objectives, targets and spending, but overshadow the ideological postures or beliefs that guide them. Rufat is indeed right when he writes that measurement tools ultimately say more about those who produce and use them than about resilience itself (Rufat 2018). Béné (2013a) partly shares this concern when he writes that "it will soon become urgent to make these agencies and NGOs accountable for the money they are spending and more importantly for the 'experiments' they are implementing on households and communities in the name of resilience".

Resilience as a Method Rather Than Horizon

Resilience measurement is supposed to provide decision-making support, help to highlight spatial variability, to allocate needed resources or to monitor progress in capacity building at community and individual scale (Cutter 2016b). But this way of thinking conceals that resilience is primarily a political construction rather than a self-evident and desirable equilibrium that would be reached mechanically as soon as all the indicators turned in the right direction.

Defining resilience (and resilience metrics) requires trade-offs reflecting the balance of powers between the various stakeholders. Designing resilience involves competing interests, values, subjective appraisals, which can be contradictory and therefore conflictual. After storm Xynthia in 2010, the French government defined "black areas" where reconstruction was prohibited, raising a lot of protests from the inhabitants. In the aftermath of the AZF factory explosion, in 2001 in Toulouse, the continuation of industrial activities was hotly debated. The recovery plan drawn up in 2020 to deal with the impacts of the COVID-19 crisis was criticized. The decision to support activities that are high greenhouse gases emitters shows that short-term resilience may be incompatible with medium- and long-term resilience. As such, defining resilience is a political process: goals, targets and priorities must be discussed.

In a word, resilience should be considered more as a method, than as a bright (and distant) horizon. Resilience measurement should be regarded as a tool that contributes to resilience building. Pfefferbaum et al. (2013)

consider, for example, that resilience assessment is a component of a broader process that supports the improvement of community resilience. The 100 Resilient Cities network supported by the Rockefeller Foundation shows how each city has appropriated resilience. Starting from a "city resilience framework" based on a "city resilience index", localities designed their own strategy, adapted to their vulnerabilities and needs, through collaborative and participatory processes.

Resilience estimate allows individuals or communities to take ownership of security issues, exchange views and build their own strategic plan. In the DRR field, practitioners indicate that the various existing frameworks are less useful to give content to resilience than to enable stakeholders to acknowledge their vulnerability, accept it and develop strategies to reduce it. They insist that systemic approach provided by the resilience offers a strong incentive to de-compartmentalize public policies, integrate the long-term perspectives or consider more participatory and multi-scale governance.

Giving metrics to resilience finally provides an opportunity to gather stakeholders and transform security governance toward more sustainability. In France, even though resilience does not exist in everyday vocabulary, the development of resilience strategies by cities or local authorities or, more recently, by the "Citizens' convention for climate" convened in 2020, demonstrate that resilience can help stakeholders to acknowledge their vulnerability and collectively agree on priority targets, based on the resources, goods, services and values they consider essential for their well-being. In the end, it appears that resilience can turn the ecological constraint into an opportunity to strengthen justice and democracy.

CONCLUSION

Giving resilience an operative content is anything but obvious: there is no universally accepted resilience metric. The failure to measure resilience certainly demonstrates the weakness of the theoretical foundations of the various frameworks that try to grasp it. Indices and indicators are surely a mandatory tool for assessing the relevance of the policies implemented, but tend to overwhelm the complexity of the processes and social determinants. Moreover, the relevant debates on methods, choice of indicators, construction of frameworks, overshadow the core problem: designing resilience is not a technical issue, but it is a political choice. Social and individual determinants of resilience only make sense within a dynamic perspective and according to the overarching context. Indicators of resilience can therefore be neither totally generic nor absolutely universal.

Resilience is not *a priori* given; it is a social construction, both political and discursive, whose content is produced by stakeholders in a quasi-performative way. Giving substance to resilience, in particular when applied to social systems, implies to respect the willingness of stakeholders. Resilience frameworks must address both the economic, social and environmental impacts of the policies implemented and their ethical dimensions. As such, resilience building is an integral part of the concern for a fair transition that aims to improve well-being and foster sustainable development.

References

Bahadur, A., Wilkinson, E., & Tanner, T. M. (2015). Measuring resilience: An analytical review. Climate and Development.

Béné, C. (2013a). Towards a quantifiable measure of resilience. *IDS Working Papers, 2013*(434), 1–27.

Béné, C. (2013b). Can we actually measure resilience vulnerabilityandpoverty. blogspot.com.es/2013/10/can-we-actually-measure-resilience.html

Cumming, G. S., Barnes, G., Perz, S., Schmink, M., Sieving, K. E., Southworth, J., & Van Holt, T. (2005). An exploratory framework for the empirical measurement of resilience. *Ecosystems, 8*(8), 975–987.

Bourbeau, P. (2017). Resilience, security and world politics. In D. Chandler & J. Coaffee (Eds.), *Routledge handbook of international resilience* (pp. 26–37). London: Routledge.

Chandler, D., & Coaffee, J. (Eds.). (2017). *The Routledge handbook of international resilience*. London / New York, NY: Routledge / Taylor & Francis Group.

Cutter, S. L. (2016a). Resilience to what? Resilience for whom? *The Geographical Journal, 182*(2), 110–113.

Cutter, S. L. (2016b). The landscape of disaster resilience indicators in the USA. *Natural Hazards, 80*(2), 741–758.

Cutter, S. L., Barnes, L., Berry, M., Burton, C., Evans, E., Tate, E., & Webb, J. (2008). A place-based model for understanding community resilience to natural disasters. *Global Environmental Change, 18*(4), 598–606.

Gaillard, J. C. (2010). Vulnerability, capacity and resilience: Perspectives for climate and development policy. *Journal of International Development, 22*(2), 218–232.

Guivarch, C., & Taconet, N. (2020). Inégalités mondiales et changement climatique. *Revue de l'OFCE, 165*(1), 35–70.

Fisichelli, N. A., Schuurman, G. W., & Hoffman, C. H. (2016). Is 'resilience' maladaptive? Towards an accurate lexicon for climate change adaptation. *Environmental Management, 57*(4), 753–758.

Fiksel, J. (2006). Sustainability and resilience: Toward a systems approach. *Sustainability: Science, Practice and Policy, 2*(2), 14–21.

Joseph, J. (2013). Resilience as embedded neoliberalism: A governmentality approach. *Resilience, 1*(1), 38–52.

Meerow, S., Newell, J. P., & Stults, M. (2016). Defining urban resilience: A review. *Landscape and Urban Planning, 147,* 38–49.

Pfefferbaum, R. L., Pfefferbaum, B., Van Horn, R. L., Klomp, R. W., Norris, F. H., & Reissman, D. B. (2013). The Communities Advancing Resilience Toolkit (CART): An intervention to build community resilience to disasters. *JPHMP, 19*(3), 250–258.

Pugh, J. (2014). Resilience, complexity and post-liberalism. *Area, 46*(3), 313–319.

Quinn, T., Adger, W. N., Butler, C., & Walker-Springett, K. (2020). Community resilience and well-being: An exploration of relationality and belonging after disasters. *Annals of the American Association of Geographers, 1,* 1–14.

Reghezza-Zitt, M., & Rufat, S. (2019). Disentangling the range of responses to threats, hazards and disasters. Vulnerability, resilience and adaptation in question. Cybergeo.

Reghezza-Zitt, M., & Rufat, S. (2016). *Resilience imperative: Uncertainty, risks and disasters.* Oxford: Elsevier.

Reid, J. (2012). The neoliberal subject: Resilience and the art of living dangerously. *Revista Pléyade, 10,* 143–165.

Schipper, E. L. F., & Langston, F. (2015). A comparative overview of resilience measurement frameworks analysing indicators and approaches. ODI. https://www.odi.org/sites/odi.org.uk/files/odi-assets/publications-opinion-files/9754.pdf

Rufat, S. (2018). Estimations de la résilience des territoires, sociétés, villes. Méthodes, mesures, validations. VertigO 30

Tierney, K., & Bruneau, M. (2007). Conceptualizing and measuring resilience: A key to disaster loss reduction. TR news 250.

UNDP. 2014. *Human Development Report 2014: Sustaining Human Progress – Reducing Vulnerabilities and Building Resilience.* New York.

Winderl, T. (2014). Disaster resilience measurements: Stocktaking of ongoing efforts in developing systems for measuring resilience. UNDP, http://www.preventionweb.net/files/37916_disasterresiliencemeasurementsundpt.pdf.

Weichselgartner, J., & Kelman, I. (2015). Geographies of resilience: Challenges and opportunities of a descriptive concept. *Progress in Human Geography, 39*(3), 249–267.

PART V

Conclusion

CHAPTER 15

Taking Care of Essential Well-being in the "Century of the Environment"

Éloi Laurent

The Coronavirus disease 2019 (Covid-19) crisis and the subsequent lockdowns of large parts of humanity have triggered and renewed fundamental questions about the true finality not only of the economy but also of human existence, many of which were initiated well before this crisis. Among those, the need to define or redefine what is really essential to human well-being stands out: What do we really need? What can we actually do without? What should we do without? In closing of this volume, I will try to shed light on these complex questions that will determine in the very short-run public policies and shape them for years to come in the perspective of the well-being transition.

What is really essential to human life? In 1819, French philosopher and economist Saint-Simon attempted to set apart essential and non-essential social classes in industrial revolution France: "Suppose that France suddenly loses … the essential French producers, those who are responsible for the most important products, those who direct the works most useful

É. Laurent (✉)
OFCE/Sciences Po, Ponts ParisTech, Paris, France

Stanford University, Stanford, CA, USA
e-mail: eloi.laurent@sciencespo.fr

É. Laurent (ed.), *The Well-being Transition*,
https://doi.org/10.1007/978-3-030-67860-9_15

to the nation and who render the sciences, the fine arts and the crafts fruitful, they are really the flower of French society, they are of all the French the most useful to their country, those who procure the most glory, who add most to its civilization and its prosperity: the nation would become a lifeless corpse if it lost them... It would require at least a generation for France to repair this misfortune". It is in the mode of the parable that Saint-Simon then tried to explain the hierarchical reversal that the new world of the industrial revolution implied for the country's prosperity, which could henceforth do without the monarchical classes, in his view, whereas "Science and the arts and crafts" had become essential.

Adapting Saint-Simon's parable to our world and peculiar situation at the beginning of the twenty-first century amounts to recognizing that we cannot do without the people who provide healthcare, guarantee the food supply, maintain the rule of law and public services in times of crisis, as well as those among us who operate the infrastructure (water, electricity, digital networks). This implies that in normal times all these professions must be valued in line with their vital importance.

But it is necessary to flush out this elementary definition by referring to the numerous studies carried out over the decades on the measurement of human well-being, work which has greatly accelerated in the last ten years. We can start by considering what is essential in the eyes of those surveyed about the sources of their well-being. Two priorities then emerge: health and social connections. In this respect, the current situation offers a striking "well-being paradox": drastic measures of lock-downs are sometimes being taken to preserve health, but they in turn lead to the deterioration of social connections due to the imposed isolation.

But how better to begin to positively identify the different factors in "essential well-being" that should now be the focus of public policy? The measurement of deprivation can be very helpful in attempting to measure wealth. The pioneering empirical work by Amartya Sen and Mahbub ul Haq in the late 1980s resulted in a definition of human development that the Human Development Indicator, first published by the United Nations in 1990, reflects only in part. In France several studies have been undertaken in recent years by the National Observatory of Poverty and Social Exclusion (ONPES) on reference budgets and extended in particular by INSEE with its "indicator of poverty in living conditions", which has led to defining the essential components of an "acceptable" life (or "a decent life").

Yet the definition of essential well-being implies two other categories that are even more difficult to delineate, let alone assess empirically: useless (or artificial) well-being, that which can be dispensed with harmlessly; and harmful well-being, which we must do without in the future because in addition to being ancillary it harms essential well-being, in particular because it may undermine the foundations for well-being by accelerating the crisis of the Biosphere and its ecosystems.

Let's start with useless well-being. How do we know what we can do without while continuing to live well? To clarify this sensitive issue, economic analysis offers a central criterion, that of the useful, which itself refers to two related notions: use and utility.

First of all, and faithfully to the etymology, what is useful is what actually serves people to meet their needs. From the human point of view, then, something is useless if it doesn't serve to meet people's needs. In the midst of the Covid-19 crisis, Amazon announced on 17 March 2020 that its warehouses would now store only "essential goods" and defined these as follows in the context of the health crisis: "household staples, medical supplies and other high-demand products". The ambiguity of the criterion for the useful is tangible in this definition, which conflates primary necessity and the interplay of supply and demand. While giving the appearance of civic behaviour, Amazon is also resolutely in line with its commercial purpose.

Furthermore, this first criterion of the useful leads into the oceanic variety of human preferences. As Aristotle notes in the first chapter of the *Nicomachean ethics*, the founding text of the well-being economics written almost two and a half millennia ago, we find among individuals and groups a multiplicity of conceptions of what constitutes a good life. But contrary to Aristotle's views, who erected his own concept of happiness as a superior form of well-being, it is not legitimate to prioritize the different conceptions of a happy life among humans. Conversely, the Aristotelian conception of happiness, which emphasizes study and the culture of books, is no less worthy than any other. Rather, a political regime based on liberty is about ensuring the possibility that the greatest number of "pursuits of happiness" is conceivable and attainable so long as none of them harms others.

Hence, the importance of the second criterion, that of utility, which measures not only the use of different goods and services but also the satisfaction that individuals derive from them. But this criterion turns out to be even more problematic than that of use from the point of view of public policy.

Classical analysis, as founded, for example, by John Stuart Mill following up on Jeremy Bentham, supposes a social welfare function, aggregating all individual utilities, which it is up to the public authorities to maximize in the name of collective efficiency, understood here as the optimization of the sum of all utilities. Being socially useful means maximizing the common well-being thus defined. But from the beginning of the twentieth century, neoclassical analysis called into question the validity of comparisons of interpersonal utility, favouring the ordinal over the cardinal and rendering the measure of collective utility largely ineffective, as shown convincingly by Robbins (1938).

This difficulty with comparison, which necessitates the recourse to ethical judgement criteria to aggregate preferences, in particular greatly weakens the use of the statistical value of a human life ("value of statistical life", or VSL) in efforts to base collective choices on a cost-benefit monetary analysis, for example in the area of environmental policy. Do we imagine that we could decently assess the "human cost" of the Covid-19 crisis for the different countries affected by crossing the VSL values calculated, for example by the OECD, with the mortality data compiled by John Hopkins University to determine which country should receive the most efficient vaccines? The economic analysis of environmental issues cannot in fact be limited to the criterion of efficiency, which is itself based on that of utility, and must be able to be informed by considerations of justice (see Introduction of this volume).

Another substantial problem with the utilitarian approach is its treatment of natural resources, resources that have never been as greatly consumed by economic systems as they are today—far from the promise of the dematerialization of the digital transition underway for at least the last three decades (IRP 2017).

The economic analysis of natural resources provides of course various criteria that allow us to understand the plurality of values of natural resources. But when it comes to decision-making, it is the instrumental value of these resources that prevails most of the time, because these are both more immediate in terms of human satisfaction and easier to calculate. This myopia leads to monumental errors in economic choices.

This is particularly the case for the trade of live animals in China, which is at the root of the Covid-19 health crisis (as well as that of 2002–2003 SARS zoonosis). The economic utility of the bat or the pangolin can certainly be assessed through the prism of food consumption alone. But it turns out both that bats serve as storehouses of coronavirus and that pangolins, fur animals and others can act as intermediary hosts between bats and humans. So the disutility of the consumption of these animals (measured by the economic consequences of global or regional pandemics caused by coronaviruses) is infinitely greater than the utility provided by their ingestion. It is ironic in this respect that the bat was precisely the animal chosen by Thomas Nagel in a classic article (Nagel 1974) aimed at tracing the human-animal border, which wondered what the effect was, from the point of view of the bat, of being a bat.

Finally, there appears, halfway between the useless and the harmful, a criterion other than the useful: that of "artificial" human needs, recently highlighted by French sociologist Razmig Keucheyan (Keucheyan 2019). Artificial is understood here in the dual sense that these needs are created from scratch (especially by the digital industry) rather than spontaneously, and that they lead to the destruction of the natural world. They contrast with collectively defined "authentic" needs, with a concern for preserving the human habitat.

Let's turn finally to the difficult question of harmful well-being and ask a candid question: Is humanity a pest? For the other beings of Nature who find it increasingly difficult to coexist with humans on the planet, the answer is unambiguous: without a doubt. Life on earth, 3.5 billion years old, can be estimated in different ways. One way is to assess the respective biomass of its components. It can then be seen that the total biomass on Earth weighs around 550 Gt C (giga tonnes of carbon), of which 450 Gt C (or 80%) are plants, 70 Gt C (or 15%) are bacteria and only 0.3% are animals. Within this last category, humans represent only 0.06 Gt C. And yet, the 7.6 billion people accounting for only 0.01% of life on the globe are on their own responsible for the disappearance of more than 80% of all wild mammals and half of all plants (Bar-On et al. 2018).

This colossal crisis in biodiversity caused by humanity, with premises dating back to the extermination of megafauna in the prehistoric age (Pleistocene), started with the entry into the regime of industrial growth in the 1950s, with the onset of the "great acceleration".

This is now well documented: while nearly 2.5 million species (1.9 million animals and 400,000 plants) have been identified and named, convergent studies suggest that their rate of extinction is currently 100 to 1000 times faster than the rhythms known on Earth during the last 500 million years. This could mean that, due to human expansion, biodiversity is on the brink of a sixth mass extinction. Whether we observe these dynamics in cross-section or longitudinally, at the level of certain key species in certain regions or by turning to more or less convincing hypotheses on the total potential biodiversity sheltered by the Biosphere (which could amount to eight million species), the conclusion is obvious: while humans are thriving, the other species are withering away, with the exception of those that are directly useful to people.

But this destruction of biodiversity is of course also an existential problem for humans themselves. According to a causal chain formalized two decades ago during an evaluation of ecosystems for the millennium, biodiversity underpins the proper functioning of ecosystems, which provide humans with "ecosystem services" that support their well-being (recent literature evokes in a broader and less instrumental way "the contributions of Nature", a concept taking centre stage in the IPBES first global assessment; IPBES 2019). This logic naturally also holds in reverse: when humans destroy biodiversity, as they are massively doing today through their agricultural systems, they degrade ecosystem services and, at the end of the chain, undermine their own living conditions. The case of mangroves is one of the most telling: these maritime ecosystems promote animal reproduction, store carbon and constitute powerful natural barriers against tidal waves. By destroying them, human communities are becoming poorer and weaker.

The start of the 2020 decade, the first three months of which were marked by huge fires in Australia and the Covid-19 pandemic, is clearly showing that destroying Nature is beyond our means. The most intuitive definition of the unsustainability of current economic systems can, therefore, be summed up in just a few words: as economic systems work against their own perpetuation, human well-being destroys human well-being.

How do we get out of this vicious spiral as quickly as possible? One common sense solution, known since Malthus and constantly updated since then, is to suppress humanity, in whole or in part. Some commentators are taking note of how much the Biosphere, freed from the burden of humans, is doing better when they are being locked-down. In reality, even if lock-downs have led to a constrained and temporary sobriety, their long-term impacts are working fully against the well-being transition. All the mechanisms of social cooperation that are essential to transition policies have been put to a standstill. The point is that it is not a matter of neutralizing or even freezing social systems to "save" natural systems, but of working over the long term on their social-ecological articulation, which is still a blind spot in contemporary economic analysis.

The fact remains that the current social emergency is forcing governments around the world to work here and now to protect their populations, particularly the most vulnerable, from the colossal shock that is simultaneously hitting economic systems around the world. The notion of essential well-being can rightly serve as a compass guiding these efforts, which could focus on sectors vital to the whole population in the months and years to come, subject to the imperative of not further accelerating the ecological crisis. Essential well-being and non-harmful well-being could converge to meet the present urgency and the needs of the future. How, precisely?

Public health and the care sector are clearly at the centre of essential well-being, understood as human well-being which works for its perpetuation rather than for its loss. The medical journal *The Lancet* has highlighted in recent years the increasingly tangible links between health and climate, health and various pollutants, health and biodiversity, and health and ecosystems.[1] Care for ecosystems and care for humanity are two sides of the same coin. But the issue of environmental health must be fully integrated, including here in France, with the new priority on health. Investing in public services beyond the health system is also a guarantee that essential well-being is shared most equitably.

This time consistency is complicated by the necessary reinvestment in essential infrastructure. Food supply systems in France and beyond, from agricultural production to retail distribution, are today far too polluting and destructive to both human health and ecosystems. Food systems already engaged in the ecological transition should be given priority in order to promote their generalization. Likewise, the energy required for infrastructure, particularly urban infrastructure (water, electricity, waste, mobility, etc.), is still largely fossil-fuelled, even though in just five years a global metropolis like Copenhagen has given itself the means to obtain supplies from 100% renewable energy. We must, therefore, accelerate the move for energy and carbon sobriety—we have all the means needed. Finally, the issue of the growing ecological footprint of digital networks can no longer be avoided, when essential infrastructures, such as heating networks and waste collection, work very well in a "low-tech" mode.

---

[1] See https://www.thelancet.com/commissions.

Finally, two practical steps can be taken to foster the well-being transition. The first is to get rid of the macroeconomic objectives of the twentieth century, which now form a "mystic square" relying on the false belief that economic growth is the ultimate goal and universal solution to all human needs. The second is to adopt a well-being golden rule for economic policies: from now onward, any economic decision must simultaneously improve present and future well-being.

REFERENCES

Bar-On, Y. M., Phillips, R., & Milo, R. (2018). The biomass distribution on Earth. *Proceedings of the National Academy of Sciences, 115*(25), 6506–6511.

IPBES. (2019). In E. S. Brondizio, J. Settele, S. Díaz, & H. T. Ngo (Eds.), *Global assessment report on biodiversity and ecosystem services of the Intergovernmental Science-Policy Platform on Biodiversity and Ecosystem Services.* Bonn, Germany: IPBES Secretariat.

IRP. (2017). Assessing global resource use: A systems approach to resource efficiency and pollution reduction. In S. Bringezu, A. Ramaswami, H. Schandl, M. O'Brien, R. Pelton, J. Acquatella, et al. (Eds.), *A Report of the international resource panel.* Nairobi, Kenya: United Nations Environment Programme.

Keucheyan, R. (2019). *Les besoins artificiels: comment sortir du consumérisme.* Paris: Zones.

Nagel, T. (1974). What is it like to be a bat? *The Philosophical Review, 83*(4), 435–450.

Robbins, L. (1938). Interpersonal comparisons of utility: A comment. *The Economic Journal, 48*(192), 635–641.

INDEX[1]

[1] Note: Page numbers followed by 'n' refer to notes.